DATE DUE

~~OC 25 05~~			

DEMCO 38-296

Encyclopedia of
Third Parties
IN THE UNITED STATES

Encyclopedia of

Third Parties

IN THE UNITED STATES

Earl R. Kruschke, Ph.D.

Professor of Political Science
California State University, Chico

ABC-CLIO
Santa Barbara, California
Denver, Colorado
Oxford, England

Library of Congress Cataloging-in-Publication Data

Kruschke, Earl R. (Earl Roger), 1934–
   Encyclopedia of third parties in the United States / Earl R. Kruschke.
     p. cm.
   Includes index.
   1. Third parties (United States politics)—Encyclopedias.
  I. Title
   JK2261.K78   1991   324.273—dc20   91-6659

ISBN 0-87436-236-9 (alk. paper)

98 97 96 95 94 93 92 91   10 9 8 7 6 5 4 3 2 1

ABC-CLIO, Inc.
130 Cremona Drive, P.O. Box 1911
Santa Barbara, California 93116-1911

This book is Smyth-sewn and printed on acid-free paper ⊗.
Manufactured in the United States of America

To My Grandchildren

Ryan Miles Ruch
Jonathan Louis Roohy
Claire Amelia Kruschke
Loren Dean Kruschke

With Love from Papa

Contents

Preface

I have been interested in the subject of minor, or "third," parties in American politics for at least a quarter of a century. Their uniqueness, their usually short duration (although a few have continued to persist for remarkably long periods of time), the variety of their causes and candidates, and the frequency of their appearance and disappearance on the American political scene all serve to stimulate examination not only of the minor parties themselves but of their role and impact on what is generally regarded as a two-party system.

The literature on third parties is extensive and diverse, yet it remains largely uncollected. Although there have been some excellent scholarly studies dealing with the theory of third parties in the American two-party context, such as Daniel A. Mazmanian's *Third Parties in Presidential Elections* (Washington, DC: Brookings Institution, 1974) and Steven J. Rosenstone, Roy L. Behr, and Edward H. Lazarus's *Third Parties in America* (Princeton, NJ: Princeton University Press, 1984), and some outstanding work on specific third parties and their activities in the American party and electoral system, such as John D. Hicks's *The Populist Revolt* (Minneapolis: University of Minnesota Press, 1931) and David A. Shannon's *The Socialist Party of America* (New York: Macmillan, 1955), much of the literature has been journalistic and of checkered quality. In general, it may be said that third parties have been treated as largely inconsequential by both scholars and journalists alike.

In this book, I make no claims about either adding to the theory of third parties in the United States or advancing and increasing our knowledge about any of the specific third parties dealt with in this listing. This book is clearly descriptive; I have drawn information from the most readily available sources of information on each of the parties discussed.

This is a book for the interested general reader and student; it should be viewed as a source to which such persons can turn in order to *begin* their study of third parties—as a reference with which they can whet their appetites for further inquiry. The book is, quite frankly, intended to be a kind of "laundry list" consisting of examples of third parties that have existed throughout American history, ranging from some of the most important (e.g., the Populist, American

Independent, Libertarian) to some of the most frivolous (e.g., American Vegetarian, Jobless, Universal). Of the hundreds of such parties that have proliferated down through American history, I have chosen 81 that I feel represent and reflect the gamut of issues, causes, and personalities that third parties have espoused and/or spawned over the years. My decisions to include the parties discussed in the following pages were made on the basis of such criteria as the number of votes the party received; the number of states in which the party candidates received support or, indeed, the concentration of support for a party within a state or even part of a state; the duration or intensity of activity engaged in by the party; its influence—or lack thereof—on the political and legislative process; the prominence or utter obscurity of its candidates; and the general flamboyance or, in some cases, obscurity of the party. In short, I have attempted to include what in my judgment constitutes a reasonable representation of the types of minor parties that have played a role in American political history.

Sources and references cited after each entry are those that should be of use to the general reader; these lists are made up largely of materials that are probably readily available in good libraries throughout the world. Perhaps most important, this book is intended to fill a gap in the literature by providing a handy first reference to third parties as they exist—and have existed—as part of the American political culture.

Conducting research in a university that does not possess a fully comprehensive library and gathering materials needed to write even a survey such as this presents some obvious obstacles. These obstacles cannot be overcome without the assistance of others. I wish especially to acknowledge the assistance of Sylvia Jones, Lorraine Mosely, and Karen Seaman of the California State University, Chico, Meriam Library Inter-Library Loan Department, whose efforts to locate books and periodicals not in the local collection have been singularly helpful. The assistance of librarians Peter Anderson and William Stuve must likewise be acknowledged; their abilities to ferret out sources that most persons would not even think about have never ceased to amaze me. Likewise, the Library of the State of California in Sacramento has proven of considerable value in researching this volume. To the many students who have collected bibliographies over the years, and to the reviewers of this manuscript, both known and unknown, I extend my thanks.

As is customary, I alone assume responsibility for errors of omission or commission.

Introduction

Conventional wisdom in the United States—indeed, perhaps even the conventional wisdom among scholars—holds that the American political party system is a "two-party" system. It is, of course, correct that two political parties have tended to dominate the American political system almost from its beginning. Still, hundreds of minor parties— generally referred to, although perhaps incorrectly, as "third parties" (we do not refer to "fourth parties" or "fifth parties," for example)— have risen and fallen (and some have even persisted for relatively long periods of time) throughout the course of American history. On the national level, for example, given the fact that the Constitution requires only that a presidential candidate be native born, 35 years of age, and a U.S. resident for 14 years, dozens of candidate nominations have been made, either by parties of one type or another or by self-nomination of the candidates—both serious and otherwise— themselves. In 1988, for example, at least 17 presidential candidates other than George Bush and Michael Dukakis received votes. (See Table 1.)

But even Table 1 does not begin to suggest the plethora of candidates running for the presidency in 1988. According to one source, a total of at least 187 minor presidential candidates were in the field (see Day, 1988). Needless to say, none of the candidates running against George Bush and Michael Dukakis had even the remotest possibility of winning the election. Of the more than 91 million votes cast by the electorate in 1988, all of the minor candidates listed in the table received a combined total of fewer than 1 million votes, or, to put it another way, less than 1 percent.

There have been many minor, or "third," parties, as this book suggests. To attempt to classify them is no easy undertaking. They have run the gamut from the absurd (e.g., advocating that immediate contact be made with residents of outer space) to the sublime (e.g., advocating that all countries be governed by men of God). Literally dozens of other parties have existed, however, whose far more rational policies have been given a relatively serious hearing by comparatively large populations or whose platform proposals have, more often, been virtually ignored.

1

Table 1
Votes Received in the 1988 Presidential Election

Candidate, Party	Popular Vote	Percentage
George Bush, Republican	48,881,011	53.37
Michael Dukakis, Democrat	41,828,350	45.67
Ron Paul, Libertarian	431,499	0.47
Lenora Fulani, New Alliance	218,159	0.24
David Duke, Populist	48,267	0.05
Eugene McCarthy, Consumer	30,510	0.03
James Griffin, American Independent	27,818	0.03
Lyndon LaRouche, National Economic Recovery	25,082	0.03
William Mara, Right to Life	20,497	0.02
Ed Winn, Workers League	18,579	0.02
James Warren, Socialist Workers	13,338	0.01
Herbert Lewin, Peace and Freedom	10,312	0.01
Earl Dodge, Prohibition	7,984	0.01
Larry Holmes, Workers World	7,719	0.01
Willa Kenoyer, Socialist	3,800	0.00
Delmar Dennis, American	3,456	0.00
Jack Herer, Grassroots	1,949	0.00
Louie Youngkite, Independent	372	0.00
John Martin, Third World Assembly	236	0.00
None of these candidates	6,934	0.01

Data from Associated Press; *New York Times*, December 29, 1988, p. B6. Reprinted with permission.

Perhaps the first "third party" in the United States was the Tertium Quids (a "third something"), which emerged in the recently established country between 1804 and 1808 and which was led by John Randolph of Roanoke in opposition to President Jefferson's policies, especially as they related to the purchase of Louisiana—an act that Jefferson admitted was one for which he had no constitutional power—and Florida. This "party" thus came between the Federalists and the Republicans of the time. Although the Quids were short-lived, their existence contributed to the rise in power of James Monroe and kept the idea of states' rights alive for development by future generations—especially those of the southerners (see Hicks, 1933).

Some third parties have been doctrinaire or ideological (e.g., the American Communist Party, the Socialist Party, the Socialist Labor Party, and the Socialist Workers Party). In 1988, the efforts of the Communist Party were probably primarily propagandistic. Letting people know that the Communist Party was still in existence served an important purpose as far as the party was concerned. Most doctrinaire or ideological parties in the United States have been Marxist in their orientation, but some analysts would also include the more recent Libertarian Party in this classification.

Other parties, such as the Progressives of 1912 and the States' Rights, or "Dixiecrat," Party of 1948, have been described as "splinter" or factional parties, having split off from one of the major parties for reasons of dissatisfaction of one kind or another. Other examples of this type of party would include the La Follette Progressives of 1924, the Henry Wallace Progressives of 1948, and the George Wallace American Independent Party of 1968. Classified similarly would be the so-called Mugwumps, a group of Republicans who seceded from their parent party to protest the nomination of James G. Blaine as presidential candidate. Derived originally from an Indian word, the label *mugwump* soon became something of a brand of criticism: "My mug is on one side of the fence and my wump is on the other."

Still other parties have used the electoral process to gain a public forum for their philosophical viewpoints. One might refer to these as single-issue parties. Examples would include the Vegetarian Party, the Prohibition Party, the Free Soil Party, the Anti-Masonic Party, and the Know-Nothings, a nativist, anti-Catholic, and anti-Irish party especially vocal during the 1850s.

Another way to classify minor parties would be on the basis of economic protest. One of the most impressive of these parties—even if of short-term existence—was the Populist Party, which was made up of agricultural and labor groups that achieved particular success from the 1890s up to about 1908.

Other terms that have sometimes been used to classify third parties have been *episodic, spin-off, hybrid,* and *personality.* And there have been still other classifications as well.

Although on the national level the success of third parties has been feeble, on the state and local levels of politics the success of third parties has been better, even if mixed. Socialists have been able to elect mayors in such places as Bridgeport and Hartford, Connecticut, and Milwaukee, Wisconsin. The Farmer-Labor Party, moreover, has been especially successful in Minnesota, particularly during the 1920s and 1930s. Indeed, it won the governorship of that state in the 1940s. And in New York, for example, the Conservative Party elected James Buckley to the U.S. Senate in 1970.

The degree of success of some of the major third parties in American history is indicated in Table 2.

Many questions may, of course, be raised about third parties. Exactly what *are* third parties? Why do they come into existence?

4   *Introduction*

Table 2
Examples of Third Party Vote, 1832–1988 (in percentages)

Election Year	Party	Popular Vote
1832	Anti-Masonic	8.0
1844	Liberty	2.3
1848	Free Soil	10.1
1852	Free Soil	4.9
1856	American ("Know-Nothing")	21.4
1860	Constitutional Union	12.6
1880	Greenback	3.4
1884	Greenback	1.7
1888	Prohibition	2.2
1892	Populist	8.5
1904	Socialist	3.0
	Prohibition	1.9
1908	Socialist	2.8
	Prohibition	1.7
1912	Progressive (Bull Moose)	27.4
	Socialist	6.0
1916	Socialist	3.2
1920	Socialist	3.4
1924	Progressive	16.6
1932	Socialist	2.2
1936	Union	2.0
1948	States' Rights (Dixiecrats)	2.4
	Progressive	2.4
1968	American Independent	13.5
1972	American	1.4
1976	American Independent	0.2
1980	Libertarian	1.1
	John Anderson National Unity Movement	6.6
1984	Libertarian	0.3
1988	Libertarian	1.2

What is their relationship to the two major parties and to the political system in general? What role do they play in the stream of American politics? What functions do they perform? To whom do they appeal? What is their organizational structure? How do we measure their success? Are third parties to be defined more as interest groups than as political parties? Are they something of both? What can we say about their role in terms of the future of American politics? Obviously, I cannot attempt to answer all of these questions between the covers of this brief book. My concern in this volume is to give only some examples of the considerable number of so-called third parties or nonmajor party support movements that have existed in American politics down through time.

Leon Epstein (1967), one of the leading scholars of political parties, defines political parties as "any group, however loosely organized, seeking to elect governmental office-holders under a given label" (p. 9). He goes on to offer a type of definition of a third party as "any party that regularly breaks the two-party competitive pattern by winning or threatening to win enough offices to influence control of the government" (p. 64). It would seem that his general definition of political parties is more descriptive of third parties in the United States than his more specific definition of them. That is the case at least with respect to the inclusion of third parties in this book. If a nondominant party or group has nominated or even supported a presidential candidate, or even if a person from such a group has nominated him- or herself, it has qualified as a third party for inclusion in this volume. Thus, I might have included many more so-called parties than I did. Or, as others will argue, some might have been excluded. Ultimately, inclusion was based on an arbitrary decision. Yet, the parties and organizations described in this book are only illustrative of the hundreds of candidate-nominating and -supporting groups that have in fact appeared intermittently throughout American history.

I feel that the parties that have been included here are "representative" of the many that have appeared because they reflect such criteria as the number of votes cast for them (for example, some 13.5 percent of the popular vote for the American Independent Party in 1968, and virtually no popular votes—let alone electoral votes—for the Universal Party); the number of states in which the candidate qualified to run; the duration and intensity of the party's activities (e.g., the Prohibition Party compared with the Poor Man's Party); the influence of the party on other parties and the national legislative process (e.g., the Populist Party); the prominence of their candidates (e.g., Robert La Follette compared with Kirby Hensley); and the general flamboyance or reticence of the party (e.g., the Black Panther Party compared with the American Vegetarian Party).

The limited success of third parties in the United States—given its vast diversity of interests, geographic differences, varied ethnic and racial groups, and economic variations, for example—seems highly unusual. As William B. Hesseltine (1962) once pointed out, it is a paradox that in the United States, with its many contrasts, that a two-party system should have come to dominate the nation's politics. Logic would inform us that, given the country's diversity, a multiparty system would more reasonably reflect the many hopes, fears, aspirations, and concerns of the dozens of different subcultures flourishing in the country. The expectation might be that we would, in fact, have a multiparty system. Nevertheless, the United States is one of the limited number of democracies of the world where a multiparty system has not been established.

Moreover, the two major parties that have come to dominate the system—the Democratic and Republican parties—appear, at least superficially, to be surprisingly similar to each other. Although political scientists and sociologists have produced a substantial body of literature that demonstrates that the two major parties draw their support from largely different constituencies, are different in their internal makeup, and take essentially different positions during election campaigns, when appealing to the American electorate—the members of which do not differ as much from one another as do the leaders and most active members of the respective parties—they make similar appeals for votes. From a party perspective, this would, in fact, be a logical position to assume. Indeed, to provide alternatives calling for widely different decisions on the part of the American electorate would be irrational from a partisan point of view; American voters are not significantly different from one another ideologically on most variables. Given the objective of the major parties to win elections, for them to create intense ideological differences would likely lead to defeat. (For highly useful studies of ideological orientations among the mass public and party elites, see, for example, Jackson, Brown, and Bositis, 1982; Pierce and Hagner, 1982; Smith, 1980.) Thus, Jefferson could declare, "We are all Republicans, all Federalists," and a contemporary American politician might assert that we are all Democrats, all Republicans—even though we now, as then, obviously are and were not. Each of the major parties has evolved into what might be described as a large umbrella under which are sheltered a number of disparate elements, each of which has been able to express its goals and objectives with the protection of the party label. From the time of the Patriots at the end of the American Revolution to the Federalist/Anti-Federalist period, on through the birth of the Democratic-Republicans and later the Jacksonian Democrats, then the Whigs, and still later the Republican Party, dissension has been largely settled by internal party compromise. In short, a third party has rarely threatened one of the major parties for survival.

Among the reasons given for the domination of a two-party system in the United States, one of the most compelling is that of the existence of the single-member district system of election by plurality. This system permits the election of only one person from a congressional district, for the Senate, for state offices, and for local political positions, regardless of the actual number of candidates running. The winner is, simply, the individual who receives the most votes, even if that number is not a majority. The same is true in the case of the presidential election. That is, the candidate in a multicandidate race who receives the most votes (a plurality) wins a majority of the electoral votes. Consequently, even those candidates who might win significant percentages of the popular vote will wind up with no electoral votes. Thus, the electoral system provides minor party candidates no real opportunity to win seats in state and local offices or the Congress, let alone a true opportunity to win the presidency.

Other explanations suggest that there has generally been a historical tradition of two-party voting in the United States that started with the British tradition and continued through the establishment of the Federalists and Anti-Federalists in the United States. The argument is that a two-party tradition became a habit from the earliest inception of political divisions in the United States. Voter loyalty to the two major parties over the years has been difficult, if not impossible, for minor parties to overcome. This fact, coupled with the uniqueness, "extremeness," or otherwise unusual character of many of the third parties or their candidates, has served to undercut their ultimate chances for success in the American political system. Relatively strong and unique interests have usually been played out through interest group politics in the United States, and minor political parties have not benefited from such philosophical or other attachments, at least on a grand scale.

Minor parties face other obstacles in the United States also, not the least of which are financial obstacles. Although the Federal Election Campaign Act provides for public funding of candidates for the Democratic and Republican parties, minor party candidates may receive government support only if they received at least 5 percent of the total vote cast in the preceding presidential election. This percentage results in the exclusion from such aid for most minor parties and their candidates.

Another difficulty faced by third party candidates is that they are not covered by the media to the same degree that the candidates from major parties are covered; without such coverage, relatively few Americans may actually know of the existence of their candidacies, and relatively few Americans are ready to vote for candidates about whom they have heard very little. Moreover, state legislative practices control which party candidates may in fact appear on the ballot. In other words, state legislation may require petitions or fees to gain access to the ballot—requirements that the minor parties are often unable to meet, given their limited financial and popular support.

Although the U.S. Supreme Court has intervened in some of these difficulties, the situation remains sufficiently problematic to make it difficult for minor parties to get on the ballot.

There is another aspect of third party difficulties that must be addressed, although it is somewhat less subject to empirical support. That is that the major parties have often taken over the proposals made by the minor parties, thus weakening them. For example, the major parties assimilated the ideas of the direct election of senators, the notion of the progressive income tax, the regulation of banks, and the ideas of initiative, referendum, and recall—all of which were ideas advocated by so-called third parties in earlier election campaigns. The appeals of the third parties have to that extent been undermined, and the major parties, given their broad bases of political, legal, and financial support, have been able once again to undercut the efforts of minor parties. It is, of course, possible, and quite logical, to argue that simply because third parties seemed to have adopted many of these proposals first, it does not necessarily follow that they were the cause of the adoption of such ideas by the major parties. The major parties might have adopted them in any event. In other words, simply because A precedes B does not mean that A caused B. Nevertheless, it is a distinct possibility that such co-optation practices by the major parties are a contributing cause of third party weakness.

It might also be argued that the introduction of the direct primary election and the machinery of the national nominating convention have provided devices to keep dissident elements *within* the major party structures. That is, unless there is a truly *major* point of discontent (for example, the civil rights issues of 1948 that led to the disaffection of the Dixiecrats from the Democratic Party), dissenters are likely to remain within a party, recognizing that they will probably do better by attempting to influence their own party colleagues than by striking off completely on their own in a separate cause.

What, then, do minor parties add to the American political scene? No one can give a definitive answer to this question, of course, but some contributions of these parties can be identified. For instance, the existence of many minor parties is evidence of the dissatisfaction of millions of Americans with the current status of political reality in the United States. If nothing else, minor parties provide a means of expression of "alternative" ideas and alternative policies for American government. Were it not for the existence of third parties, it is possible that even more Americans would abstain from voting during presidential elections.

Controversy is sometimes shunned by the major parties; certain topics (e.g., dealing with the budget deficit, "liberal" versus "conservative" approaches to government, the question of the necessity of increasing taxes) are often avoided or completely ignored until it becomes absolutely necessary, from a political perspective, to deal with them. Then the minor parties, or minor candidates, see their ideas placed on the public agenda. Those third parties that have been the most long-lasting have been those with an enduring philosophical or ideological foundation largely inconsistent with attitudes held by the majority of Americans. Thus, it may be ideology that holds those at the fringes of American society most closely together.

In addition, minor parties have traditionally played what has come to be called a safety-valve function: the disaffected and the alienated in American society may express their dissatisfaction with the prevailing realities of politics by supporting dissident candidates. How similar is this to the "letters to the editor" column of one's local newspaper? And how much violence may be prevented by providing such an outlet for the angry or those otherwise unhappy with pre-vailing political conditions? Third parties and their candidates may thus be said to provide an outlet for frustrations while simultaneously giving their members an opportunity to voice ideas.

Third parties might also actually mobilize some persons who might otherwise not vote. Democrats and Republicans may be unap-pealing to some Americans; not offering fully viable alternatives to voters—whether sophisticated or relatively ignorant—the major par-ties are not supported by a number of Americans who see an advan-tage in expressing outrage, frustration, or idealism through their support of optional parties and candidates. Third parties may be viewed by some as actually more responsive to voters than the two major parties. As one scholar has summarized it:

> The entry of minor candidates into a normal two-party electoral contest can influence the outcome of the election in any of three distinct ways: by influencing who turns out to vote, by altering individual voters' preferences for candidates, or by splitting one or more of the major candidates' vote. (Mauser, 1983, p. 113)

The study of third parties is thus useful from a variety of per-spectives. Third parties teach us, for example, that the two-party system remains imperfect and that alternative parties have ideas and policies that might be implemented to ameliorate the two-party sys-tem's deficiencies. Some of the tactics employed by third parties dem-onstrate that the usual avenues provided by the major American parties are sometimes inadequate (as in the case of the Mississippi Freedom Democratic Party, for example). Third parties also serve as a forum for a cause (as in the case of the Liberty Party, for example). Studying third parties can also help to reveal how they have influenced and sometimes altered presidential election outcomes. And, also important, the existence of third parties has been largely influential in keeping alive the continued efforts to reform or even abolish the electoral college.

The importance of third parties, in and of themselves, has been succinctly stated in one of the now classic books on the subject. William B. Hesseltine, in 1962, stated:

> Despite the number of third parties and the often small vote which they polled, the minor groups played a significant role in American political history and made their contribution to the maintenance of the American system of government by unanimity. Often third parties voiced dissents and made sufficient headway at the polls to force the attention of the political managers of the major parties. Often the threat of a third party modified the program of a controlling group. Frequently third parties were the vehicle through which a new idea or policy was launched and tested. When a new proposal met a favorable reception it was adopted by a major party. In a negative sense, too, third parties served to test new programs, and many of their proposals failed to win support and were discarded. Some third parties could list the number of their proposals that were later enacted into law by other parties. At the same time the pathway of American political history was littered with discarded ideas that were once the darlings of third parties. Such, too, was the record of candidates, politicians, and managers. Some won their spurs in third parties and rose to power in major parties, while unresponsive voters retired other hopeful leaders from the political arena.
>
> Third Parties played a significant part in American political history—even in the maintenance of the traditional "two-party" system. An understanding of their rises and falls contributes depth and meaning to the American democratic system. (pp. 13–14)

What, then, of the future? This book provides a list of some of the more conventional and unconventional third parties or movements that have either run or supported various candidates. What are the possibilities for the emergence of a meaningful third party in the future?

Paul R. Abramson, John H. Aldrich, and David W. Rohde (1990) provide an interesting and highly useful discussion of this point in their recent book, *Change and Continuity in the 1988 Elections.* Recognizing that "no new political party" has arisen since the ascendancy of the Republicans in the 1850s, future possibilities for third parties seem to emerge from three particular realities: the lack of party affiliation on the part of many Americans, the relatively weak attachment of most Americans to the two dominant parties, and the existence of a vast reservoir of nonvoters. In these authors' words:

Third parties have three sources of hope. First, approximately one-third of all Americans of voting age claim to have no party ties. Second, and perhaps more important, only three adults in ten claim to be strongly committed to either of the two major parties. Third, there are more than 80 million nonvoters, who, if brought to the polls, could transform any political movement into a majority party. Even though all minor party candidates together won only 900,000 votes in 1988 (just under 1 percent of the votes cast), eight years earlier John B. Anderson, an independent candidate, won 5,700,000 votes or 6.6 percent of the total. Clearly, a new political party could emerge, but how likely is such a development, and what would such a party's ideological stripe be? (p. 295)

Their assessment of the likelihood of future success of a third party is bleak. Although the minor parties receiving even one electoral vote during the entire period following the Second World War have been right-wing parties, Abramson and his colleagues cite a variety of reasons—economic, social, and moral—that it becomes "hard to see how a conservative political party can compete with the Republicans" (p. 296). But a third party attempting to occupy the center may face even more difficult obstacles.

[John] Anderson's candidacy of 1980 illustrates the problems facing a third party of the center. According to Anthony Downs, the center is the logical place for each party to strive toward, but one of the two major parties is likely to hold that space already. A third party of the center finds it difficult to present a distinctive policy agenda. . . . A centrist party has a chance only if the two major parties veer too far to the right and left simultaneously, or if both major parties nominate unpopular candidates. Moreover, even when the major parties have moved to the right or left, it is usually easy for at least one of them to recapture some of the center ground. (p. 296)

A leftist party would have a better opportunity, particularly if the Democratic Party became more centrist. But the problems of organizing such a party would be immense—and have, indeed, been demonstrably so even when such comparatively popular candidates as Eugene McCarthy and Barry Commoner ran as candidates for the presidency, and especially when suggestions are made to organize a black third party. Indeed, according to Abramson et al., "A black political party running a national campaign would probably win only the three electoral votes of the District of Columbia" (p. 297). To win, a leftist party would have to be multiracial in makeup. But even if this were accomplished, the authors maintain that it would be "extremely unlikely that such a coalition could actually win a general election for the presidency" (p. 297). Trade unions might provide the necessary multiracial social structure, but they have usually supported the Democratic Party and are likely to be disinclined to support a party without any track record at the polls. Thus, the authors conclude, "The absence of any social structure that could provide the organizational basis for a third party of the left greatly reduces the chances that there will be a successful third party movement—even if the Democrats clearly move to the political center in 1992" (p. 298).

These realities, when coupled with the impediments faced by third parties mentioned earlier, make it extremely unlikely that a viable third party movement will be successful, if, indeed, it appears at all. There is no reason to believe that it will suddenly become easier for third party candidates to get on the ballot. There is no reason to believe that it will suddenly become easier for third parties to raise the amounts of money needed to launch an even marginally successful assault on the major party structure. There is no reason to believe that the media will suddenly become sufficiently interested in them to give to the third parties an amount of coverage even minimally approaching that given to the candidates of the major parties. Lacking a base of support, it is simply more logical for candidates who might actually wish to run as independents or as third party candidates to seek nomination by one of the major parties. The habituation of Americans to the two-party system is deeply rooted, the sense of dualism perhaps growing out of traditional American values and institutions. The probability that adherence to such values will change abruptly is low; relatively moderate parties will continue to dominate the great middle ground from which most of the votes are drawn. And the middle ground of American politics is Democratic and Republican territory. Although there has been erosion in major party affiliation, the political socialization process may very well ensure the perpetuation of the two major parties into the future. Finally, it can be argued that even if a third party emerges, the chances of its survival are dim because its policies, if shown to be appealing to a large number of voters, may almost immediately be taken over by the major parties in order to siphon off voter support. Barring the adoption of a system of proportional representation in the United States or amendment of the Constitution in such a way that a parliamentary system combined with such representation would be introduced, the prospect of future success for third parties on any significant level continues to be dim. As long as this is the case, most American voters will probably continue to believe that to vote for a third or minor party candidate is to waste their votes. To them, it is simply better to vote for the "lesser of two evils," and those two "evils" continue to reside in the Democratic and Republican parties. (For a comparative study of the development of new parties, see Harmel and Robertson, 1985.)

References

Abramson, Paul R., John H. Aldrich, and David W. Rohde. *Change and Continuity in the 1988 Elections.* Washington, DC: Congressional Quarterly Press, 1990.

Day, Glenn. *Minor Presidential Candidates and Parties of 1988.* Jefferson, NC: McFarland, 1988.

Epstein, Leon D. *Political Parties in Western Democracies.* New York: Praeger, 1967.

Harmel, Robert, and John D. Robertson. "Formation and Success of New Parties: A Cross-National Analysis." *International Political Science Review,* 6 (October), 1985: 501–523.

Hesseltine, William B. *Third Party Movements in the United States.* Princeton, NJ: D. Van Nostrand, 1962.

Hicks, John D. "The Third Party Tradition in American Politics." *Mississippi Valley Historical Review,* 20 (June), 1933.

Jackson, John S., III, Barbara Leavitt Brown, and David Bositis. "Herbert McClosky and Friends Revisited: Party Elites Compared to the Mass Public." *American Politics Quarterly,* 10 (April), 1982: 158–180.

Mauser, Gary. *Political Marketing: An Approach to Campaign Strategy.* New York: Praeger, 1983.

Mazmanian, Daniel A. *Third Parties in Presidential Elections.* Washington, DC: The Brookings Institution, 1974.

Mazmanian, Daniel A. "Third Parties in Presidential Elections," *Parties and Elections in an Anti-Party Age.* Bloomington and London: Indiana University Press, 1978.

Pierce, John C., and Paul R. Hagner, "Conceptualization and Party Identification: 1956–1976." *American Journal of Political Science,* 26, 1982: 377–387.

Rosenstone, Steven J., Roy L. Behr, and Edward H. Lazarus. *Third Parties in America.* Princeton: Princeton University Press, 1984.

Smith, Eric R. A. N. "The Levels of Conceptualization: False Measures of Ideological Sophistication." *American Political Science Review,* 74, 1980: 685–696.

Afro-American Party

Established in 1960 in Alabama by the Reverend Clennon King.

The primary objective of the party was to stimulate greater activity on the part of blacks in political affairs. Given the then overwhelmingly racist character of the Democratic Party in the South, the Afro-American Party was perceived as a potential alternative for black involvement in state and national politics.

Conventional wisdom long suggested that black voters had historically been solidly wedded to the Democratic Party. To a considerable extent this contention may be said to have been demonstrably true, especially in the northern cities, where blacks had been encouraged in varying degrees to join the political machines and political clubs, and where a comparatively large number of blacks were elected to city councils, state legislatures, and other offices. It is important to note, however, that before 1936, blacks had solidly supported the Republican Party, their allegiance to that party based largely on the fact that it was under Republican administrations (especially that of Lincoln) that they had won whatever new freedoms they possessed. But the advent of the administrations of Franklin D. Roosevelt seemed to cement once and for all the allegiance of blacks to the Democratic Party. Their ties to the Democrats emerged mainly as the result of the adverse economic conditions to which they had been subjected, and the policies of Roosevelt and his "New Deal" served to attempt to change their condition. This general allegiance continued under the administrations of Harry Truman, John Kennedy, and Lyndon Johnson, although during the Eisenhower administration increased black support for the Republicans was notable, even if more or less temporary.

Yet, this loyalty to the Democratic Party was also to a considerable extent illusory. Many blacks, rebuffed by Democrats and Republicans alike, had joined third parties in the past. Moreover, the slow progress blacks had made on the national level while the Democrats were in office (many Democrats in national office were, after all, demonstrably hard-core segregationists and anti-civil rights advocates) and the continued practices of white supremacy, segregation, and other forms of racial prejudice, most notable in the Democratic Party's southern contingents, provided blacks with stimuli to attempt

15

to formulate an organization that would accomplish black objectives more swiftly and with broader application than had been the case when blacks relied primarily on working through the Democratic Party.

The Afro-American Party put forth Clennon King as its presidential nominee in 1960 and selected Reginald Carter as the party's vice presidential candidate. Some candidates for local office were also nominated. However, not even one candidate of the party was elected. Indeed, the ticket received under 1,500 popular votes. Thus, efforts on the part of Alabama blacks to establish an alternative to the Democratic Party turned out to be nothing more than a futile gesture.

By 1964, the feeble electoral support the party had achieved, the passage of more stringent civil rights legislation by the U.S. Congress, and the efforts of the Democratic Party to win the support of increasing numbers of blacks led to the disappearance of the party.

Sources/References

Schapsmeier, Edward L., and Frederick H. Schapsmeier. *Political Parties and Civic Action Groups*. Westport, CT: Greenwood, 1981.

Walton, Hanes, Jr. *Black Political Parties: An Historical and Political Analysis*. New York: Free Press, 1972.

_____. *Black Politics: A Theoretical and Structural Analysis*. Philadelphia: J. B. Lippincott, 1972.

American Beat Party

Also known as the American Beat Consensus, established in Chicago in 1959.

The American Beat Party's objectives were to advance the beliefs and life-style of the so-called beatniks—or beat generation—as well as to change American culture.

William Lloyd Smith proclaimed himself the party's presidential nominee in 1960. Smith's plan or "platform" proposed elevating the working class and advocating the rights of all persons to pursue their own individual life-styles. His platform also urged federal government subsidies for artists, and, among other things, making "peace with everybody, because all beatniks are cowards," and the legalization of "nepotism, favoritism, excess profits, and mink coats."

The beats were composed largely of artists and authors who expressed a generally anarchical point of view. They glorified intense and beatific experiences, noncomplex speech forms, and, to some extent, nihilism. Among the leading exponents of the beats were Jack Kerouac, Chandler Broussard, Kenneth Rexroth, Allen Ginsberg, Lawrence Ferlinghetti, Gregory Corso, and William Burroughs.

The beats were only one element of a general avant-garde movement under way in Western society at the time. One of their major objectives was to return the arts and literature to the masses. Their works represented a deep alienation from contemporary American culture in general and a call for establishing a new sense of community in America. Establishment writers railed vehemently against the works of the beats, citing their alleged promotion of promiscuity; their physical, literary, and artistic vulgarities; and their attacks on the generally accepted civilities and mores of civilized society. The hostile reaction to the beats was picked up by the popular media, which often referred to them as dirty people wearing sandals, and as "sick," offensive, and otherwise emotionally unstable. One of the major centers of beat activity in the United States was San Francisco, California.

Even though the "party" ran a candidate, it was never officially listed on the ballot of any state. Yet, the movement it represented probably was influential in affecting the life-styles of many individuals during the 1950s and 1960s and therefore probably had an impact far beyond its immediate environment. The movement was a forerunner of the broader New Left and other similar protest movements that appeared later and that had an effect on many people's consciousness. Eventually, the beat movement was absorbed by other cultural forces. As a distinct movement, it no longer survives.

Sources/References

Cook, Bruce. *The Beat Generation.* New York: Charles Scribner's Sons, 1971.

Miller, Douglas T., and Marion Nowak. *The Fifties.* Garden City, NY: Doubleday, 1975.

Parkinson, Thomas F. (Ed.). *Casebook on the Beat.* New York: Crowell, 1961.

Schapsmeier, Edward L., and Frederick H. Schapsmeier. *Political Parties and Civic Action Groups.* Westport, CT: Greenwood, 1981.

American Independent Party

Established in Montgomery, Alabama, in 1968, largely as the personal organizational vehicle by which Governor George C. Wallace of Alabama hoped to gain the presidency that year.

Having been elected governor in 1962 as a Democrat and as an ardent segregationist, Wallace had gained wide media attention when, on the campus of the University of Alabama, he proclaimed his support of segregation "now," "tomorrow," and "forever."

Wallace's entry into presidential politics had actually occurred in 1964, when, to the surprise and in some cases dismay of his colleagues in the Democratic Party, he challenged the Democratic front-runners in three major presidential primaries—those of Wisconsin, Indiana, and Maryland. Wallace's vehement opposition to the Civil Rights Act of 1964 had already become well known and had dramatically propelled him onto the national political scene. Opinion surveys had indicated that there existed among Americans a residue of substantial and deep-seated opposition to both the tactics and the substance of the entire civil rights movement during this period of American history, but Wallace's astonishingly strong support in the three primaries—he received 34 percent of the Democratic primary vote in Wisconsin, 31 percent in Indiana, and about 43 percent in Maryland—lent credence to speculation about an even greater "white backlash" than had earlier been thought likely. Wallace thus sought to capitalize on the undercurrent of racial prejudice reflected in the politics of the 1964 campaign. He coupled his attack on civil rights with vehement opposition to the "Great Society" programs being advocated by the incumbent Democrat, President Lyndon Johnson.

In 1968, Wallace broke with the Democratic Party and sought the presidency as the candidate of the American Independent Party. He established its headquarters in Montgomery. The party apparatus was sustained largely by the personal strength, will, and magnetism of George Wallace himself, through his sheer political skill and his unflagging optimism about his possibilities of success in the quest of the presidency.

The apparent inability and unwillingness of the national government to deal successfully with the country's basic problems (especially the war in Vietnam), the political turbulence that shattered the academic atmosphere on dozens of college campuses, the rash of assassinations of some of the leading political figures of the generation, the apparent desire of middle Americans to get back to a "simpler" way of life, the continuing reaction against some vague and undefined "establishment," the seemingly ever-increasing tax burden, and the general social and political malaise that seemed to have affected the country—on these and on racial strife in particular George Wallace built his movement. To all of these difficulties he offered simple solutions.

"Knock some heads together!" "Law and order!" "Keep the races apart!" "Get the federal government out of people's lives!" "Get the U.N. out of the U.S.!" "Pinkos!" "The Supreme Court!" "Fuzzy-headed professors!" "Pseudointellectuals!" Using these and other slogans, Wallace went forth under the guise of an old-time populist, attacking real or imagined villains for their alleged elitism, arrogance, and support of what he considered unconstitutional positions, and sometimes charging them with outright treason. He enjoyed confronting those who on the one hand supported the right to read pornographic literature and on the other urged the prohibition of prayer in public schools. These and other shibboleths were offered by Wallace as answers to the complex difficulties facing U.S. society in the 1960s and 1970s.

The American Independent Party platform of 1968 began:

> A sense of destiny pervades the creation and adoption of this first Platform of the American Independent Party. . . .
> As this great nation searched vainly for leadership while beset by riots, minority group rebellions, domestic disorders, student protests, spiraling living costs, soaring interest rates, a frightening increase in the crime rate, war abroad and loss of personal liberty at home; while our national political leaders paid homage to the legions of dissent and disorder and worshipped at the shrine of political expediency, only this Party, the American Independent Party, and its candidates . . . possessed the courage and fortitude to openly propose and advocate to the nation those actions which are necessary to return this country to its accustomed and deserved position of leadership among the community of nations and to offer hope to our people of some relief from the continued turmoil, frustration and confusion brought about through the fearful and inept leadership of our national political leaders.

Among the planks included in the platform were pledges to restore power to the state and local levels of government, to provide greater support for law enforcement, to reduce taxes, to create incentives for industry, to provide aid to the elderly, to provide farm price supports, to establish an equitable minimum wage, to develop low-cost mass transportation, to give support to NATO and the creation of a "balance of force" in the Middle East, and to negotiate a settlement in Vietnam. It should be emphasized that the party advocated total victory in Vietnam and, indeed, that use of low-yield nuclear weapons was not ruled out as a way to achieve that objective. The platform opposed gun control and foreign aid to those countries opposing the United States militarily. It suggested that members of the U.S. Supreme Court and other federal judges be elected and then reconfirmed at intervals, the durations of which were to be established.

The platform concluded, in part, by stating:

> We believe that our analysis of the nature of these problems is in keeping with the feelings of the great majority of our people. We

further feel that our approach to solution of these matters is sound, logical, practical and attainable and in keeping with the basic, inherent good judgment of the American people.

Although a jerry-built organization run mainly from the governor's mansion in Montgomery, the American Independent Party eventually qualified for inclusion on the ballot in all 50 states—a fairly extraordinary achievement given the diversity and discriminatory language of most state statutes dealing with third parties. Winning a position on the ballot was brought about largely by lawsuits in such populous states as Ohio. But to a considerable extent, too, Wallace and his movement achieved eminence because of the news media, which seemed awestruck by Wallace's garrulousness and behavior, which sometimes bordered on the vulgar. His every move seemed to be reported somewhere. In short, his pronouncements were considered "news." His audaciousness was perceived as worth covering. His inflammatory statements, spoken so pugnaciously, were demanding of media attention. Thus, Wallace and his campaign soon skyrocketed to national and international attention.

Initially choosing Marvin Griffin of Georgia as his running mate, Wallace ultimately selected Curtis LeMay, a retired Air Force general, as vice presidential candidate of the party. Although not as much in the public eye as Wallace, General LeMay had become especially widely known for his outspoken comments on the Vietnam War and had a wide following among a conservatively oriented group of the electorate who were especially concerned with our policy in Southeast Asia.

Although Wallace's self-professed sole aim in 1968 was to get on the ballot and to reserve the real fight for the presidency until 1972, as the autumn of 1968 approached, public opinion polls seemed to suggest that victory in November might be possible after all—even if remote. And, even if victory remained impossible, Wallace might still be able to play the role of spoiler—that is, he might deny each of the major candidates sufficient votes in the electoral college so that the election would have to be decided by the House of Representatives. Candidates of both major parties were concerned that a substantial third party vote presented at least the possibility of such an event.

Although coming close, Wallace did not achieve even this degree of success. But his accomplishment was nevertheless remarkable: he received nearly 10,000,000 popular votes—or 13.5 percent of the votes cast—the largest popular vote ever received by a third party candidate in American history. His 46 electoral votes, from the states of Alabama, Arkansas, Georgia, Louisiana, and Mississippi, were more than Republican candidate Barry Goldwater received in the election of 1964. In general, the performance of the American Independent Party was the best by a minor party since Robert La Follette's Progressive Party effort in 1924. Wallace's electoral vote contributed significantly to the election of Richard Nixon by denying Hubert Humphrey, the Democratic candidate, more votes in the electoral college.

After his defeat, Wallace once again returned to the fold of the Democratic Party, winning reelection to the governorship of Alabama. With Wallace no longer at the helm of the American Independent Party, the party lost much of its unity in the 50 states.

The entire character and momentum of Wallace's political effort changed dramatically, however, when, while campaigning in a Maryland shopping center in May 1972, he was shot by Arthur H. Bremer of Milwaukee—an assassination attempt that left Wallace permanently paralyzed from the waist down. Not only did this effectively remove him from being considered a true presidential contender in the Democratic Party, it also forced those thinking of his running as a third party candidate to restructure their entire strategy. Although some supporters of Wallace remained optimistic about his national political future, the realities brought about by his physical condition caused Wallace himself to refuse even a draft movement in behalf of his candidacy.

The remnants of Wallace's old party held a convention in Louisville, Kentucky, in 1972 and, although the delegates wanted to renominate Wallace (he declined in a statement from his hospital bed), they nominated instead John G. Schmitz, former congressman from California's conservative Orange County and a member of the John Birch Society, for president, and Thomas Anderson, a right-wing journalist from Tennessee, for vice president. The party appeared under the shorter title of the American Party in many states. In the November election, Schmitz and Anderson were able to attract only about 1,100,000 votes—only about 1.4 percent of the popular vote, mainly from the West and the South—and no electoral votes.

The 1972 platform had repeated many of the positions taken by the party in the 1968 platform: support for school prayer; opposition to antigun laws; and opposition to the women's movement, abortion, the use of drugs, sex education, deficit spending, and U.S. involvement in international organizations. The platform supported reforms in the social security system, protection of the neighborhood school concept, greater national defense spending, reduction of unemployment and taxes, and a vigorous reassertion of the Monroe Doctrine.

A factional struggle in the party continued after the defeat in November. Anderson and William K. Shearer, the chair of the California section of the party, fought a bitter battle for the chairmanship of the entire party, a battle ultimately won by Anderson, who retained the title American Party for the organization. Shearer, using his California organization, expanded his efforts to a national scale and retained the name American Independent Party for his group. Thus, by 1976 there were two well-defined factions made up of disparate elements of the once-united Wallace organization.

In 1976, the American Independent Party held its convention in Chicago, where it chose as its presidential nominee Lester Maddox, the ex-governor of Georgia, and William Dyke, Republican ex-mayor of Madison, Wisconsin, as its vice presidential candidate. The Maddox supporters at the convention were able to repel a takeover attempt at the convention on the part of a number of well-known conservatives, including Richard Viguerie, who had established himself as an expert mail-order fund-raiser; William Rusher, publisher of the leading conservative magazine *National Review*; and Howard Phillips, a leader of the Conservative Caucus and the former head of the Office of Economic Opportunity. But their efforts to make the party over into a more legitimate and comfortable vehicle for conservatives with a well-established and highly respected philosophical point of view failed when they were unable to attract well-known figures such as Senator Jesse Helms or Representative Philip Crane to run under the party label.

By 1980, the American Independent Party had declined to the point where it was able to run in only eight states. Its candidate in 1980 was John C. Rarick, former Democratic congressman from Louisiana. He was able to muster only 41,268 votes, mostly in the states of Alabama, Louisiana, and California, the home state of his running mate, Eileen M. Shearer.

In 1984, the American Independent Party did not run a candidate, having effectively withdrawn from presidential politics. Yet, in 1988, James Griffin, running under the label of American Independent, received 27,818 votes, 0.03 percent of the vote.

Sources/References

Carlson, Jody. *George C. Wallace and the Politics of Powerlessness: The Wallace Campaigns for the Presidency, 1964–1968*. New Brunswick, NJ: Transaction, 1981.

Congressional Quarterly, Inc. *National Party Conventions, 1831–1984*. Washington, DC: Congressional Quarterly, Inc., 1987.

Frady, Marshall. "The American Independent Party." In Arthur M. Schlesinger, Jr. (Ed.), *History of U.S. Political Parties: Vol. 4, 1945–1972*. New York: Chelsea House, 1973.

Johnson, Donald Bruce (Comp.). *National Party Platforms: Vol. 2, 1960–1976*. Urbana: University of Illinois Press, 1978.

Lipset, Seymour Martin, and Earl Raab. "The Wallace Whitelash." *Trans-Action*, 7 (December), 1969.

Rogin, Michael. "Politics, Emotion, and the Wallace Vote." *British Journal of Sociology*, 20 (March), 1969.

Schapsmeier, Edward L., and Frederick H. Schapsmeier. *Political Parties and Civic Action Groups*. Westport, CT: Greenwood, 1981.

Schoenberger, Robert A., and David R. Segal. "The Ecology of Dissent: The Southern Wallace Vote in 1968." Paper presented at the annual meeting of the American Political Science Association, Los Angeles, September 9, 1970.

Smallwood, Frank. *The Other Candidates: Third Parties in Presidential Elections*. Hanover, NH: University Press of New England, 1983.

White, Theodore. *The Making of the President, 1968*. New York: Atheneum, 1968.

Wicker, Tom. "George Wallace: A Gross and Simple Heart." *Harper's Magazine*, 234 (April), 1967.

American Labor Party

Established in New York City in 1936.

The American Labor Party was composed largely of dissident socialists, some communists, many ardent anticommunists, liberals, and labor leaders seeking to elect Franklin D. Roosevelt to the presidency by wresting electoral support from the Socialist Party candidacy of Norman Thomas. The party hoped also to elect state and local leaders of the liberal-labor persuasion; for example, it endorsed Herbert Lehman, the Democratic candidate for governor of New York.

Among the first leaders of the party were David Dubinsky, president of the International Ladies' Garment Workers' Union, and Emil Rieve, who was head of the American Federation of Hosiery Workers. Dubinsky, who had been born in Brest-Litovsk, Poland, and who had escaped from a prison in Siberia, had come to the United States in 1911. Becoming a cloak cutter and member of the International Ladies' Garment Workers' Union, he rose rapidly in its ranks. He became president of the union in 1932. He was a vice president of the American Federation of Labor, and he was instrumental in linking that union with the Congress of Industrial Organizations. When the AFL disaffiliated CIO unions, Dubinsky resigned. He himself broke with the CIO in 1938 and made the ILGWU an independent organization. He helped to form the Liberal Party in New York in 1944, and remained active in the ILGWU and the labor movement (AFL-CIO) until 1966, when he retired.

The American Labor Party's activities were confined mainly to New York, and, more specifically still, to New York City. The party proved to be especially influential in electing Fiorello La Guardia mayor in 1937 and in 1941, and Vito Marcantonio to Congress in

1938. The party also endorsed and worked for the election of Henry A. Wallace to the presidency in 1948.

The party was soon beset with internal bickering and "ideological warfare," much of it stemming from arguments over appropriate policy positions it should take toward the Soviet Union.

David Dubinsky, Alex Rose, and Professor George Counts (a Columbia University professor of education who became president of the American Federation of Teachers, serving from 1939 to 1942 in that capacity) had come to control the party by the early 1940s. But in 1944, Sidney Hillman defeated Dubinsky for the position of state party chair. Hillman—although himself not a communist—had often been branded as a collaborator with, or a sycophant of, the communists. He had been born in Lithuania and emigrated to the United States in 1907. He began his career as a garment worker and in 1914 became president of the Amalgamated Clothing Workers. He was later one of the founders of the CIO, and he was vice president of that union from 1935 to 1940. But his earlier efforts to bring all trade unionists into affiliation with the American Labor Party had been vehemently opposed on the grounds that this would bring the party under the control of well-known procommunists. His idea was therefore defeated, and, after making concessions to various factions in the party ranks, he became American Labor Party chair. He was joined by such left-wing leaders as Michael Quill (president of the Transport Workers Union, an Irish immigrant who had worked in the subways of New York and who developed a reputation for being a particularly fiery speaker) and Joseph Curran (president of the National Maritime Union). But they themselves later quit the party, reiterating Dubinsky's earlier argument that communists and communist sympathizers had come to dominate it. Dubinsky and other notable members of the left of the time—for example, Adolf Berle (a professor of law at Columbia University who later became a member of Franklin Roosevelt's "brains trust" and who served in a number of diplomatic positions throughout his career) and George Counts—left the American Labor Party and formed the Liberal Party in 1944.

In 1948 the American Labor Party supported Henry A. Wallace (the former cabinet secretary in the Truman administration who had been fired for his alleged support of Soviet foreign policy positions) for the presidency and for the formation of a third party. Wallace, the logical successor to Franklin D. Roosevelt, became a controversial figure because of his efforts to achieve a type of early "detente" with the Soviet Union. Still, Wallace's opposition to the atheism of the Bolsheviks, his deep Christianity, his revulsion at Stalin's treatment of the Kulaks, and his opposition to recognition of the Soviet Union all seemed to suggest that his views were at least ambiguous, and not necessarily procommunist. The American Labor Party was able to muster slightly over 500,000 votes for Wallace in New York, but many members of the party withdrew because of fear and concern over his left-wing candidacy and the party's more radical proposals, for example, doing away with the House Un-American Activities Committee and opposition to the Marshall Plan, the Truman Doctrine, and the draft. Achieving cooperation with the Soviet Union was among the party's most important objectives. Even with the party's support, however, Henry Wallace lost the election in 1948, and Vito Marcantonio— a leading member of the party who had been a candidate for both the Democratic and Republican parties from time to time as well as of the Fusion ticket, and who had been a protégé of Fiorello La Guardia and assistant district attorney—lost the fight for both the mayoralty of New York City and later for his congressional position.

In 1952, Vincent Hallinan of California was supported (as the Progressive Party candidate) by the American Labor Party, but his vote totaled only slightly more than 140,000. By 1954, not having received the requisite 50,000 votes under the law in that year's election, the American Labor Party was removed from the ballot in New York State. It passed out of existence in 1956 as a result of a vote by its New York State committee.

Sources/References

Danish, Max D. *The World of David Dubinsky*. Cleveland: World, 1957.

Dubinsky, David, and A. H. Raskin. *David Dubinsky: A Life with Labor*. New York: Simon & Schuster, 1977.

Josephson, Matthew. *Sidney Hillman: Statesman of American Labor*. Garden City, NY: Doubleday, 1952.

Laslett, John H. M., and Seymour Martin Lipset. *Failure of a Dream*. Garden City, NY: Anchor/Doubleday, 1974.

Shaffer, Alan. *Vito Marcantonio: Radical in Congress*. Syracuse, NY: Syracuse University Press, 1966.

Schapsmeier, Edward L., and Frederick H. Schapsmeier. *Political Parties and Action Groups*. Westport, CT: Greenwood, 1981.

Walton, Richard J. *Henry Wallace, Harry Truman, and the Cold War*. New York: Viking, 1976.

American Party

Established in 1972 in Louisville, Kentucky, by one faction of the divided American Independent Party of Alabama's governor, George Wallace.

Governor Wallace, because of the paralysis resulting from his having been shot while campaigning as a candidate for the Democratic Party's presidential nomination, withdrew from the 1972 presidential campaign. His withdrawal prompted a number of his supporters to call a convention in Louisville, where they nominated John G. Schmitz, a conservative Republican from California, and Thomas J. Anderson, a Tennessee journalist, as candidates for president and vice president, respectively. Mr. Schmitz received 1,099,482 popular votes in 1972.

The party was not to survive intact, however. Two factions emerged after the 1972 election, one in California, which chose to use the label American Independent Party, originally employed by Wallace, and the other in Utah, which continued under the name American Party. The American Independent Party nominated Lester Maddox, former governor of Georgia, as its presidential nominee in 1976; the American Party, meanwhile, nominated Thomas Anderson. The factionalism led to disputes and quarrels among both candidates and parties, and both contenders for the presidency consequently did very poorly. Maddox received only 170,000 votes and Anderson even fewer, with only about 160,000.

Deep internal divisions continued after the 1976 election, and monetary support for the party virtually disappeared. Nevertheless, the American Party nominated Percy L. Greaves, Jr., a lecturer and author, as its candidate in 1980. Greaves's performance at the polls was feeble—he received only 6,647 votes and was on the ballot in only five states. In the state of Kansas, where Frank Shelton ran under the party label (receiving only 1,555 votes), and in Minnesota, where the party fielded electors without specifically named candidates, only 6,139 votes were cast in their support.

The party had generally advocated the concepts of free enterprise, "the Constitution," a free market economy, little or no federal intervention in personal matters, a sound currency, and a return to the gold standard. It also advocated doing away with many of the rights of labor unions and the elimination of minimum-wage laws, and argued for taking a strong position in international affairs.

The party ceased to function as a viable entity after 1980, although, for example, Delmar Dennis, ran in 1984 and 1988 under the label of the American Party and received 3,456 votes in 1988.

Sources/References

Day, Glenn. *Minor Presidential Candidates and Parties of 1988.* Jefferson, NC: McFarland, 1988.
See also references listed under *American Independent Party.*

American Party (Know-Nothings)

Established in New York City in 1849.

The Know-Nothing movement had its origins in New York and grew out of the establishment of various secret societies (such as the Order of the Star Spangled Banner and the Order of United Americans) in the 1840s. At that time, fraternal organizations with membership restricted to native-born Protestants staged elaborate rituals and held secret meetings. Their members were told to answer "I know nothing" when they were queried about activities of the group. Thus, they became known as "Know-Nothings."

In 1852, leadership of the Order of the Star Spangled Banner was taken over in New York by James W. Barker; under him, the Know-Nothings became nationally organized, and by 1854, state and local councils of the organization came together to form a National Council. Recruitment was a state-level function even though requirements for membership were set by the National Council.

The roots of the American (Know-Nothing) Party lay in the soil of "nativism"—a belief that there exists a unique and fundamental *American* tradition that must be preserved and defended, especially against "foreign" influences. This sentiment had asserted itself early on in American history. In the period of the 1830s through 1850s, for example, many citizens of the United States became frightened and alarmed over the influx of "foreigners"—immigrants who were slow to become assimilated into American culture. Especially feared were the Irish and Catholics in general. An idea particularly widely held at the time was that "popery" was seeking absolute political control in the United States. In response to this fear, a flood of antipapal literature swept the country. Many Americans believed that Catholic priests were dictating the political behavior of their parishioners and were requiring them to pay allegiance to the pope in Rome rather than to American political institutions. So enraged had some Americans become that on the night of August 11, 1834, a nativist mob set fire to a Catholic convent in Charlestown, Massachusetts. Police were unable to contain the mob's fury, and the convent as well as a farmhouse owned by the nuns were burned to the ground.

In further response to this fear of Catholicism and foreign immigration, nativists in New York and elsewhere established societies that opposed entry of foreigners, who, they maintained, were among other things a major source of poverty in the United States, a wellspring of moral bankruptcy, a major cause of political corruption, and one of the main causes of high unemployment. Some of the critics went so far as to advocate a 25-year residence qualification for citizenship.

The American Party was based on an elaborate organizational pyramid that followed a federal structure. Consistent with its secret nature, intricate and esoteric rituals and procedures were employed at its meetings. Membership at the level of the first degree, for example, required that a person be of proper age, that he had been born in the United States, that his parents were Protestant, and that, if married, his spouse was not a Catholic. Organizational rules also required that members be willing to use their personal influence to gain support for only native-born Americans who were running for public office and to make every effort to keep foreigners and Roman Catholics out of public office. In addition, members had to renounce allegiance to any other party and to promise to obey American Party principles and objectives. Having achieved the second degree in the ritualistic hierarchy, one could hold office in the Order and also serve as one of the party's nominees for political office. Among instructions to candidates were charges to make every effort to remove foreigners, aliens, and Catholics from political power and never to appoint, under any circumstances, such persons to positions of public trust.

Although united in their opposition to Catholicism, the actual political character of the Know-Nothings varied from one region of the country to another. In California, for example, the party was concerned more with reform than with vehement opposition to immigration in general and to Catholics in particular. Indeed, in the western states generally, Know-Nothings were more fearful of immigration than they were of Catholic influence. In the South, Know-Nothings were concerned mainly with opposition to the Democratic Party. In the border states—Missouri, Tennessee, Kentucky, and Maryland—the impact of the Know-Nothings was greater, and their opposition was vented especially toward Irish Democrats. Yet here they were also the party of union, fearful of the rise of sectionalism and the difficulties likely to follow domination by a sectional party.

But the greatest power of the Know-Nothings lay in the Northeast. In 1854, the Know-Nothings elected 40 members to the New York State Legislature and won the governorship as well. Centers of Know-Nothing strength included Pennsylvania and Delaware; the party's other notable successes included the election of Know-Nothing governors in Rhode Island, New Hampshire, and Connecticut. The state of Massachusetts proved to be the greatest center of their power, however. There the governor, all state officers, and the entire State Senate were members of that movement and there, also, with the exception of one Whig and one Free-Soiler, the State House of Representatives was made up of Know-Nothings.

Other examples of Know-Nothing strength were evidenced by the fact that 48 Know-Nothings served in the 34th Congress of the United States—43 in the House and 5 in the Senate. Eight state legislatures were dominated by members of the organization.

The American Party had thus become almost something of a fad. "Know-Nothing Candy," "Know-Nothing Tea," "Know-Nothing Toothpicks," and various other nativist-oriented literature and paraphernalia flooded the country, very much as bumper stickers and other types of campaign paraphernalia make their frequent appearance during the latter part of the twentieth century. Nativism seemed to be moving toward national triumph, and the successes of the movement suggested the possibility that it could mount a serious threat to the presidency in the election of 1856.

Aside from virulent anti-Catholicism, the Know-Nothings attracted support for other reasons. The major parties were deeply divided on the slavery issue, the Democrats proslavery, the Republicans opposed to it. Thus, many citizens who found themselves either uncommitted or "in between" on this issue were left without a party. The Know-Nothings, professing neutrality on the slavery issue, nevertheless pledged themselves to preserve the Union. Thus, thousands flocked to their support, having in their view nowhere else to go. Adding further frustration and confusion to the voters' decision-making processes was the large number of other political parties in the field. Voters opposed to the Know-Nothings scattered their strength in voting for those parties, not one of which could hope to gain enough support for victory. These factors, coupled with the growth of nativist sentiment in the United States and Know-Nothing willingness to compromise on the slavery question, brought the party to the apex of its success.

But that success was not to last. Although hundreds of Know-Nothing candidates had been elected to state and national office, the movement was essentially unable to implement its policies. Because they were unable to dominate the policy-making process, Know-Nothings found it necessary to compromise and cooperate with the major parties, thus seriously eroding their own principles. As a national movement, moreover, the Know-Nothings themselves eventually fell victim to the slavery issue. In 1855, a party convention adopted a prosouthern stand on the slavery issue, and the antislavery members of the party bolted in anger. The party never fully recovered from this split. This fundamental schism, coupled with the party's minority status among the electorate, its historic and overt encouragement of violence against Catholics and foreigners, the backfiring reaction and ridicule of its secrecy and its rituals, and internal dissension, eventually led to the party's collapse.

In 1856, in the only national nominating convention held by the organization, the Know-Nothings nominated Millard Fillmore, the former Whig president, on the second ballot, as their candidate for president and Andrew Jackson Donelson of Tennessee as vice presidential candidate.

The Know-Nothing platform proclaimed, among other things:

> Americans must rule America; and to this end, native-born citizens should be selected for all state, federal, or municipal offices of government employment, in preference to naturalized citizens—nevertheless,
>
> Persons born of American parents residing temporarily abroad, shall be entitled to all the rights of native-born citizens; but
>
> No person should be selected for political station (whether of native or foreign birth), who recognizes any alliance or obligation of any description to any foreign prince, potentate or power, who refuses to recognize the federal and state constitutions (each within its own sphere), as paramount to all other laws, as rules of particular [political] action.

With respect to the formation of state and territorial constitutions and laws, the platform stated,

> None but those who are citizens of the United States, under the Constitution and laws thereof, and who have a fixed residence in any such territory, are to participate in the formation of the constitution, or in the enactment of laws for said territory or state.

Other planks indicated that a period of 21 years' residence should be required for naturalization, declared opposition to "any union between Church and State," and included comments related to the "reckless and unwise policy of the present administration in the general management of our national affairs."

By 1857, most of the northern members of the Know-Nothing movement had transferred their allegiance to the Republican Party. By 1860, remnants of the party could be found only in the border states. Americans began to reassert their belief that their country should be free and open, and that immigration and Catholicism need not be feared.

Sources/References

"American Ritual: Constitution of the National Council of the United States of North America." In M. W. Cluskey (Ed.), *The Political Text-Book or Encyclopedia*. Philadelphia: James B. Smith, 1860.

Baker, Jean H. *Ambivalent Americans: The Know-Nothing Party in Maryland.* Baltimore: Johns Hopkins University Press, 1977.

Beals, Carleton. *Brass-Knuckle Crusade: The Great Know-Nothing Conspiracy 1820–1860.* New York: Hastings House, 1960.

Billington, Ray A. *The Protestant Crusade, 1800–1860.* New York: Macmillan, 1938.

"A Calm Discussion of the Know Nothing Question." *Southern Literary Messenger,* 20 (September), 1854.

Congressional Quarterly, Inc. *National Party Conventions, 1831–1984.* Washington, DC: Congressional Quarterly, Inc., 1987.

Haynes, George C. "The Causes of Know-Nothing Success in Massachusetts." *American Historical Review,* 3 (October), 1897.

Johnson, Donald Bruce (Comp.). *National Party Platforms: Vol. 1, 1840–1956.* Urbana: University of Illinois Press, 1978.

"Know-Nothingism." *United States Democratic Review,* 37 (June), 1856.

"The Know Nothings." *Brownson's Quarterly Review,* Whole Vol. 17, Being Series III, Vol. 3 (January), 1855.

Mandelbaum, Seymour. *The Social Setting of Intolerance.* Glenview, IL: Scott, Foresman, 1964.

Schapsmeier, Edward L., and Frederick H. Schapsmeier. *Political Parties and Civic Action Groups.* Westport, CT: Greenwood, 1981.

Schlesinger, Arthur M., Jr. (Ed.). *History of U.S. Political Parties: Vol. 1, 1789–1860.* New York: Chelsea House, 1973.

American Vegetarian Party

Established in Chicago in 1948 by 85-year-old Dr. John Maxwell, a naturopathic physician, who owned a vegetarian restaurant in which he reportedly served 500 persons a day, and Symon Gould, editor of *American Vegetarian* magazine.

Vegetarianism is of ancient origin. It was a subject of philosophical debate in ancient Greece for nearly 1,000 years, and the notion that it was morally wrong to eat animals was argued by such eminent philosophers as Pythagoras, Empedocles, Theophrastus, Plutarch, Plotinus, and Prophyry. The idea lay dormant for hundreds of years, but in the twentieth century it has again become a topic of some interest.

Maxwell and Gould ran as candidates for president and vice president, respectively, in 1948. Their primary objective was the promotion of vegetarianism in the United States. Thus, the party platform included a plank dealing with banning the consumption of meat. It opposed the slaughter of livestock, use of liquor and tobacco, use of medicine, and vivisection. The party advocated the idea that farmers should be forbidden from spending more than one-fifth of their efforts in the raising of poultry and cattle for slaughter. It also included calls for government ownership of natural resources and advocated pensions of $100 per month for citizens over 65 years of age.

Although their supporters thought they would probably receive some 5,000,000 votes, the Vegetarian candidates reportedly received the astoundingly low total of only 4 votes in 1948.

Undeterred, the party's candidates continued to run until 1960, when Gould died. The actual number of votes received by the party in any election was invariably insignificant. With the death of Gould, the party likewise ceased to exist. Given the narrowness of the appeal of the single issue on which the party was built, its hopes for any success were doomed from the start.

Sources/References

Barkas, Janet. *The Vegetable Passion: A History of a State of Mind.* New York: Charles Scribner's Sons, 1975.

Dombrowski, Daniel A. *The Philosophy of Vegetarianism.* Amherst: University of Massachusetts Press, 1984.

Dyer, Judith C. *Vegetarianism: An Annotated Bibliography.* Metuchen, NJ: Scarecrow, 1982.

Giehl, Dudley. *Vegetarianism: A Way of Life.* New York: Harper & Row, 1981.

Mason, James B. "Vegetarianism Is a Human Rights Struggle." *Vegetarian Times* (June), 1980.

"Meatless Tuesday," photo of John Maxwell, "Transition" column. *Newsweek* (August 11), 1947, p. 52.

"The Real Dark Horses Start Running for the Presidency," photo of John Maxwell, "People" column. *Life* (April 26), 1948.

Schapsmeier, Edward L., and Frederick H. Schapsmeier. *Political Parties and Civic Action Groups.* Westport, CT: Greenwood, 1981.

Vegetarian Information Service. *Vegetarian Information Sources.* Washington, DC: Vegetarian Information Service, 1980.

"What Is a Vegetarian?" *Vegetarian Messenger and Health Review,* 45 (March), 1948.

Anti-Masonic Party

Established in Batavia, New York, in 1826, in reaction to the death of William Morgan, who was allegedly murdered by a member of the Masonic Lodge.

The Masonic fraternity, an ancient organization founded on the principles of reform, reason, philanthropy, morality, and brotherhood, probably had its modern origins in early eighteenth-century England.

The exact date of its earliest origins remains uncertain. This fraternal organization, whose members believed essentially in the philosophical tenets of the Age of Enlightenment, and among whose members could be counted some of the most prominent, brilliant, and socially oriented citizens of their time, became the object of vilification and defamation. So severe was the reaction of some persons to the existence of the order that a political party—the Anti-Masonic Party—was formed to oppose its alleged antidemocratic views and its so-called secret rituals.

    A single event is usually suggested as responsible for igniting the movement that led to formation of the party, but the roots of the party probably lie more deeply in the soil of hostility and paranoia that was being cultivated at the time. As stated above, the event stimulating formation of the party involved the kidnapping and, allegedly, the ultimate murder, of one William Morgan, a disgruntled Freemason who, it was alleged, in order to avenge an affront by some of his fellow Masons, threatened to write and publish an exposé of the rituals of the organization. Morgan, who had been imprisoned for a minor debt in Batavia, New York, was released on the night of September 11, 1826. He was seen entering a carriage—and from that point was never seen again. About a week after his disappearance, the local newspaper published a story suggesting that Morgan had been kidnapped and murdered by a group of Masons attempting to protect the secrecy of their fraternity. This story touched off a series of vehement reactions: vocal public demands that the kidnappers be brought to justice, scathing condemnations of the Masonic order, a New York State legislative inquiry, and finally the formation of the Anti-Masonic Party.

    But the rise of the Anti-Masonic Party can be traced to other sources as well. There had long existed in the United States a latent general hostility toward so-called secret societies. Frontiersmen in particular considered them undemocratic and un-American. Moreover, many shopkeepers, ministers, politicians, and businessmen saw it to their advantage to disassociate themselves from the fraternity, even though they had never become members. Some churches prohibited Masons from joining their congregations, and those ministers who were found to be Masons were often expelled. So intense had the fear of secret societies become that such nationally prominent figures as ex-President John Quincy Adams and Supreme Court Justice Joseph Story attempted to force Harvard College to banish Phi Beta Kappa, the scholastic society, from its campus.

    The American historian Richard Hofstadter has referred to "the paranoid style in American politics." This paranoid style involves an unreasonable and irrational fear that some ill-defined group is intent on threatening and ultimately destroying basic American traditions, values, and institutions. In this sense, then, the rise of anti-Masonry may fall into the same category as the phenomena that came to be called McCarthyism of the 1950s, the Red Scare of the 1920s, and the Know-Nothing movement of the 1820s. Persons characterized by this paranoid style are said to possess intense fears of the unknown, of the "foreign," of those things they vaguely regard as "un-American," and about which, because of their ignorance, they express deep suspicion. Such fears are based on sociopsychological factors not yet fully understood. The history and organizational structure of Freemasonry fit well into the general classification of those groups held suspect by the paranoid. The Morgan incident served only to touch off these fears.

Over a year after the disappearance of Morgan, a corpse was discovered on the shore of Lake Ontario. A coroner's jury ruled that the person had died by accidental drowning. However, a committee organized by Thurlow Weed, editor of the *Albany Evening Journal*, held another, unofficial inquest and came to the conclusion that the remains were none other than those of William Morgan—although it was later discovered that the body was in fact that of a Canadian. This contrived inquest and false identification were enough to make it possible for Weed to organize an Anti-Masonic Party in Ontario County, New York, in 1827. These efforts proved successful enough to garner the party 4 senate seats and 17 assembly seats in the New York Legislature in 1828. Based on its success in New York, the party grew into a national entity, largely attracting to its ranks poor farmers, laborers, evangelical Christians, and others to whom a sense of egalitarianism had wide appeal. Within months, the party had gathered enough adherents to enable it to hold a national nominating convention in 1830.

The Anti-Masonic Party thus became the *first* American political party to hold a convention to nominate candidates for national office. Party caucuses and state legislatures had been the usual devices used to nominate national candidates; the convention had been used only on state and local levels. The Anti-Masonic Party also had the distinction of being the first party to adopt an "address to the people," a written statement that was to become the precursor to the party platform as we now know it, and also established a correspondence committee that laid the framework for national campaign organizations of parties to follow.

Attendance at the Philadelphia convention was lower than had been anticipated; fewer than 100 delegates appeared. Because of the low turnout, no nominations for president or vice president were made. A declaration of principles was adopted, however, and a call for a second convention, this one for September 1831, was issued. The second convention took place in Baltimore.

The party had great difficulty in finding a presidential candidate. Although an attempt was made to induce ex-President John Adams to run as the party's nominee, he did not wish to seek office again, despite his intense opposition to Masonry. Associate Supreme Court Justice John McLean, John Marshall, and John C. Calhoun were also considered.

The Anti-Masons finally turned to William Wirt, a Pennsylvanian who had formerly served as attorney general of the United States. Wirt's nomination was ironic—he had himself been a Mason and had never renounced his membership in the order. Wirt had also proclaimed that he would not denounce other Masons or attempt to drive them from office. The party was thus split from the start; yet, since it was apparent they had no choice, many delegates reluctantly voted for Wirt. This reluctance notwithstanding, he was a first-ballot winner and nearly the unanimous choice of the delegates, receiving 108 of 111 votes cast. Wirt's letter of acceptance of the nomination was apparently prepared in advance; after a strong defense of Masonry, he declared that if the delegates felt they had nominated him without full understanding of his position on Masonry, they could feel free to select someone else. Amos Ellmaker of Pennsylvania was chosen as the party's vice presidential nominee.

In its "address to the people," the party made many appeals to the paranoia of the times. A few excerpts follow.

> The existence of secret and affiliated societies is hostile to one of the principal defences of liberty,—free discussion,—and can subserve no purpose of utility in a free government. . . .
>
> . . . the organization of the anti-masonic party is founded upon the most satisfactory and undeniable evidence, that the masonic institution is dangerous to the liberties, and subversive of the laws of the country. . . .
>
> . . . where evils of this nature are found existing in a free government, holding, by means of a secret combination, a majority of the civil, judicial, and military offices in the country, there are but two modes of redressing the grievance—either by revolution, or by an appeal to the ballot boxes.
>
> . . . the anti-masonic party, in choosing the latter remedy, have taken up the peaceful and legitimate weapons of freemen, and that they ought never to lay them down in this cause, until the liberty of the press, the liberty of speech, equal rights, and an entire overthrow of masonic usurpations, are fully and completely achieved.

Wirt proved to be a weak candidate in 1832. Receiving less than 8 percent of the vote, and carrying only Vermont's seven electoral votes, he lost overwhelmingly to Henry Clay and Andrew Jackson, the candidates of the two major parties. He received less than 8 percent of the popular votes. The Anti-Masonic Party never fully recovered from this defeat. It soon disappeared as an influence in national party politics, although its lingering impact was felt in some states, notably Vermont. In addition, the Anti-Masons were occasionally able to act as the determining influence in the outcome of close elections, and, with the help of the Whigs, were able to elect an Anti-Mason governor of Pennsylvania in 1835, where they also controlled the lower house of the state legislature. In those parts of New England where absolute majorities were needed to elect candidates, Anti-Masons were able to prevent either major party from receiving a majority of the votes cast; election outcomes were therefore sometimes delayed for months.

These limited successes aside, the Anti-Masonic Party had been dealt its death blow in the election of 1832. The anti-Masonic movement had by that time already lost much of its impetus. Many fraternities and other "secret societies" had disbanded; others began to be viewed in a more favorable light. Emphasis was being placed on other areas of politics; it was characteristic that some of the leading Anti-Masonic journals were soon attacking Democrats as the main villains. In 1836, the Anti-Masonic Party endorsed William Henry Harrison, the Whig candidate, and within a short time most of those who had been Anti-Masons entered into the ranks of that organization. Thus, the Anti-Masonic Party died almost as quickly as it had appeared.

Sources/References

Congressional Quarterly, Inc. *National Party Conventions, 1831–1984*. Washington, DC: Congressional Quarterly, Inc., 1987.

Hesseltine, William B. *Third Party Movements in the United States*. Princeton, NJ: D. Van Nostrand, 1962.

Holt, Michael F. "The Antimasonic and Know Nothing Parties." In Arthur M. Schlesinger, Jr. (Ed.), *History of U.S. Political Parties: Vol. 1, 1789–1860*. New York: Chelsea House, 1973.

Johnson, Donald Bruce (Comp.). *National Party Platforms: Vol. 1, 1840–1956*. Urbana: University of Illinois Press, 1978.

McCarthy, Charles. "The AntiMasonic Party: A Study of Political Antimasonry in the United States, 1827–1840." In *Annual Report of the American Historical Association for the Year 1902* (Vol. 1). Washington, DC: U.S. Government Printing Office, 1903.

Ratner, Lorman. *Antimasonry: The Crusade and the Party*. Englewood Cliffs, NJ: Prentice-Hall, 1969.

Vaughn, William Preston. *The Antimasonic Party in the United States, 1826–1843*. Lexington: University Press of Kentucky, 1983.

Anti-Monopoly Party

Established in Chicago in 1884 by the Anti-Monopoly Organization of the United States.

Establishment of this party can be linked to a number of state parties formed in reaction to the so-called economic Panic of 1873 and to the Granger movement—the latter consisting of farmers and debtors who were angrily reacting to the economic domination and exploitation being perpetrated by the railroads, banks, and big business interests of the time.

The national convention of the Anti-Monopoly Party was held on May 14, 1884, in Chicago. Attendance was not impressive; indeed, its Platform Committee was composed of delegations from only 17 states and the District of Columbia.

The party's platform advocated mutual cooperation between labor and capital, that corporations be placed under legal regulations, and that public expenditures be reduced. It urged the national government to increase significantly its regulation of commerce among the various states and to break the power of monopolies. To that end, it advocated the establishment of bureaus of labor statistics, the use of arbitration in labor disputes, enforcement of the national eight-hour law, a graduated income tax, passage of an interstate commerce law, direct election of senators, making illegal the importation of foreign contract labor, the elimination of grants of public lands to corporations, and doing away with discrimination against agriculture.

Benjamin F. Butler of Massachusetts was nominated as the party's presidential candidate. General Absolom M. West of Mississippi was selected as its vice presidential nominee. Interestingly, the Greenback Party also nominated Butler and West as its national candidates.

Benjamin Butler was one of the most controversial men of his time. Born in Deerfield, New Hampshire, in 1818, he was described as a homely child; he had a deformity of the eyelids and otherwise allegedly unpleasant physical features. These physical handicaps, coupled with several other behavioral idiosyncrasies that emerged during his political career, plagued him virtually all of his life. It is said that he was often attacked vehemently only because of his allegedly unattractive facial features.

Butler's political reputation rested on his widely recognized great political ability, the largely unprincipled pursuit of his goals, and his almost studied proclivity to arouse the antagonisms of others and hence to stimulate controversy. It is said that he delighted in conflict. His memory was reported to be prodigious and his intellect capacious. He was also reputed to be both tremendously egotistical and delightfully humorous. He began his political career as a Democrat (but also as a strong Unionist), became a Republican, later returned to the Democratic Party, and then ran as the presidential candidate of the Anti-Monopoly and Greenback parties.

Butler practiced law in Lowell and in Boston. As a lawyer, he was willing to work for those who could not afford his services. He was elected to the Massachusetts State Legislature in 1852 and 1858, but was defeated in his race for the governorship in 1859–1860. He was elected governor 24 years later, after seven more attempts to win that office.

He was active as a military officer during the Civil War in Washington, D.C., in Maryland, and especially in New Orleans. There he was military governor and the object of intense vilification and sometimes even physical attacks because of his highly unpopular policies and activities. He was eventually removed from his position there and, ultimately, from his military command in 1864.

He continued his career in politics, however, serving from 1867 to 1875 in Congress as one of the most radical of Republicans. He helped to conduct the impeachment of President Andrew Johnson and ardently advocated the policies of Reconstruction. From 1877 to 1879, he was an independent Greenback member of Congress. He was elected *as* a Greenback in 1882. After his presidential nomination in 1884, he lost to Grover Cleveland, receiving only 175,066 votes, or 1.8 percent of the popular vote. Undoubtedly, he would have received even fewer votes had the Greenbackers not supported him. After the election, many of his supporters switched their allegiance to the Populist Party.

Although Butler would never live to see their enactment, many of the policies and principles he advocated through his political efforts were eventually adopted by the major political parties and have long since become the law of the land.

Sources/References

Bland, T. A. *Life of Benjamin F. Butler*. Boston: Lee & Shepard, 1879.

Butler, Benjamin F. *Butler's Book*. Boston: A. M. Thayer, 1892.

Dewitt, David Miller. *Impeachment and Trial of Andrew Johnson*. New York: Macmillan, 1903.

Nash, Howard P., Jr. *Stormy Petrel: The Life and Times of Benjamin F. Butler, 1818–1893*. Rutherford, NJ: Fairleigh Dickinson University Press, 1969.

Parton, James. *General Butler in New Orleans*. New York: Mason Brothers, 1864.

Rhodes, James Ford. *History of the United States*. New York: Macmillan, 1899–1919.

Schapsmeier, Edward L., and Frederick H. Schapsmeier. *Political Parties and Civic Action Groups*. Westport, CT: Greenwood, 1981.

Stanwood, Edward. *A History of the Presidency from 1788 to 1897* (Vol. 1). Boston: Houghton Mifflin, 1892, 1896, 1898, 1920, 1924.

Trefousse, Hans L. *Ben Butler: The South Called Him BEAST*. New York: Octagon, 1974.

Black Panther Party

Established in Oakland, California, in 1966 by Bobby Seale and Huey P. Newton. Others who were to become prominent in the party were

Eldridge Cleaver, Bobby Rush, Elaine Brown, Elmer Pratt, Raymond Hewitt, and Johnny Spain.

From its inception, the Black Panther Party was a militant, black nationalist organization replete with paramilitary infrastructure, uniforms, and a revolutionary rationale that justified the use of violence to accomplish its objectives. The primary aims of the party included liberation of blacks from what the party labeled their "colonial status" in American capitalist society. The party's ideology rested on a platform adopted largely from the works of Karl Marx, Vladimir Lenin, Mao Zedong, and Frantz Fanon. The party also derived much of its ideological foundation from the work and thought of Malcolm X. Apropos of its Marxist-military organization, its leaders were given such titles as supreme commander, chairman, minister of defense, minister of information, chief of staff, field marshal, minister of education, minister of finance, minister of justice, minister of foreign affairs, and prime minister.

Although the party at various times had organizational operations in some 15 states, it can be said to have represented only a very small fraction of the black community in the United States. Its militancy and armed confrontations with police in such communities as Oakland, Chicago, Los Angeles, and New York City were viewed by many mainstream black civil rights leaders as counterproductive and harmful generally to attempts by blacks to achieve a greater share of civil rights. Violent confrontations between party members and the police led to the death of party leaders Fred Hampton and Mark Clark in Chicago, and Bobby Hutton in Oakland. Moreover, both Huey Newton and Eldridge Cleaver were indicted for allegedly shooting several police officers, although the charges were ultimately dropped. Bobby Seale, charged as one of the "Chicago Seven" in disrupting the 1968 Democratic Convention, was convicted, but the conviction was later overturned, and, later still, after being charged with murder as a codefendant in a Connecticut case, he was acquitted in 1971. In 1971, also, 13 Panthers were accused of conspiring to bomb public places, but they, too, were eventually acquitted. These mistrials and acquittals were viewed by many as good evidence that the Black Panthers were in fact being unduly harassed by police and the court system in the United States. Adding to this notion was the fact that Fred Hampton and another Panther were shot—apparently without provocation—in their beds in Chicago during a police raid. Huey Newton later fled to Cuba after being charged with another shooting; he eventually returned to the United States and then took over leadership of the Black Panther Party.

Eldridge Cleaver ran for president of the United States as the candidate of the Peace and Freedom Party (q.v.) in 1968. In 1973, he went to Algeria to avoid imprisonment for a parole violation, but in 1975 he voluntarily returned to the United States to face the charges against him. In 1972, four members of the Black Panther party hijacked a Delta Airlines plane and forced its pilot to fly to Algeria, demanding $1 million in ransom money.

In 1973, the Black Panther Party renounced the use of guns and violence. Bobby Seale in that year ran unsuccessfully for the office of mayor of Oakland, California. The party began to emphasize programs such as providing free breakfasts for schoolchildren and health clinics, which had been among Panther practices earlier in the party's development. Moreover, party members from then on had to accept 26 rules of discipline involving matters ranging from polite speech and payment for anything damaged by a member to not taking liberties with women and no ill treatment of any captives the party might take.

Statements made by the party during its early stages of development emphasized its perceptions of the alleged racist nature of the California legislature, the federal government's oppression of black people, the necessity of using guns to achieve the party's goals, the role of the party as a vanguard group required to exercise prolonged resistance to the state, the need for suffering and bloodshed, and the need for a class struggle and for revolution. The party also emphasized the need for black people to arm themselves and had advocated before the legislature the constitutional right to keep and bear arms; the use of guerrilla tactics; and the need to manufacture bombs, grenades, and other types of firearms. There were frequent references to Marx, Lenin, Stalin, Mao, Kim Il Sung, Ho Chi Minh, and other major Marxist and communist revolutionary figures.

The Black Panthers developed relationships with many left-wing and radical groups in the United States, ranging from the Communist Party of the United States (q.v.), the Socialist Workers Party (q.v.), the Progressive Labor Party, and Students for a Democratic Society to the "Red Guards" organization in San Francisco, the Young Lords (a Latino revolutionary group working in Chicago), and the American Servicemen's Union.

The party had also established relationships with international groups. For example, the organization had communication with the Association of Democratic Jurists of North Korea, the Korean Democratic Lawyers Association, the Committee for the Peaceful Unification of the Fatherland in North Korea, the Palestine National Liberation Movement, the French Federation of Black African Students, the German Socialist Students' League, the South Vietnam People's Committee for Solidarity with the American People, and the Solidarity Committee for Third World People's Liberation Struggle in

Scandinavia, as well as groups in Cuba, Tanzania, Mozambique, Angola, South Africa, and elsewhere. The party also professed anti-Zionist views, denouncing Israel and maintaining a position of support for the Al Fatah, the Arab guerrilla organization, and for Yasser Arafat.

On August 22, 1989, Huey P. Newton, one of the cofounders of the Black Panther Party, was shot to death in a west Oakland, California, neighborhood. He had been released from San Quentin Prison in spring 1989. Huey Newton was born in Monroe, Louisiana, and was named after the populist governor of that state, Huey Long. Most of his life was spent in Oakland, and it was at Merritt College there that he met Bobby Seale, with whom he founded the Black Panthers on October 22, 1966.

It was the Black Panther Party that was largely responsible for placing the word *pig* into the American vernacular as a reference to the police. Some blacks regarded Newton and the Panthers as the most significant force ever to strike back at the white power structure; others regarded them as nothing more than urban terrorists. In any event, they were deemed important enough that the Federal Bureau of Investigation, then led by J. Edgar Hoover, led a secret operation against the Panthers to discredit their movement.

The Black Panther Party is no longer a significant force in American politics, but it is important to emphasize that the Panthers were an expression of the widespread anger and concern of thousands of black Americans over questions related to police brutality and the inability of blacks to gain significant social and political power.

It should also be noted that the Black Panther Party described here is not the same as the Lowndes County (Alabama) Freedom Organization (q.v.), which also was once known as the Black Panther Party.

Sources/References

Cleaver, Eldridge. *Soul on Ice*. New York: McGraw-Hill, 1967.

Heath, G. Louis (Ed.). *The Black Panther Leaders Speak*. Metuchen, NJ: Scarecrow, 1976.

_____ (Ed.). *Off the Pigs! The History and Literature of the Black Panther Party*. Metuchen, NJ: Scarecrow, 1976.

Marine, Gene. *The Black Panthers*. New York: New American Library, 1969.

Newton, Huey P. *To Die for the People: The Writings of Huey P. Newton*. New York: Random House, 1972.

San Francisco Chronicle. August 23, 1989.

Schanche, Don A. *The Panther Paradox: A Liberal's Dilemma*. New York: David McKay, 1970.

Schapsmeier, Edward L., and Frederick H. Schapsmeier. *Political Parties and Civic Action Groups.* Westport, CT: Greenwood, 1981.

Christian Nationalist Party

Established in 1947 in Eureka Springs, Arkansas, by the Reverend Gerald Lyman Kenneth Smith, a minister who captivated thousands of Americans through his spellbinding, vehemently racist, and anti-Semitic speeches and magazine.

The Christian Nationalist Party was a by-product of the Christian Nationalist Crusade, a fervently fundamentalist religious movement composed of the Christian Youth for America, the Christian Veterans of America, the Christian Veterans Intelligence Service, the Salt Lake City Pro-American Vigilantes, and a group led by the Reverend Arthur Terminiello, the "Father Coughlin of the South." Smith also used "front groups" to advance his cause. Examples include the Patriotic Tract Society, Midwestern Political Survey Institute, the Committee of California Pastors, and the Radio Petition Committee.

Born in a small Wisconsin town, himself the son of a minister, Smith eventually attended Valparaiso University, where one of his majors was drama. For a time, Smith provided his services to the Disciples of Christ in Indiana and later in King's Highway Christian Church of Shreveport, Louisiana.

The Reverend Smith's entry into politics came in 1933, when he became a member of the Silver Shirts—also known as the Christian American Patriots—an organization that had been founded by William Dudley Pelley in Asheville, North Carolina. This group once claimed as many as two million members. Smith later joined forces with Dr. Francis E. Townsend (of Townsend Plan fame) and with father Charles E. Coughlin, the anti-Semitic priest whose radio broadcasts from Royal Oak, Michigan, influenced millions of Americans during the middle and late 1930s and after the beginning of World War II. Forming the Committee of One Million, Smith attempted to forge lower- and middle-class Americans into an extremist right-wing movement similar to what Hitler was able to develop in Germany.

Smith ran for president in 1944, but received only 1,780 votes. After his defeat, he continued to attack Negroes and Jews and turned his wrath against the United Nations and internationalists in general, who he claimed were under the influence of "international Jewry."

Running as the presidential candidate of the Christian Nationalist Party in 1948 (with Henry A. Romer as his vice presidential running mate), he advocated the deportation of Jews, the legal segregation of Negroes and their return to Africa, the closure of the United Nations (which he labeled the "Jew-N" and the "Jew-nited Nations"), and total opposition to communism, which he insisted was organized by Jews. He attacked the severe treatment given the defeated Germans, and supported aid to the elderly and infirm, increased veterans benefits, and subsidies to farmers. In the 1948 election, he received only 42 votes.

In 1952, the Christian Nationalist Party nominated General Douglas MacArthur for president (although MacArthur rejected its support) and supported Jack B. Tenney of California as its vice presidential candidate (Tenney had been former chairman of the "Tenney Committee" in California, a group organized to look into un-American activities). Smith during that year supported the Protestant fundamentalist campaign to "Stop Ike-the-Kike," viciously attacking General Dwight D. Eisenhower with his anti-Semitic outbursts.

The campaign of 1952 brought Smith to his most active involvement in politics. He vehemently attacked both Democrats and Republicans—maligning the characters of Dwight Eisenhower, Thomas E. Dewey, Averell Harriman, Alben Barkley, Richard Russell, Adlai Stevenson, and Estes Kefauver. But the Christian Nationalist Party ticket received only 13,883 popular votes in 1952.

Smith again ran for the presidency in 1956, this time choosing Charles F. Robertson of California as his running mate. The ticket received an incredibly modest total of eight votes! Although the party essentially ceased to exist after this election, Smith's virulent attacks continued through his writings and lectures.

Sources/References

De Lorme, Roland L., and Raymond G. McInnis. *Antidemocratic Trends in Twentieth-Century America*. Reading, MA: Addison-Wesley, 1969, pp. 188–192.

Roy, Ralph Lord. *Apostles of Discord*. Boston: Beacon, 1953.

Schapsmeier, Edward L., and Frederick H. Schapsmeier. *Political Parties and Civic Action Groups*. Westport, CT: Greenwood, 1981.

Smith, Gerald L. K. "We Take Our Stand." Editorial from *The Cross and the Flag* (April 1942), *Congressional Record*, 88 (March 26), 1942.

Thayer, George. *The Farther Shores of Politics*. New York: Simon & Schuster, 1967.

Christian Party

Established in Asheville, North Carolina, in 1936 by William Dudley Pelley.

Born in New England, the son of a Methodist minister, Pelley was catapulted to national attention by way of a magazine article in which Pelley alleged that his spirit had at one time left his body and had carried on communication with the dead. But Pelley's even greater notoriety came as a result of his open racism and his practice of what came to be known as the "ministry of hate." Pelley bombarded the country with a barrage of anti-Semitic, racist, and antidemocratic tracts and speeches.

Pelley moved to Asheville, North Carolina, in 1932, where he opened Galahad College—an institution established to further what he called "Christian economics." In 1933 he established an organization known as the Silver Shirts, or the Christian American Patriots, whose members' costumes included silver shirts, blue corduroy trousers, and gold stockings. Versions of this organization were founded throughout the United States. Pelley also published a weekly magazine called *Liberation.*

The objective of the Christian Party, according to Pelley, was to help extricate the nation from the Great Depression. The major need of the country, he claimed, was a dictatorial president who would take the strong measures necessary to lead the country back to prosperity. To do this, Pelley said, he would engage in the traditional "Robin Hood approach"—take from the rich and give to the poor. He ran as the presidential candidate of the party with the slogan "For Christ and the Constitution." His running mate was Willard W. Kemp.

Pelley's anti-Semitism was evidenced in his comments during the campaign. He wanted to "defranchise" all Jews and prohibit them from owning property in the United States unless a licensing system specifically designed for that purpose was established. He also had as a goal limiting their numbers in various professions to a proportion that would reflect their actual numbers in the American population as a whole. His party's platform advocated redistribution of wealth and racial segregation, and was generally pro-Nazi in its point of view. In the 1936 election, Pelley received 1,598 votes.

Pelley was later placed in federal prison on a sedition charge. He was released in 1950. He never achieved his objective of winning a campaign for national office. The Silver Shirt organization came to an end. After World War II, Pelley continued to publish fanatical tracts. He died in 1965.

Sources/References

Roy, Ralph Lord. *Apostles of Discord.* Boston: Beacon, 1953.

Schapsmeier, Edward L., and Frederick H. Schapsmeier. *Political Parties and Civic Action Groups.* Westport, CT: Greenwood, 1981.

Thayer, George. *The Farther Shores of Politics*. New York: Simon & Schuster, 1967.

Citizens' Party

Founded in 1979 in Washington, D.C., by Barry Commoner—a professor of environmental science at Washington University in St. Louis, Missouri—and by dissident liberals in reaction to what they perceived to be failures in Jimmy Carter's presidency.

The Citizens' Party advocated left-wing, liberal positions focused mainly on environmentalist and populist-oriented programs that members hoped would lead to what they termed "economic democracy." The attitude of the founders of the party—who included such persons as Maggie Kuhn of the Gray Panthers; Archibald Gillies, former chairman of the John Hay Whitney Foundation; Harriet Barlow, of the Institute for Local Self-Reliance; Adam Hochschild, publisher of *Mother Jones* magazine; and Don Rose, the former manager of Jane Byrne's mayoral campaign in Chicago—was that the Democrats and Republicans—given their traditional support of capitalism and the prevailing economic status quo—were both unwilling and unable to deal with the critical difficulties being faced by the country. The major parties were perceived as being fearful of discussing such issues as the dangers of nuclear power and the need for a significant decrease in defense spending so that monies used for these purposes could be allocated for more urgent social programs domestically.

Commoner was—and perhaps continues to be—one of the best-known environmentalists of the last 20 years. In addition to serving as a university professor, Commoner had worked as an editor for *Science Illustrated* magazine, for the Scientists' Institute for Public Information, and for the American Association for the Advancement of Science, and had run the Center for the Biology of Natural Systems. Born in Brooklyn, Commoner had received his undergraduate training at Columbia University and his doctorate from Harvard. His view of politics embraced the idea that as a scientist he had a public responsibility, particularly with respect to social and political issues.

The party advocated, among other goals, the nationalization of railroads, the restructuring of oil companies to public utility status, the freezing of oil prices, passage of the Equal Rights Amendment, guaranteed full employment, drastic reductions in defense spending, establishment of a national health insurance program for all Americans, creation of worker-management operations in the automobile industry, federal government policies to seek alternatives to then current nuclear energy policy, and price controls on such things as food, fuel, and housing. Perhaps the major argument of the party was that the United States was controlled by its major industrial corporations and that the decisions of these institutions, and not those of the common people, dominated American affairs.

The Citizens' Party convention in Cleveland did not actually adopt a platform; proposals presented at the convention reportedly numbered some 300 items, a list largely irreducible to a manageable platform, as platforms are usually understood. Units of the party organization on the state level thus became more or less responsible for delineating their own briefer versions of the list of goals and for establishing their own "platforms."

Barry Commoner was nominated as the party's presidential candidate in 1980. Commoner's running mate was LaDonna Harris, wife of former Oklahoma Senator Fred Harris, who himself later ran as a presidential candidate under the slogan of "new populism." Harris, who was a leading feminist and a Comanche Indian, labeled herself as "a woman of color." She had already established a reputation for herself as an activist in behalf of Native American, civil rights, and feminist causes. She had helped found the National Women's Political Caucus and had served on the board of the National Organization for Women. She was president of the Americans for Indian Opportunity. Although she had been a lifelong Democrat, she too had become disillusioned with the party and thus sought political alternatives to the traditional party organizations.

The Citizens' Party was able to muster enough support to enable it to qualify for the ballot in 29 states and the District of Columbia. The major campaign activities of the party were expended in California, Illinois, Michigan, New York, and Pennsylvania, states with large electoral votes and a large working-class element to whom the candidates presumably could appeal best. In particular, the party attempted to gain the support of environmental and antinuclear activists.

The Citizens' Party also ran 22 other candidates, including two for the Senate and seven for the House of Representatives. Still, the Citizens' Party candidates received only 234,294 votes in the election—less than 1 percent. They received no electoral votes.

Commoner often charged that his campaign was largely ignored by the major news media mainly because the media felt that he was not a serious candidate and that he was running merely to attract attention to certain issues. The media, Commoner argued, were mainly concerned with the possibility of a candidate's winning the election; if they perceived victory as unlikely, coverage either was not extended or was very limited.

In 1984, the party selected feminist Sonia Johnson of Virginia as its presidential nominee and Richard J. Walton of Rhode Island as her vice presidential running mate. Johnson had received national press coverage in 1979 when she was excommunicated from the Mormon church for her outspoken support of the Equal Rights Amendment. She had also received attention for her 37-day fast in 1982, when she used this tactic as a means to get the Illinois State Legislature to pass the ERA. In 1984, the party received only 72,200 votes, some 0.1 percent of the total votes cast.

Sources/References

Congressional Quarterly, Inc. *National Party Conventions, 1831–1984.* Washington, DC: Congressional Quarterly, Inc., 1987.

New York Times. October 27, 1980.

San Francisco Chronicle. August 2, 1979; November 13, 1979; April 14, 1980.

Schapsmeier, Edward L., and Frederick H. Schapsmeier. *Political Parties and Civic Action Groups.* Westport, CT: Greenwood, 1981.

Smallwood, Frank. *The Other Candidates: Third Parties in Presidential Elections.* Hanover, NH: University Press of New England, 1983.

"The Third Party Challengers." *Newsweek* (October 20), 1980.

von Hoffman, Nicholas. "The Third Man Theme." *New York Times Magazine* (September 28), 1980.

Communist Party of the United States of America (CPUSA)

Born as two parties in 1919 as a result of factional divisions among members of the Socialist Party.

One "party" was established in Chicago under the leadership of John Reed and Benjamin Gitlow. This group labeled itself the Communist Labor Party (CLP) and based its organizational structure on the Soviet model of the Communist Party. The first executive secretary of the Communist Labor Party was Alfred Wagenhaupt. Cleveland, Ohio, was chosen as its national headquarters.

The other "party" meeting in Chicago—the city that became its national headquarters—labeled itself the Communist Party of America. It was the larger of the two factions. It chose as its national secretary Louis C. Fraina. This group had been organized under the auspices of the Russian Federation (one of the foreign-language federations of the Socialist Party) and of elements of the Michigan Socialist Party.

The two factions had early on differed over the subject of working with members of the Socialist Party and with trade and labor unions—the CLP favoring such interaction and the CPA opposing it. Both groups, however, followed the tenets of the philosophy of Karl Marx and Friedrich Engels and the revolutionary Bolshevik ideology as preached by Vladimir Lenin and Leon Trotsky. Both factions also joined the Communist International (Comintern).

Both parties were almost immediately subjected to harassment by agents of A. Mitchell Palmer, then attorney general of the United States. Local authorities also intervened against the two groups. Because of these investigations, significant reductions in party membership occurred. Indeed, in 1920 the Communists went underground. But based on the urging of the Third International (Comintern), the Communists in December of 1921 established the Workers Party of America—a legally recognized organization. It thus qualified for the ballot. The party then emerged in 1923.

The party nominated William Z. Foster for president and Benjamin Gitlow for vice president in the 1924 presidential election. Among its platform resolutions were calls for the nationalization of U.S. industry, diplomatic recognition of the Soviet Union, government aid for the unemployed, an end to the policies of U.S. "imperialism," and, in general, the establishment of a Communist social system in the United States. The platform proclaimed:

> There is only one way in which the exploitation of the workers and farmers of this country can be ended. That is through the workers organizing their mass power, ending the capitalist dictatorship and establishing the Workers' and Farmers' Government.
> In place of the capitalist dictatorship there must be established the rule of the workers. The governmental power must be used in the interest of the workers and farmers as it is now used by the capitalist dictatorship in the interest of the capitalist class.
> The Russian workers and peasants have established their rule in the form of the Soviet government and are using their power against the capitalists and for themselves—to build a Communist social system which will give the workers and farmers the fruits of their toil.

The platform devoted sections to discussing a "farmer-labor party"; industrial nationalization; unemployment compensation; doing away with labor injunctions, militarism, and imperialism; and the recognition of the Workers and Peasants' Government of Russia, among other points.

Throughout the 1920s, the Communists attempted to expand their influence by working through the farmer-labor movement, but they met with little success. Pursuit of their objectives was impeded by most farmer-labor leaders and especially by such Progressives as Robert M. La Follette of Wisconsin. Strikes instigated by Communists among textile and garment workers during the middle and latter years of the decade of the 1920s also led to decreased support from workers throughout the labor movement. The defections from the Workers (Communist) Party were evidenced by the fact that it was able to attract the support of only 36,386 voters in the 1924 election.

In 1928, the party again ran the same two candidates as it had in 1924. During this so-called Third Period of Communist Party development the party enunciated the theory of "social fascism." Labor leaders and socialists were attacked as being more dangerous than the fascists themselves, and Communist leaders made a strong appeal to American Negroes, advocating that they establish their own national republic in the South. In an extraordinarily long platform, the party discoursed on an almost incredible array of real and alleged social, political, and economic ills. The platform again attacked the "concentration of capital" and what it referred to as "trustification." It treated the subjects of wealth, poverty, imperialism, and the major political parties. It particularly attacked the Socialist Party, which, it said, "still claims to be a working-class party," but which "is in fact a party of the lower middle class. Its leadership has become part of the bureaucracy of the A.F. of L." It excoriated Norman Thomas by stating:

> The presidential candidate of the Socialist Party. . . is the worst kind of pacifist, a typical preacher, who performs the greatest service for American imperialism by creating illusions about the League of Nations, about the possibility of preventing wars by peaceful means. . . . The Socialist Party of today is for the protection of capitalist law and order, is against revolution, is against the working-class government of Soviet Russia, and supports every measure of the A.F. of L. bureaucracy for class collaboration.

Lauding the Soviet Union, the platform suggested that it was the only nation in which workers had gained control over their own destiny. It proclaimed:

> Forward to a Workers' and Farmers' Government! Forward by means of relentless class struggle! The Workers (Communist) Party is the party of the class struggle. It is the deadly enemy of capitalist society. It fights for the complete unity of the working class, for the united struggle of native-born, foreign-born, and Negro workers against the common enemy: trustified capital.

But these pronouncements seemed only to isolate the Communists more, and, even though membership in the party had increased, the actual influence of the Communists remained limited. Thus, in the 1928 election, the party, running Foster and Gitlow, received fewer than 50,000 votes.

The greatest electoral success achieved by the Communists was in 1932. In that election, the party put forth William Z. Foster as its presidential candidate and selected James W. Ford as his running mate. In its platform for that year, the party candidly proclaimed that it was "the political party of the oppressed masses of the people—the industrial workers, the persecuted Negroes, the toiling farmers." It also suggested that "the Communist party enters this election campaign explicitly to rally the toilers of city and country, Negro and white, in a united struggle for jobs and bread, for the fight against imperialist war." It also called upon "the oppressed masses to rally under Communist leadership in the revolutionary struggle to overthrow capitalism and to establish a government in the United States of workers and farmers." It included sections dealing with food, police behavior, behavior of the dominant and traditional two parties, a call for a "Soviet America," and others. The platform concluded:

> Support the Communist Election Campaign! Rally behind its platform and candidates! Make this the starting point of a gigantic mass movement against starvation, terror and war! Resist with all your energy and strength the brutal attacks of the capitalists! Fight for unemployment insurance against wage cuts, for relief for the farmers, for equality for the Negroes, against the murderous capitalist terror and against the plans for a new bloody imperialist war. Resist the carrying through of the capitalist way out of the crisis! Fight for the workers' way—for the revolutionary way out of the crisis—for the United States of Soviet America! Vote for the workers' candidates—the Communist candidates! Vote Communist!

Yet, even given the fact that the party was waging this campaign during the very depths of the Great Depression, it managed to attract only some 102,221 votes out of the 40 million cast, a showing of 0.3 percent of the popular vote.

In 1935, another shift in the official view of the party was declared at the Seventh World Congress of the Comintern. The new line emphasized the need to develop a "popular front"—an effort to bring together all antifascist groups. The Communists thus abandoned their opposition to the policies of the New Deal under Roosevelt and became involved in mainstream union activities, especially in the Congress of Industrial Organizations (CIO). Through their efforts, they gained some significant positions of authority in the unions.

In the 1936 campaign, the Communist Party ran Earl Browder and James W. Ford as its candidates for president and vice president, respectively. The party's slogan that year was "Communism is twentieth-century Americanism." Among its platform planks were those that advocated opposition to German, Italian, and Japanese imperialism; passage of a graduated income tax; independence for the commonwealth of Puerto Rico; increased taxation on high incomes; a guaranteed minimum wage; a reduction of the workweek to 30 hours; keeping the United States out of Latin American affairs; and maternity and health insurance.

The platform concluded its appeal to the American voters with the following exhortation:

> Communism is Twentieth-century Americanism. The Communist party continues the traditions of 1776, of the birth of our country, of the revolutionary Lincoln, who led the historic struggle that preserved our nation. In the greater crisis of today only the Communist party shows a way to a better life now, and to the future of peace, freedom, and security for all.
>
> By supporting, working with, and voting for the Communist party. . . ; by organizing the mass-production industries into powerful industrial unions. . . ; by independent political action and by building the American people's front—the Farmer-Labor party— the toilers of America can best fight for the realization of their aims in 1936.
>
> Forward to a progressive, free, prosperous, and happy America.
>
> Vote Communist!

Once again, however, the American people appeared unimpressed with these exhortations. The landslide victory scored by Democratic candidate Franklin Delano Roosevelt over his Republican opponent Alfred M. Landon left the Communists far behind, with only slightly more than 80,000 votes.

In 1940, Earl Browder and James Ford were once again the nominees of the Communist Party. The party had been parroting the official dogma as established in Moscow, especially in 1939, when a nonaggression agreement was signed between Stalin and Hitler. With the signing of this treaty, the CPUSA reversed its earlier position, which had advocated military intervention against Hitler. The party now said nothing when Germany invaded Poland and when the Soviet Union took Latvia, Lithuania, and Estonia and a part of Finland, making those areas part of the Soviet Union. The party also supported American isolationists in opposing aid to Great Britain when Germany set out to conquer that country, and opposed both the military draft and the mobilization of industry to prepare for war. Thus the Communist Party's campaign in 1940 emphasized keeping the United States out of what the party labeled the "imperialist war."

The 1940 Communist platform also attacked the Democratic administration for sacrificing social welfare programs and insisted that "Wall Street" advocated war but that "The People" desired peace. It put forth a so-called People's Program, which denounced the "imperialist policies and acts" of the American government, the major political parties, and Wall Street's alleged "imperialist policy of economic and political domination." It called for the democratization of the armed forces. It demanded "full rights" for blacks; work, job security, and a high standard of living for all "toilers"; and the curbing of the "monopolists." It also advocated "building up of a united mass party—a national Farmer-Labor Party, an anti-imperialist third party of the people." It concluded with a vehement attack on both the Democratic and Republican parties and insisted that a vote for the Communist Party would be a vote against "imperialist war" and "Wall Street's imperialist adventures," and for "peace, freedom and socialism." Once again, however, American voters rejected the Communist Party, casting fewer than 50,000 votes for its candidates.

In 1941, after Germany invaded the Soviet Union, the Communist Party yet again turned about-face, and, instead of urging isolationism, called for American assistance to the Soviets and to Great Britain, which had become an ally of the Soviet Union. Because of the passage of the Smith Act in the United States, moreover, the CPUSA had earlier withdrawn from the Comintern, which Stalin had dissolved in 1943. As a result of its action, the party insisted that there no longer existed an international revolutionary organization and that it had become a more or less loyal and otherwise respected American political group. Following this line of reasoning, it began to urge cooperation with liberal and other legitimate left-of-center groups. In the spring of 1944, furthermore, Earl Browder dissolved the Communist Party; the organization adopted, instead, the name Communist Political Association. It did not nominate candidates for the presidency that year, although it did throw its support to President Franklin Roosevelt, who repudiated their endorsement.

The American Communist Party continued to suffer problems. For example, after World War II, Earl Browder was vehemently denounced by Kremlin forces and was removed as party leader; he was later expelled from the party altogether. The term *Browderism* had become synonymous with tactics of accommodation that the Soviet leadership no longer found useful to the party. William Z. Foster became chair of the party, and Eugene Dennis was chosen as national secretary. The Communist International was renamed the Cominform and was reactivated in 1947. Reasserting its zigzagging philosophical and pragmatic behavior pattern, which reflected the official party dogma of the time, the American Communist Party now once again began rigidly to assert the principles of the Cominform. Thus it attacked the Truman Doctrine, American assistance to Greece and Turkey, the Marshall Plan, and NATO; in general, the party's pronouncements reflected the intensification of what had been dubbed the Cold War.

In 1948, the Communist Party again did not nominate candidates. It chose instead to support the candidacy of Henry Wallace, former vice president in the Democratic administration and the 1948 candidate of the Progressive Party. Even though it did not choose to nominate candidates, it did write a platform that called for a "peace program," and that included the following objectives, among others:

> End the 'cold war,' the draft, and the huge military budget.
> Restore American-Soviet friendship, the key to world peace and the fulfillment of the people's hope in the United Nations.
> Conclude a peace settlement for a united, democratic Germany and Japan based on the Yalta and Potsdam agreements. Guarantee the complete democratization and demilitarization of these Countries.
> Stop military aid and intervention in China, Korea, and Greece.
> Break diplomatic and economic ties with Franco Spain.
> Scrap the Marshall Plan and the Truman Doctrine. Furnish large-scale economic assistance to the war-ravaged victims of fascist attack. Give this aid through the United Nations without political strings.
> Lift the embargo on, and extend full recognition to Israel.
> Give immediate, unconditional independence to Puerto Rico.
> Aid the economic development of the colonial and semi-colonial countries of Asia, Africa and Latin America on the basis of full support to their fight for their national independence. Defeat the Truman Arms Standardization Plan.
> Abandon economic, political and military pressures on the countries of Latin America.

Other planks in the platform dealt with proposals to repeal the Taft-Hartley Act, price controls, a wage freeze, education and health insurance, and especially with demands for the abolition of the House Committee on Un-American Activities. Throwing its support to the newly formed Progressive Party, the platform proclaimed:

> The Communists, who support every popular progressive movement, naturally welcome this new people's party. We supported progressive features of Roosevelt's policies, domestic and foreign. We helped organize the C.I.O. in the 1930's. We have supported every democratic movement since the Communists of Lincoln's generation fought in the Union cause during the Civil War.

On most immediate questions before the people of the country
the Progressive Party has offered detailed platform planks
around which all forward-looking people can unite. . . .
The Progressive Party is by its very nature a great coalition of
labor, farmers, the Negro people, youth, and professional and
small business people. It is anti-monopoly, anti-fascist, anti-war.
By its very nature it is not an anti-capitalist party. It is not a
Socialist or a Communist Party and we are not seeking to make it
one. It is and should develop as a united front, broad, mass people's party.
There is only one Marxist Party in America, one party dedicated to replacing the capitalist system with Socialism—and that is
the Communist Party.

Its protestations to the contrary notwithstanding, the Communist Party's difficulties continued. The Taft-Hartley Act of 1947 required labor unions—if they wished to use the facilities of the
National Labor Relations Board—to file affidavits stating that their
officers were not members of the Communist Party. During
1949–1950, moreover, the CIO expelled unions that continued to be
communist dominated. President Truman, in 1947, declared that
communists, or those sympathetic to communism, would be barred
from employment in the executive branch. Revelations about party
activities by such ex-Communists as Whittaker Chambers, the inquir-
ies by federal grand juries into party affairs, passage of "little Smith
Acts" in some of the states, and, ultimately, the provision in the
Communist Control Act of 1954 that denied "rights, privileges, and
immunities" to the Communist Party as a legal entity, all of these and
other impediments added to the party's plight.
Places on the ballot were also denied to candidates of the
Communist Party in many states. Later, the rise of Senator Joseph R.
McCarthy from Wisconsin, and his intense and highly publicized tactics in search of communists in the federal government, took its toll on
the party. In 1949, 11 party officials were convicted under the Smith
Act. In addition, the McCarran Internal Security Act of 1950 (the
McCarran-Walter Act) and the Communist Control Act of 1954 were
passed by the Congress. The party was further weakened by revelations of communist espionage against the United States, the increasingly widespread use of loyalty programs and the requirement of
loyalty oaths in many occupations, intensified labor-union activities
against infiltration by communists into their ranks, the outbreak of
the Korean War (which brought anticommunist opinion to still
greater intensity), and a highly successful effort on the part of the FBI
to infiltrate the party itself. The rise of Khruschev in the Soviet Union
and his subsequent attacks on Stalinism likewise had adverse effects
upon party activities. The crushing of the Hungarian uprising in 1956

by the Soviet Union stimulated further defection by party members; indeed, even the party's main publication, the *Daily Worker*, suspended publication in 1958.

During the 1960s, with the rise of the New Left, the rebirth of radicalism, and the easing of restrictions on left-wing activities, the Communist Party was once again revived. Gus Hall ran for the presidency in 1968, with Charlene Mitchell as his running mate. But even with the general revival of radicalism in the United States, the party received only a little in excess of 1,000 votes.

In 1972, the party nominated Gus Hall and Jarvis Tyner. The party's platform for that year again urged many of the same political, economic, and social changes that it had espoused in the past. The platform began with the statement, "The United States of America is a deeply troubled nation—more troubled than ever before." After a lengthy introduction attacking armaments, the military establishment, the Nixon-imposed wage freeze, "oppression of minority peoples," and big business, among other of its usual scapegoats, it devoted sections to ending war, militarism, and poverty; improving the right of labor to organize; freedom for minorities; recognizing the needs of youth; and equality for women—among other points. The platform urged the following:

> We call for the largest possible vote for Gus Hall and Jarvis Tyner. . . . This will be the most meaningful and forceful electoral protest against the reactionary policies and rule of monopoly capitalism. This will be the most affirmative and effective vote for peace, jobs, freedom and socialism. Only a determined people, united in struggle, can win a society that truly provides for their needs.

The party, in 1972, polled 25,229 votes.

In 1976, the party ran the same candidates as in 1972. In an uncharacteristically brief platform, the opening statement declared, "Nine-tenths of the U.S. people have no confidence in either the Republican President or the Democratic Congress. Why? Because both major parties serve big business. They put profits before people."

The platform then went on to devote comments to cutting the "bloated military budget by 80%"; reducing the "work week by law to 30 hours at 40 hours' pay"; "end[ing] all cold war policies"; calling for "independence for Puerto Rico"; demanding the "outlaw[ing] of racism, which has poisoned the life of our nation"; calling for a "guarantee [of] a secure future for our youth"; doing away with "discrimination and establish[ing] equality for women in social, political and economic life"; calling for a "guarantee [of] justice to our senior citizens"; asking to "make the people's health care a No. 1 priority"; and "abolish[ing] all anti-democratic and repressive laws." The platform ended with the following comment: "You wouldn't elect your boss as your shop steward. Why elect his stooge to public office?" The party managed to muster only 58,992 votes in that campaign.

In 1980, the party ran Gus Hall and Angela Davis, the latter a lecturer at San Francisco State University. Hall had expressed his position in his book *Basics for Peace, Democracy, and Social Progress*, published in 1980. Its contents repeated the usual charge that capitalism is oppressive and contained the customary communist railings against capitalist imperialism. Davis did little campaigning beyond issuing occasional press releases. In 1980, the party received only 43,871 votes.

Since that time, the party has been largely unable to capture significant attention among the American people. Indeed, from 1968 through 1984, the party was able to garner only less than one-tenth of 1 percent of the popular vote.

Some scholars have argued that those involved in the Communist Party in the United States were indeed legitimate trade unionists and that the traditional interpretation of the U.S. communist movement is based on simplistic thinking. For example:

> The Communist party had a dual character. It was a blend of national and international radicalism. The party was formed mainly by former members of the Socialist party, who were inspired by the Russian revolution and committed to making an American socialist revolution. . . . The Communists saw no conflict between their commitment to internationalism (and the Soviet Union) and the interests of the American workers. The Communists' ties to an international movement did not keep them from being leading fighters for industrial unionism in the auto industry. The moral and intellectual strength that the Communists derived from their international ties made them better fighters than they otherwise would have been. (Keeran, 1980, p. 3)

Even if this revisionist interpretation is adopted, it is not likely that the Communist Party will be able to attract a wide following in the United States. The dilemma of the party has resided in the fact that while advocating a revolutionary philosophy and ideology, it has had to operate within a system emphasizing democracy, open elections, and majority rule, and an economic system that invites competition based on the belief that one can achieve personal wealth if one puts one's mind to it and works, generally speaking, by the rules of the game.

The frequent on-again, off-again, reverse and forward gear pattern of the official party line as enunciated by either Moscow or Peking has led to deep schisms in the party and to the rise and fall of party leaders on a not infrequent basis. In short, the very legitimacy of communist factions in the United States has been seriously questioned and, indeed, seriously undermined, for the most part as a result of party policy or of the actions of party members themselves.

The Communist Party of the United States has, nevertheless, occupied a place of unique distinction down through time: it is the only major third party in the United States to have had ties internationally and to have expressed allegiance to the policies of a foreign— and for much of the time, an "enemy"—government.

Given the apparent decline of Marxism around the world in recent years, and, especially, the fragmentation of the Soviet empire in Eastern Europe, the future of the communist movement in general would appear to be in some jeopardy. There is no reason to believe that its future in the United States—as articulated by the remnants of the Communist Party of the United States—will be any brighter.

Sources/References

Browder, Earl R. *What Is Communism?* New York: Vanguard, 1936.

Bullush, Bernard, and Jewel Bullush. "A Radical Response to the Roosevelt Presidency: The Communist Party (1933–1945)." *Presidential Studies Quarterly*, 10 (Fall), 1980: 645–661.

Congressional Quarterly, Inc. *National Party Conventions, 1831–1984.* Washington, DC: Congressional Quarterly, Inc., 1987.

Delaney, Robert F. *The Literature of Communism in America: A Selected Reference Guide.* Washington, DC: Catholic University of America Press, 1962.

Draper, Theodore. *American Communism and Soviet Russia.* New York: Viking, 1960.

Foster, William Z. *History of the Communist Party of the United States.* New York: Greenwood, 1952.

Howe, Irving, and Lewis Coser. *The American Communist Party: A Critical History 1919–1957.* Boston: Beacon, 1958.

Isserman, Maurice. *Which Side Were You On?* Middletown, CT: Wesleyan University Press, 1982.

Jaffe, Philip J. *The Rise and Fall of American Communism.* New York: Horizon, 1975.

Johnson, Donald Bruce. *National Party Platforms* (2 vols.). Urbana: University of Illinois Press, 1978.

Keeran, Roger. *The Communist Party and the Auto Workers Unions.* Bloomington: Indiana University Press, 1980.

Klehr, Harvey. *Communist Cadre.* Stanford: Hoover Institution Press, 1978.

_____. *The Heyday of American Communism: The Depression Decade.* New York: Basic Books, 1984.

Oneal, James, and G. A. Werner. *American Communism: A Critical Analysis of Its Origins, Development and Programs.* New York: E. P. Dutton, 1947.

Schapsmeier, Edward L., and Frederick H. Schapsmeier. *Political Parties and Civic Action Groups.* Westport, CT: Greenwood, 1981.

Seidman, Joel (Ed.). *Communism in the United States: A Bibliography.* Ithaca, NY: Cornell University Press, 1969.

Smallwood, Frank. *The Other Candidates: Third Parties in Presidential Elections.* Hanover, NH: University Press of New England, 1983.

Starobin, Joseph. *American Communism in Crisis, 1943–1957.* Cambridge, MA: Harvard University Press, 1972.

Conservative Party

Established in New York City in 1962; sometimes referred to as the Conservative Party of New York.

Made up of conservatively oriented citizens, the Conservative Party had as its primary objectives when it was established to blunt the impact of the Liberal, Democratic, and Republican parties in New York. Such influential Republicans as the late Governor Nelson Rockefeller and the late Senator Jacob Javits, as well as liberal Mayor of New York John Lindsay, became particularly favorite targets of the conservative movement.

The Conservative Party has articulated policies aimed at reducing taxes and balancing the budget. It has also been especially concerned with such major issues as crime control, the development of right-to-work laws, maintaining the concept of the neighborhood school, reducing the number of social welfare programs, and reducing foreign aid. It has argued in support of a strong posture in national defense based on nuclear weaponry, and has urged diplomatic nonrecognition of communist-controlled governments and military assistance to U.S. allies and to those other nations that oppose communist regimes.

Drawing its support mainly from solid middle-class voters, the Conservative Party came into national prominence in 1965, when it ran as its candidate for mayor of New York City William F. Buckley, Jr. Buckley had developed—and continues to maintain—an international reputation as a novelist, essayist, journalist, publisher, lecturer, and talk-show host. Running against liberal Republican John Lindsay, Buckley was able to attract some 341,226 of the votes cast in the five boroughs of New York City. Moreover, the Conservative Party gubernatorial candidate, Dr. Paul L. Adams, achieved a major "upset" of sorts when he was able to capture the third-highest vote tally in 1966, exceeding the total received by Franklin D. Roosevelt, Jr. (the Liberal Party candidate), and coming in behind only the major candidates of the Republican and Democratic parties themselves. Perhaps the singularly most impressive achievement of the party was the election in 1970 of James Buckley, the less well-known brother of William, to the U.S. Senate. Once in the Senate, however, James Buckley voted with the Republican Party to organize that body, and was later appointed by the Republican leadership to various committee assignments, even serving as vice chair of the Republican Senate Reelection Committee in 1974. The continued working relationship between the Conservative Party and the Republicans during this period was emphasized in 1980, when James Buckley received the state Republican nomination for the Senate.

The Conservative Party was originally established by such well-known figures as Kieran O'Doherty, a Republican committeeman from the borough of Queens and a one-time candidate for the U.S. Senate; Suzanne La Follette, the niece of the former famous Progressive senator from Wisconsin, Robert M. La Follette; William F. Rickenbacker, son of the famous World War I pilot Captain Eddie Rickenbacker; J. Daniel Mahoney, a New York City attorney; Frank S. Meyer of conservative journal *National Review* fame; and Professor Henry Paolucci, a member of the staff of Iona College of New Rochelle and a one-time challenger of the late Robert F. Kennedy for a U.S. Senate seat.

The future of the Conservative Party will undoubtedly depend on its capacity to attract candidates similar in stature to that of the Buckleys and those others who were instrumental in its original formation.

Sources/References

Carroll, Maurice. "New York State's Conservative Party, Near Its Goals, Ponders Future Roles." *New York Times* (February 22), 1981.

Mahoney, J. Daniel. *Action Speaks Louder—The Story of the New York Conservative Party*. New Rochelle, NY: Arlington House, 1968.

Schapsmeier, Edward L., and Frederick H. Schapsmeier. *Political Parties and Civic Action Groups*. Westport, CT: Greenwood, 1981.

Constitution Party

A generally right-wing conservative party established in Los Angeles, California, in 1952.

The Constitution Party was probably never remotely of national importance, even though it from time to time supported such widely known personalities and politicians as Douglas MacArthur and William E. Jenner.

Among the objectives of the party were many of those included on the usual agenda of the politically far right in the United States. For example, the party urged restrictions on the use of federal power, especially in the area of civil rights legislation; opposed expansion of welfare programs; and rejected most activities of the federal government in the area of business regulation. In addition, party pronouncements called for a balanced federal budget, tax cuts, reducing federal costs (all of these coupled at the same time with increased military spending and larger defense budgets and a policy of total victory in the event of warfare), and the application of rigid restrictions on immigration. The party was vehement in its demands for the right to conduct prayer in public schools and advocated U.S. withdrawal from the United Nations, reduction of U.S. foreign aid, and renouncing of U.S. recognition of communist governments.

The party nominated candidates in 1952, 1956, 1960, 1964, and 1968. Douglas MacArthur, its 1952 choice, rejected the nomination. In that year, three candidates—Vivian Kellums, Jack Tenny, and Harry F. Byrd—ran as the party's vice presidential candidate, their names appearing on various ballots in various states. Constitution Party candidates ran in Arkansas, California, Colorado, Missouri, New Mexico, North Dakota, Tennessee, Texas, and Washington, and in some other states as candidates of the America First Party. But they received a total of only some 17,220 votes, most of those from California, the state where the party saw its birth.

In 1956, William E. Jenner, a former Republican senator from Indiana, was nominated as the party's presidential candidate, and Mayor J. Bracken Lee, the conservative mayor of Salt Lake City, Utah, was the party's vice presidential candidate. The party that year ran candidates only in Texas. The candidates of the States' Rights Party (q.v.)—T. Coleman Andrews and Thomas H. Werdel—were endorsed by Constitution Party organizations in some other states. The Constitution Party's ticket nevertheless managed to garner some 30,999 votes in Texas, even under these adverse circumstances.

In 1960, the Texas element of the Constitution Party chose Charles L. Sullivan of Mississippi and Merritt B. Curtis of the District of Columbia as its nominees. In the state of Washington, however, the Constitution Party chose Merritt B. Curtis as its presidential candidate and B. N. Miller as its vice presidential nominee. The split in the party, and the fact that it was on the ballot in only two states, was reflected in its poor showing at the polls: the Sullivan-Curtis campaign resulted in 18,169 votes, while Washington voters gave Curtis and Miller only 1,240 votes.

The fate of the Constitution Party in 1964 continued to reflect its insignificance nationally. Offering candidates Joseph B. Lightburn of West Virginia as its presidential nominee and Theodore C. Billings for vice president, the pair were able to attract only 5,090 votes.

By 1968, the party was on the ballot in only one state, North Dakota, where it ran Richard K. Troxell of Texas and Merle Taylor of Iowa for president and vice president, respectively. Only 34 votes were cast for their candidacy. The party has not been active since that time.

Sources/References

Schapsmeier, Edward L., and Frederick H. Schapsmeier. *Political Parties and Civic Action Groups.* Westport, CT: Greenwood, 1981.

Constitutional Union Party

Established in 1859 by factions of both the Whig and American (Know-Nothing) (q.v.) parties in Baltimore, Maryland.

The primary objective of the party was to attempt to preserve the Union in face of the growing debate over sectionalism between North and South, the increasingly volatile slavery issue, and secession threats being made by the South.

The only nominating convention held by the party took place in Baltimore in May of 1860 and focused on a major contest between former Tennessee Senator John Bell (who had also served as speaker of the House of Representatives and who had been both a Whig and a Democrat) and Texas Governor Sam Houston. Most states sent delegates to the convention. Southern delegates were still sentimentally attached to nativist views and tended to favor Houston. The other wing of the party was made up mainly of Whigs from the North. After a bitter debate over the voting procedure and the number of votes each delegation should be permitted to have, Bell, a moderate Whig by reputation, became the party's nominee on the second ballot, receiving 138.5 votes to Houston's 68. Edward Everett, a former senator from Massachusetts, was selected as the vice presidential nominee.

The platform of the party was brief and addressed several issues quite specifically. In its entirety, it read:

> *Whereas*, Experience has demonstrated that Platforms adopted by the partisan Conventions of the country have had the effect to mislead and deceive the people, and at the same time to widen the political divisions of the country, by the creation and encouragement of geographical and sectional parties; therefore
>
> *Resolved*, that it is both the part of patriotism and of duty to *recognize* no political principle other than THE CONSTITUTION OF THE COUNTRY, THE UNION OF THE STATES, AND THE ENFORCEMENT OF THE LAWS, and that, as representatives of the Constitutional Union men of the country, in National Convention assembled, we hereby pledge ourselves to maintain, protect, and defend, separately and unitedly, these great principles of public liberty and national safety, against all enemies, at home and abroad; believing that thereby peace may once more be restored to the country; the rights of the People and of the States re-established, and the Government again placed in that condition of justice, fraternity and equality, which, under the example and Constitution of our fathers, has solemnly bound every citizen of the United States to maintain a more perfect union, establish justice, insure domestic tranquility, provide for the common defense, promote the general welfare, and secure the blessings of liberty to ourselves and our posterity.

In the election of 1860, Bell received 590,901 votes, the least of all the candidates participating in the election campaign. His vote represented a figure just under 13 percent of the popular vote and enabled him to obtain 39 electoral votes from Kentucky, Tennessee, and Virginia. The other candidates were Abraham Lincoln, the Republican victor, Stephen A. Douglas of the Democratic Party, and John C. Breckinridge, who ran as the candidate of the National Democratic Party (q.v.).

The great American Civil War broke out soon after the election, bringing to an end the efforts of the Constitutional Union Party to conciliate the contentious political factions debating the slavery question. Having originally been hastily brought together by dissidents of two other parties representing border states, the party crumbled almost as quickly as it had emerged.

Sources/References

Congressional Quarterly, Inc. *National Party Conventions, 1831–1984*. Washington, DC: Congressional Quarterly, Inc., 1987.

Johnson, Donald Bruce (Comp.). *National Party Platforms: Vol. 1, 1840–1956*. Urbana: University of Illinois Press, 1978.

Schapsmeier, Edward L., and Frederick H. Schapsmeier. *Political Parties and Civic Action Groups.* Westport, CT: Greenwood, 1981.
Stabler, John B. *A History of the Constitutional Union Party: A Tragic Failure.* Ann Arbor, MI: University Microfilms, 1954.
Stanwood, Edward. *A History of the Presidency from 1788 to 1897* (Vol. 1). Cambridge, MA: Riverside, 1924.

Equal Rights Party (1884)

Established in San Francisco in 1884 by Belva A. Bennett Lockwood.

Like the Equal Rights Party founded by Victoria Woodhull (but which never actually developed as a party), Lockwood's party had as its major objectives the promotion of woman suffrage and feminist causes.

In 1884, Bennett (her maiden name) was nominated as the party's presidential candidate. Chosen as her running mate was Marietta Lizzy Bell Stowe. The platform was predictable. It included demands for equal rights for minorities, especially blacks; suffrage for women; a national temperance law; uniform state laws on marriage and divorce; and a pledge not to make war on others. The ticket drew only slightly more than 4,000 votes.

In 1888, Bennett once again ran for the presidency. Charles S. Wells was the vice presidential candidate. The party's platform repeated the demands of 1884, and included this time as well a plank dealing with civil service reforms. Drawing fewer than 100 popular votes, the party came to an abrupt end.

Sources/References

Schapsmeier, Edward L., and Frederick H. Schapsmeier. *Political Parties and Civic Action Groups.* Westport, CT: Greenwood, 1981.
Stern, Madeleine. *We, the Women.* New York: Schulte, 1963.

Farmer-Labor Party

Established in Chicago in 1919 by John Fitzpatrick of the Chicago Federation of Labor and Edward N. Nockels.

The party was originally named simply the Labor Party, but the organization was retitled in 1920 to reflect its broader socialist-oriented base and aspirations. It had as a main objective the unification of left-wing labor groups into a viable, full-blown third party movement.

At its Chicago nominating convention in 1920, the Farmer-Labor Party put forth the candidacy of Parley P. Christensen of Utah as its presidential nominee and Max S. Hayes of Ohio as its vice presidential nominee. Senator Robert M. La Follette of Wisconsin was touted by some as the strongest possible potential leader of the party, but attempts to nominate him were defeated.

The Farmer-Labor platform declared:

> The American Declaration of Independence, adopted July 4, 1776, states that governments are instituted to secure to the people the rights of life, liberty and pursuit of happiness and that governments derive their just powers from the consent of the governed.
>
> Democracy cannot exist unless all power is preserved to the people. The only excuse for the existence of government is to serve, not to rule, the people.
>
> In the United States . . . , the power of government, the priceless and inalienable heritage of the people, has been stolen from the people—has been seized by a few men who control the wealth of the nation and by the tools of these men, maintained by them in public office to do their bidding. . . .
>
> Having thus robbed the people first of their power and then of their wealth, the wielders of financial power, seeking new fields of exploitation, have committed the government of the United States, against the will of the people, to imperialistic policies and seek to extend these enterprises to such lengths that our nation to-day stands in danger of becoming an empire instead of a republic.
>
> . . . these masters . . . through their puppets in public office, in an effort to stifle free discussion, stripped from the inhabitants of this land, rights and liberties guaranteed under American doctrines on which this country was founded and guaranteed also by the federal constitution.
>
> These rights and liberties must be restored to the people.
>
> More than this must be done. All power to govern this nation must be restored to the people. . . .
>
> The invisible government of the United States maintains the two old parties to confuse the voters with false issues. These parties, therefore, can not seriously attempt reconstruction, which, to be effective, must smash to atoms the money power of the proprietors of the two old parties.
>
> Into this breach step the amalgamated groups of forward looking men and women who perform useful work with hand and brain, united in the Farmer-Labor Party of the United States by a spontaneous and irresistible impulse to do righteous battle for democracy against its despoilers, and more especially determined to function together because of the exceptionally brazen defiance shown by the two old parties in the selection of their candidates and the writing of their platforms in this campaign.

Having thus set the tone for the party's campaign, the platform included planks dealing with "restoration of civil liberties and American doctrines"; the election of judges to the federal courts; universal suffrage; initiative, referendum, and recall; and a provision that "war may not be declared except in cases of actual military invasion, before referring the question to a direct vote of the people." Other parts of the platform called for the abolition of "imperialism at home and abroad"; "democratic control of industry"; free coinage of silver; old-age pensions; public ownership of railroads, mines, and natural resources; "promotion of agricultural prosperity"; reduction in the cost of living; economic justice to soldiers; and a "labor's bill of rights," which included the right to organize and to bargain collectively, a maximum 8-hour workday and 44-hour workweek, abolition of labor for children under the age of 16, and the doing away with of detective and strike-breaking agencies, among a host of other requirements. The platform concluded with a call for a "federal department of education to advance democracy and effectiveness in all public school systems throughout the country, to the end that the children of workers in industrial and rural communities may have maximum opportunity of training to become unafraid, well-informed citizens of a free country."

In the 1920 election, the Farmer-Labor Party ran its presidential candidates in 17 states, but the Christensen-Hayes campaign garnered only 189,339 votes, 1 percent of the total vote. Warren G. Harding, the Republican, was the overwhelming victor; even Eugene V. Debs, the Socialist Party candidate, outpolled the Farmer-Labor Party, notwithstanding the fact that he was in prison at the time, serving a sentence for sedition.

The death knell of the Farmer-Labor Party was sounded in 1921 when communists seized control of the party apparatus. The influence of the communists caused many well-meaning liberals and other left-of-center Democrats to leave the party. The Farmer-Labor Party of Minnesota continued as a separate and independent organization and was successful in electing its gubernatorial candidate and some local officials. Hubert H. Humphrey, the late Democratic U.S. senator from Minnesota, vice president, and presidential candidate, was a long-time recipient of the party's support. The Democratic Party has continued to benefit from its assistance.

Sources/References

Johnson, Donald Bruce (Comp.). *National Party Platforms: Vol. 1, 1840–1956.* Urbana: University of Illinois Press, 1978.

Rice, Stuart A. *Farmers and Workers in American Politics* (Studies in History, Economics and Public Law, Vol. 113, Whole No. 253). New York: Columbia University, 1924.

Schapsmeier, Edward L., and Frederick H. Schapsmeier. *Political Parties and Civic Action Groups*. Westport, CT: Greenwood, 1981.

Stedman, Murray S., and Susan W. Stedman. *Discontent at the Polls: A Study of Farmers and Labor Parties, 1827–1948*. New York: Columbia University Press, 1950.

Valelly, Richard M. *Radicalism in the States: The Minnesota Farmer-Labor Party and the American Political Economy*. Chicago: University of Chicago Press, 1989.

Free Soil Party

Established at Buffalo, New York, in August 1848 by individuals dedicated to the purpose of maintaining "free soil, free speech, free labor, and free men."

Delegates to this party's convention were composed largely of persons holding antislavery views and those desiring cheap land. They were a coalition of elements of the nearly moribund Liberty Party (q.v.); the so-called Conscience Whigs, who were antislavery; and the Barnburners—a faction of the Democratic Party. The Barnburners were so fanatically antislavery that they were often compared to the Dutch farmer who burned down his barn to get rid of the rats that infested it. Hence, their appellation.

Delegates from the northern states and three of the border states were present at the convention. Martin Van Buren, the former president, was nominated as the presidential candidate and Charles Francis Adams of Massachusetts—the son of former President John Quincy Adams—was declared vice presidential nominee.

The 1848 Free Soil platform opened with these stirring words: "*Whereas*, We have assembled in Convention, as a union of *Freemen*, for the sake of Freedom, forgetting all past political differences in a common resolve to maintain the rights of Free Labor against the aggressions of the Slave Power, and to secure Free Soil for a Free People." It went on to declare a number of principles and aspirations. First denouncing the nominees of the other parties as "candidates, neither of whom can be supported by the opponents of Slavery-extension, without a sacrifice of consistency, duty, and self-respect," it was therefore necessary to require the need for the people to declare their independence from slavery and "to rescue the Federal Government from its control," and the party thus resolved to plant itself "upon the NATIONAL PLATFORM OF FREEDOM, in opposition to the Sectional Platform of Slavery."

The platform also proposed that the federal government not interfere with slavery within state limits (those laws having been passed in those areas without congressional responsibility), but that slavery no longer be extended. It suggested that the Constitution had clearly denied to the federal government "all constitutional power to deprive any person of life, liberty, or property without due legal process." In a ringing challenge, the platform declared:

> Congress has no more power to make a slave than to make a king; no more power to institute or establish slavery, than to institute or establish a monarchy. No such power can be found among those specifically conferred by the Constitution, or derived by just implication from them.
>
> Resolved, that it is the duty of the federal government to relieve itself from all responsibility for the existence or continuance of slavery wherever that government possess constitutional power to legislate on that subject, and is thus responsible for its existence.
>
> Resolved, that the true, and in the judgment of this Convention, the only safe means of preventing the extension of slavery into new territory now free, is to prohibit its existence in all such territory by an act of Congress.

In other words, the party demanded that there should be "no more slave states and no more slave territory."

Among other platform demands were those for free homesteads, a revenue-producing tariff, river and harbor improvements, and low-cost postage rates.

In the election, Martin Van Buren received 291,501 popular votes, but no electoral votes. His total, however, was large enough to derail the election victory of the Democratic nominee, Lewis Cass. Although it had lost the presidency, the Free Soil Party was nevertheless able to elect Salmon P. Chase to the U.S. Senate and also to elect nine candidates to the House of Representatives.

A second nominating convention of the Free Soil Party was held in Pittsburgh, Pennsylvania, in 1851. This time, however, the party designated itself the Free Democratic Party and nominated John P. Hale and George W. Julian as presidential and vice presidential candidates, respectively.

In its platform, the Free Democratic Party reiterated the basic objective of the 1848 platform: "no more slave States, no slave Territory, no nationalized slavery, and no national legislation for the extradition of slaves." Indeed, the platform declared that "slavery is a sin against God and crime against man, which no human enactment nor usage can make right; and that Christianity, humanity, and patriotism, alike demand its abolition." It also stated that "all men have a natural right to a portion of the soil; and that, as the use of the soil is indispensable to life, the right of all men to the soil is as sacred as their right to life itself." It demanded that public lands be preserved for the people and not be sold to individuals or corporations. It also called for the independence of Haiti and arbitration in the settlement of international disputes, and contained planks offering condemnations of the Fugitive Slave Act and the Compromise of 1850, among other matters of concern.

In the 1852 election, Hale received the fewest of all the votes cast—some 155,210 popular votes and no electoral votes. As in 1848, the Free Soil or Free Democratic Party was unable to carry a single state. This time, the Democrat, Franklin Pierce, emerged as the victorious candidate, beating the Whig, Winfield Scott. Because of its poor performance, the Whig Party was therefore defunct by 1854, and Free Soilers began to join the ranks of the Republican Party in large numbers.

Although the Free Soil Party fared poorly in its election campaigns, it was undoubtedly able to focus attention on the major emerging issue of the day—that of slavery—and it helped to galvanize public sentiment against that "peculiar institution." The issue of slavery was, of course, to emerge as the most significant political controversy in the mid-1850s and 1860s—and to lead to the ultimate break between the North and the South.

Sources/References

Bell, Howard H. "The National Negro Convention, 1848." *Ohio Historical Quarterly*, 67 (October), 1958.

Blue, Frederick J. *The Free Soilers: Third Party Politics, 1848–1854.* Urbana: University of Illinois Press, 1973.

Congressional Quarterly, Inc. *National Party Conventions, 1831–1884.* Washington, DC: Congressional Quarterly, Inc., 1987.

Foner, Eric. "Racial Attitudes of the New York Free Soilers." *New York History*, 46 (October), 1955.

_____. "Politics and Prejudice: The Free Soil Party and the Negro: 1849–1852." *Journal of Negro History*, 50 (October), 1965.

_____. *Free Soil, Free Labor, Free Men: The Ideology of the Republican Party before the Civil War.* New York: Oxford University Press, 1970.

Johnson, Donald Bruce (Comp.). *National Party Platforms: Vol. 1, 1840–1956.* Urbana: University of Illinois Press, 1978.

Mintz, Max M. "The Political Ideas of Martin Van Buren." *New York History*, 30 (October), 1949.

Schapsmeier, Edward L., and Frederick H. Schapsmeier. *Political Parties and Civic Action Groups.* Westport, CT: Greenwood, 1981.

Sewell, Richard H. *John P. Hale and the Politics of Abolition.* Cambridge, MA: Harvard University Press, 1965.

Freedom and Peace Party

Established in Chicago in 1968 by former comedian Richard (Dick) Gregory.

Gregory, a black, had been a television personality and stand-up comedian, and had also become widely known for his fasts on behalf of social and political causes. The Freedom and Peace Party should not be confused with the Peace and Freedom Party (q.v.), of which Gregory was a former member.

Never a serious contender for the presidency, Gregory's objective was to focus attention on the Vietnam War and on civil rights matters. His campaign was conducted largely on college and university campuses. Using techniques he had capitalized on as a comedian—especially the use of satire and humor—he attacked various aspects of American culture and drew particular attention to the issues of racism, the oppressive and inhumane behavior of big business, his view of what he termed "U.S. imperialism," and other aspects of American culture that in his judgment offended the basic aims of the civil rights movement.

Gregory attributed to Al Capp, the "Li'l Abner" cartoonist, his entrance into presidential politics. Capp had been writing and suggesting to others that Gregory be nominated for president.

In his platform, Gregory called for prosecution of crime syndicates, ending the war in Vietnam, expanded welfare and educational opportunities, the investigation of rural problems and of the food supply, lowering the voting age, the investigation of living conditions on Indian reservations and among the minority populations of the country, establishment of a youth commission, creation of a federal 24-hour educational television station for adults, implementation of the Kerner Commission Report, prohibition of the sale and manufacture of handguns and regulations on those who own long guns, and requiring the federal government to provide for the families of soldiers killed or wounded in the nation's wars. In the 1968 election, Gregory attracted only 47,133 votes.

Gregory was inaugurated as "president in exile" on March 4, 1969, in Washington, D.C., under plans coordinated by the New Party, a coalition of political independents, cochaired with Gregory by James P. Dixon, then president of Antioch College.

Although his party disintegrated, Gregory went on to continue to speak on college and university campuses. Most recently, he has become widely known as a leader in weight loss for obese people; as was pointed out above, he had himself fasted on several occasions in order to draw attention to various political problems he deemed of particular importance.

Sources/References

Gregory, Dick. *Dick Gregory's Political Primer*. New York: Harper & Row, 1970.
_____. *Up from Nigger*. New York: Stein & Day, 1976.
Walton, Hanes, Jr. *Black Politics: A Theoretical and Structural Analysis*. Philadelphia: J. B. Lippincott, 1972.

Freedom Now Party

Established in Washington, D.C., in August 1963.

The chairman of the party was Conrad L. Lynn, a New York lawyer. The party's major aim was to run candidates in New York, Connecticut, and California in 1963, but all of the candidates of the party were roundly defeated. In fact, few Americans probably even knew of the existence of the candidates, let alone of the party itself. Major objectives of the party were to emphasize civil rights issues and the creation of job opportunities for blacks.

In the 1964 election year, the party focused its campaign on the state of Michigan. In that state, the party fielded some 39 black candidates to compete for a variety of offices, ranging from those on the local level to those on the national. Led by the Congregationalist minister Albert Cleage, the party hoped at least to show the Democratic Party in Michigan that the candidates of the Freedom Now Party should be recognized as a political force. Another objective of the party was to educate members of the black community to involve themselves in politics and to use whatever political and social force they could muster to accomplish black objectives. But once again the party's candidates received so few votes that the party's future was never in doubt: there would be no party in the future.

Having failed in its campaign, the Freedom Now Party did not run candidates in 1966. Its inability to achieve even a modicum of success seemed to indicate conclusively that a party focused exclusively on race is probably doomed to failure, regardless of how legitimate its interests might be.

Sources/References

Jones, David R. "Negro Party Puts Strength to Test." *New York Times* (October 4), 1964.

"Negro Party Files in Michigan." *New York Times* (May 3), 1964.
Schapsmeier, Edward L., and Frederick H. Schapsmeier. *Political Parties and Civic Action Groups.* Westport, CT: Greenwood, 1981.
Walton, Hanes, Jr. *Black Political Parties: An Historical and Political Analysis.* New York: Free Press, 1972.

Greenback Party

Established in Indianapolis, Indiana, in November 1874.

Particularly influential in establishment of the Greenback Party were such groups as the National Grange, the Knights of Labor, and other farmer-labor groups. Farmers in the West and South who had been victims of a post-Civil War economic depression (known as the Panic of 1873) saw their economic salvation in the development of an inflated currency based on cheap paper money known as greenbacks (which had first been introduced during the Civil War). Their basic argument was that such currency would help to eliminate the farm debt that had been built up during periods of high prices. Those who were debtors—mainly farmers and workers—thus made an effort to have the greenbacks declared legal tender and to keep them in circulation. Thus, the Greenback Party favored an inflationary rather than a deflationary economic situation.

The Greenback Party was also known as the Greenback-Labor Party, the Independent Party, or the National Party.

In 1876, the Greenback Party ran Peter Cooper (a New York philanthropist) as its presidential candidate and Samuel Cary as its vice presidential nominee. Among the party's platform demands that year were that paper money be made legal tender, that the sale of gold bonds to foreigners be ended, that the Specie-Resumption Act of 1875 be repealed, and that the issuance of silver bonds be ended. Its platform declared:

> The Independent (Greenback) party is called into existence by the necessities of the people whose industries are prostrated, whose labor is deprived of its just reward by a ruinous policy which the Republican and Democratic parties refuse to change. . . .
> First. We demand the immediate and unconditional repeal of the Specie-Resumption act . . . and the rescue of our industries from ruin and disaster resulting from its enforcement. . . .
> Second. We believe that a United States note, issued directly by the Government, and convertible on demand into United States obligations bearing a rate of interest not exceeding one cent a day

on each $100, and exchangeable for United States notes at par, will afford the best circulating medium ever devised. . . .

Third. It is the paramount duty of the Government in all its legislation to keep in view the full development of all legitimate business. . . .

Fourth. We most earnestly protest against any further issue of gold bonds for sale in foreign markets. . . .

Fifth. We further protest against the sale of Government bonds for the purpose of purchasing silver to be used as a substitute for our more convenient and less fluctuating fractional currency.

The platform and the Greenback candidates did not attract significant support, however. In 1876, Cooper received some 75,973 votes.

Still, these issues were of importance to millions of Americans of the time. By 1878, the party had increased its base of support, receiving over a million votes and successfully putting into office 14 of its congressional candidates. But these successes marked the apogee of the party's influence.

In 1880, it nominated General James G. Weaver of Iowa and Benjamin J. Chambers for president and vice president, respectively. It had high hopes in that election year, and its platform again called for unlimited coinage of silver, issuance of paper money, the abolition of prison (contract) and child labor, and the exclusion of the Chinese. Other elements of the platform included a call for the breaking up of monopolistic industries, introduction of a graduated income tax, reduction of military expenditures, and the granting of suffrage to all American citizens. With these and other principles it went before the American people, proclaiming:

> Civil government should guarantee the divine right of every laborer to the results of his toil, thus enabling the producers of wealth to provide themselves with the means for physical comfort, and the facilities for mental, social and moral culture; and we condemn as unworthy of our civilization the barbarism which imposes upon the wealth-producers a state of perpetual drudgery as the price of bare animal existence. . . .
>
> Corporate control of the volume of money has been the means of dividing society into hostile classes, of the unjust distribution of the products of labor, and of building up monopolies of associated capital endowed with power to confiscate private property. It has kept money scarce, and scarcity of money enforces debt, trade and public and corporate loans . . . therefore we declare:
>
> First—That the right to make and issue money is a sovereign power to be maintained by the people for the common benefit. . . .
>
> Second—That the bonds of the United States should not be refunded, but paid as rapidly as practicable.

Remaining provisions of the platform dealt with a wide variety of subjects, ranging from such matters as an eight-hour law, Chinese serfs, railroad land grants, interstate commerce, discrimination against soldiers, and the relations of the major political parties to corporations and monopolies to standing armies, democratic rules for the governance of Congress, and government by, of, and for the people. To further these goals, the Greenback platform declared that it sought "the cooperation of all fair-minded people." The platform concluded with the resolution that "every citizen of due age, sound mind, and not a felon, be fully enfranchised, and that this resolution be referred to the States, with recommendation for their favorable consideration."

In the interim, however, economic prosperity had returned, and with the passage of the Bland-Allison Act in 1878 and the help of the Resumption Act, the degree of discontent and apprehension among the people had substantially abated. Thus, support for the party's presidential candidate dipped to only 308,997 votes in 1880, and only eight representatives were elected to Congress.

In 1884, the Greenback Party nominated General Benjamin F. Butler as its presidential nominee and Absolom M. West of Mississippi as its vice presidential candidate. Its platform vigorously attacked both Democratic and Republican parties, alleging that they were mere instruments of corporate wealth. Other planks denounced trusts and called for government regulation of interstate commerce. Cheap money remained one of the party's major economic objectives, and demands for a graduated income tax, a government postal telegraph system, pensions for Civil War veterans, woman suffrage, and a reduction in the length of terms for U.S. senators were among others made by the party. The platform declared, for example, "We demand the substitution of greenbacks for national bank notes and the prompt payment of the public debt. We want that money which saved our country in time of war and which has given it prosperity and happiness in peace." It castigated the major parties as well: "We denounce, as dangerous to our republican institutions, those methods and policies of the Democratic and Republican parties which have sanctioned or permitted the establishment of land, railroad, money and other gigantic corporate monopolies."

The platform insisted that the public lands are the inheritance of the people and denounced major corporations for their exploitation of them and the government for its overt and tacit approval of such exploitation. A plank stated: "All private property, all forms of money and obligations to pay money, should bear their just proportion of the public taxes. We demand a graduated income tax." After other exhortations, the platform concluded: "We appeal to all people who believe in our principles to aid us by voice, pen, and votes." Even with these calls for change, however, the party managed to muster only 175,096 votes.

The Greenback Party merged with the Union Labor Party (q.v.) in 1888 in hopes of improving its prospects at the polls. But, failing once more to have a significant impact on the election, the Greenbacks then joined forces with the Populist Party in 1892.

This move did not prove particularly advantageous. Still, it was not until 1918 that the Greenbacks once again emerged with their own party identity. In that year, John Zahnd, a reformer from Indiana, became the party's presidential candidate and continued to run on the party's ticket until 1940. By 1944, because of its very low level of support, the party did not field a candidate. In 1948, John G. Scott of New York and Granville B. Leeke of Indiana were the party's candidates. In 1952, the Greenback Party nominated Frederick C. Proehl of Washington and J. Edward Bedell of Indiana as its candidates; in 1956, Proehl ran again with Edward K. Meador of Mississippi as the vice presidential candidate. By this time the party had become so relatively unimportant that most of the electorate simply ignored it. Support for the party grew so small that it actually did not appear on the ballot in any of the states. The party thus ceased to exist.

Even during its halcyon days, the Greenback Party was not widely supported by a majority of the voters. The subject of currency reform was an important one, but inflationary policies advocated by the party would have ultimately proven ruinous for the economy. The debtor class did benefit from some legislation passed in its behalf as a result of the party's protestations, but with the rise of the Populist Party, the Greenback Party essentially lost its attraction.

Sources/References

Congressional Quarterly, Inc. *National Party Conventions, 1831–1834.* Washington, DC: Congressional Quarterly, Inc., 1987.

Johnson, Donald Bruce (Comp.). *National Party Platforms: Vol. 1, 1840–1956.* Urbana: University of Illinois Press, 1978.

Nugent, Walter T. K. *Money and American Society 1865–1800.* New York: Free Press, 1968.

Schapsmeier, Edward L., and Frederick H. Schapsmeier. *Political Parties and Civic Action Groups.* Westport, CT: Greenwood, 1981.

Unger, Irwin. *The Greenback Era: A Social and Political History of American Finance, 1865–1879.* Princeton, NJ: Princeton University Press, 1964.

Independence Party

Established by the internationally known publisher William Randolph Hearst in Chicago in 1908. Its sole objective was to support his running for the presidency.

In 1906, Hearst had run as an independent for the governorship of New York under the sponsorship of the Independence League, an organization established to advance his campaign and candidacy for that position. Hearst himself had lost the Democratic Party's nomination for the presidency by a close margin in 1904. More than 200 newspapers across the country had advocated his candidacy, and he was invited to address various state legislatures. Labor had united in his behalf, and he carried Democratic nominating conventions in some 21 states and territories. His efforts in quest of the presidency were actually aimed at testing his strength against Theodore Roosevelt, who, it had been asserted, had been "stealing his thunder." But all of Hearst's efforts proved to be of no avail. Hearst's tide appeared to be an ebb tide.

Nevertheless, given his strong support in the campaign of 1904, Hearst assumed that he would be at the head of the Independence Party ticket in 1908. However, at the party's convention, delegates instead nominated Thomas Higsen of Massachusetts (a manufacturer of kerosene and axle grease) and John Temple Graves of Georgia (an outstanding speaker and a writer for Hearst) for president and vice president. These nominations notwithstanding, Hearst's influence in the party continued to be strong.

The introductory paragraphs of the party's platform set the tone of the campaign:

> We, independent American citizens, representing the Independence party in forty-four States and two Territories, have met in national convention to nominate, absolutely independent of all other political parties, candidates for President and Vice-President of the United States.
> Our action is based upon a determination to wrest the conduct of public affairs from the hands of selfish interests, political tricksters and corrupt bosses, and make the Government, as the founders intended, an agency for the common good.

The platform then went on to denounce the Democratic and Republican parties, declaring that the new party looked to the Declaration of Independence "as the fountain-head of all political inspiration" and that it hoped to "restore the action of the government to the principles of Washington and Jefferson and Lincoln." The platform further stated:

> It is not our purpose . . . to effect a radical change in the American system of government, but to conserve for the citizens of the United States their privileges and liberties won for them by the founders of this Government and to perpetuate the principles and policies upon which the nation's greatness has been built.

The Independence party is, therefore, a conservative force in American politics, devoted to the preservation of American liberty and independence, to honesty in elections, to opportunity in business and to equality before the law.

The platform contained planks advocating the use of the initiative, referendum, and recall; use of direct primaries; imposing regulations on the stock market; improving general working conditions; establishing government ownership of utilities; and making illegal the use of child and convict labor. It advocated reducing the tariff, doing away with monopoly industries, establishing postal savings banks and enhancing the parcel post service, establishing a department of public health, admitting Arizona and New Mexico as new states, establishing a graduated income tax, excluding Asians, and implementing popular election of senators and judges. In the international arena, it advocated the construction of a powerful naval force and the use of arbitration for settling international differences. The platform concluded with the following charge:

> Equality of opportunity, the largest measure of individual liberty consistent with equal rights, the overthrow of the rule of special interest and the restoration of government by the majority exercised for the benefit of the whole community; these are the purposes to which the Independence party is pledged, and we invite the co-operation of all patriots and progressive citizens, irrespective of party, who are in sympathy with these principles and in favor of their practical enforcement.

But the Higsen-Temple campaign drew the support of only 82,537 voters—some .55 percent—lagging behind even the Socialist and Prohibition parties. Republican William Howard Taft beat Democrat William Jennings Bryan by more than a million votes to win the presidency. Thus, the Independence Party had no significant impact on the 1908 election, and it passed quickly from the political landscape.

Sources/References

Johnson, Donald Bruce (Comp.). *National Party Platforms: Vol. 1, 1840–1956.* Urbana: University of Illinois Press, 1978.

Older, Mrs. Fremont. *William Randolph Hearst: American.* New York: D. Appleton-Century, 1936.

Schapsmeier, Edward L., and Frederick H. Schapsmeier. *Political Parties and Civic Action Groups.* Westport, CT: Greenwood, 1981.

Winkler, John K. *W. R. Hearst: An American Phenomenon.* London: Jonathan Cape, 1928.

Independent Progressive Party

Established in Los Angeles in 1947 by left-wing liberals.

The party's original objective was to help elect Henry A. Wallace to the presidency. A year after its founding it thus became a state arm of the Progressive Party and undertook efforts to elect a slate of state candidates and the presidential and vice presidential candidates of the Progressive Party, Henry A. Wallace and Senator Glen Taylor (a Democrat from Idaho).

The party was highly vulnerable from its inception, especially because of the overtly pro-Soviet statements made by the party's national candidates. Its very limited appeal is revealed in the voting statistics: the party nationally received 1,157,057 votes; in California, its "birthplace," only 190,381.

In 1952, the remaining members of the Independent Progressive Party gave their support to Vincent Hallinan, a well-known left-wing radical lawyer, as presidential nominee, and to Charlotte Bass, a black female civil rights leader, as vice presidential nominee. The candidacy netted a national vote of 140,023, nearly 25,000 of which came from California alone.

California's unique system of candidate cross-filing in existence at the time of the election meant that the only significant opposition to the Democratic-Republican candidates in some districts came from the Progressive candidates. Thus voters had to vote for the Independent Progressive Party if they desired to express their rejection of the otherwise dominant candidates running on the tickets of both major parties.

The Independent Progressive Party dissolved after this election.

Sources/References

McWilliams, Carey. "California's Third-Party Donnybrook." *Nation,* 116 (April 24), 1948.

Schapsmeier, Edward L., and Frederick H. Schapsmeier. *Political Parties and Civic Action Groups.* Westport, CT: Greenwood, 1981.

Schmidt, Karl M. *Henry A. Wallace: Quixotic Crusade 1948.* Syracuse, NY: Syracuse University Press, 1960.

Wallace, Henry A. "California and the New Party." *New Republic,* 118 (June 7), 1948.

Independent Republican Party

Established by radical Republicans in Cleveland, Ohio, in 1864.

The objective of the party's membership was to prevent the reelection of Abraham Lincoln to the presidency because of their displeasure with his policies carried out during the Civil War. The party's presidential nominee was John C. Frémont, the former Republican nominee. For their vice presidential nominee, the Independent Republicans selected General John Cochrane.

Bowing to pressure, however, both Frémont and Cochrane withdrew from the presidential campaign of the Independent Republicans and decided instead to support the candidates of the National Union Party—to which the Republican party had changed its name—Abraham Lincoln and Andrew Johnson.

Sources/References

Schapsmeier, Edward L., and Frederick H. Schapsmeier. *Political Parties and Civic Action Groups.* Westport, CT: Greenwood, 1981.

Zornow, William F. *Lincoln and the Party Divided.* Norman: University of Oklahoma Press, 1954.

Internationalist Workers Party

A party on the ballot in New Jersey in 1988.

Herbert Lewin was the party's presidential candidate. A vice presidential candidate was not announced.

Arguing that the 1988 presidential election would occur in the context of growing world revolution, and maintaining that the era of Reagan was behind us, the party asserted that the American people were increasingly confronted by the dangers of American military aggression. Thus, the party argued, "our struggle is inseparable from the struggles of the working class and the oppressed around the world."

Running as candidates of the Fourth International, Lewin and his colleagues offered a "revolutionary socialist program" and the "creation of a mass independent political party of the working class and the oppressed," and for a replacement of the present government with domination by workers and "oppressed." "Our aim is the creation of a Socialist America and a Socialist World."

Their platform included calls for victory over imperialism; quashing U.S. interventionism in the world; nuclear disarmament on the part of the United States; freedom for the Palestinians; the resignation of President Reagan, Vice President Bush, and cabinet officials; doing away with the electoral college; election of the Supreme

Court; the cessation of racism and sexism; the opening of borders; defense of the sanctuary movement; opposition to racism and police oppression; defense of Native American rights; free birth control; union wages for everyone; the ending of the health care crisis; decent housing for everyone; multilingual and multicultural education; elimination of income taxes for families with incomes below $45,000; closure of nuclear plants; and opposition to the "ultra-right wing fundamentalist political movement [which] continues to be a serious threat to the working class and the oppressed despite the setbacks they have suffered since Reagangate, the Jimmy and Tammy Bakker scandal, and the resignation of Jerry Falwell from politics." The platform called for many additional similar demands as well.

Source/Reference

Day, Glenn. *Minor Presidential Candidates and Parties of 1988.* Jefferson, NC: McFarland, 1988.

Jobless Party

Established by Father James Renshaw Cox in St. Louis, Missouri, in 1932.

The Jobless Party was specifically a political organization aimed at helping to solve some of the economic problems resulting from the Great Depression. Father Cox of Pennsylvania became the party's presidential candidate at its St. Louis convention in 1932. As vice presidential candidate, the convention nominated V. C. Tisdal of Oklahoma.

Among the party's proposals to deal with the problems of the Depression were nationalization of banks, confiscation of great wealth, and the creation of public works financed by the federal government to help provide jobs. Government relief programs were also advocated.

One contemporary commentary on Father Cox's nomination is interesting. The *Christian Century* observed:

> Father Cox is the nominee of the Jobless party, Mr. Harvey of the Liberty party. It would be unfortunate to regard these futile and discordant minority movements as merely comic interludes in an otherwise serious campaign. As political organizations, of course they are nothing. As expressions of urgent need and human suffering, they are profoundly moving. . . . As a demonstration, their assembling was not without its value. Even a third party will find

it hard to make any headway against the firmly fixed bipartisan habit of our political life, but sixth, seventh and eighth parties are little more than the loosely organized desperation of discordant minorities, or commentaries on the vanity of human wishes. (*Christian Century*, August 31, 1932).

Father Cox was forced to end his campaign before the day of the election because of lack of financial support. He received only 740 votes, and the Jobless Party collapsed. Its radical proposals were soundly rejected by voters even during the Depression; their support went to Franklin Delano Roosevelt, the Democrat, whose campaign offered policies that seemed more likely to bring solutions to the problems of the unemployed.

Perhaps ironically, Father Cox was later appointed by President Roosevelt to serve as a member of the National Recovery Administration's Pennsylvania state board. Perhaps ironically, too, the various public works programs suggested by the Jobless Party were eventually incorporated into New Deal measures concerned with dealing with the problems of the Depression.

Sources/References

"Father Cox's Army at St. Louis." *Christian Century* (August 31), 1932.

"Jobless Name Cox, End Convention." *New York Times* (August 18), 1932.

McCoy, Donald R. *Angry Voices: Left-of-Center Politics in the New Deal Era*. Port Washington, NY: Kennikat, 1971.

"Priest Leads Unemployed." *Christian Century* (February 17), 1932.

Schapsmeier, Edward L., and Frederick H. Schapsmeier. *Political Parties and Civic Action Groups*. Westport, CT: Greenwood, 1981.

La Raza Unida

Established in Crystal City, Texas, in 1970.

La Raza Unida ("the united race") developed among Chicanos in the Southwest because they felt they could no longer achieve their objectives through working within the major party system and through the Democratic Party in particular. In other words, "after 1968, the Mexican-American looked at the American political system and found that the Mexican-American after almost 120 years of being an American citizen did not have any real political voice. The Mexican-American tried to work in the two-party system, but the party failed him" (Santillan, July 1971, p. 48).

In Texas, the party was led by Jose Angel Gutierrez. He emphasized the need for justice for Chicanos and the fact that Chicanos would turn against mainstream politicians who did not display concern for the welfare of the people. Gutierrez felt that Chicanos had to learn to control their own destiny, not rely on Anglo Democrats to achieve it for them. Among points he emphasized was the fact that although some 26 counties in Texas had Chicano majorities, none was controlled by Chicanos. After struggles to get on the ballot, Chicanos won seats on the council and school board of Cotulla, Texas, and in Carriza Springs and Crystal City.

The party developed in other states as well. In Colorado, for example, Chicanos held their first party conference in June 1970. The platform of the party adopted there is illustrative, generally, of the objectives of the group as a whole. For example, it called for development of "adequate housing for La Raza," that schools be made "warm and inviting," and that there exist "completely free education from kindergarten to college with no fees, no lunch charges, no tuition, no dues." The platform stated that Spanish should be "the first language and English the second," and that texts be rewritten to emphasize Mexican-American and Indio-Hispanic influences in the development of the Southwest. Other provisions dealt with economic opportunities, job development, law enforcement, redistribution of wealth, and the war in Vietnam.

The Oakland, California, area La Raza Unida platform is also revealing. It called for ending the draft and exemption of all Raza young people from military service. It sought full equality for the Spanish language and splitting away from the dominant two-party system, which Chicanos felt was oppressive to La Raza. There were also pronouncements on foreign policy, economics, education, and self-defense.

There was also a Women's Platform, which dealt with child care, work, birth control, and education. It emphasized that women are triply exploited: as women, as members of La Raza, and by poverty.

A stated objective of the party was to deemphasize election of national candidates but to seek control of offices on local, regional, and state levels. The party has been somewhat successful on the local level and has been influential on the state and national levels in terms of exerting political pressure. On the national level, some of the candidates La Raza has supported have been elected as Democrats. More important, perhaps, is the fact that La Raza has nudged the major parties in the United States toward recognizing the grievances of Chicanos throughout the country.

The philosophical foundation of La Raza Unida thus rested in the belief that the two-party system had failed them. The Spanish-surnamed politicians who had been chosen had, they felt, been chosen by dominant Anglo interests, and once they had gotten into office they had merely continued to perpetuate a system that was one of suppression to Chicanos.

For a time the movement spread into other states, including those of the Midwest. In recent years, however, the party has not been particularly active.

Sources/References

Garcia, F. Chris. *Chicano Politics: Readings*. New York: MSS Information, 1973.

———. *La Causa Politica: A Chicano Politics Reader*. Notre Dame, IN: University of Notre Dame Press, 1974.

Garcia, Richard A. (Comp. and Ed.). *The Chicanos in America 1540–1974: A Chronology and Fact Book*. Dobbs Ferry, NY: Oceana, 1977.

Martinez, Elisabeth Sutherland, and Enriqueta Longeaux y Vasquez. *Viva la Raza! The Struggle of the Mexican-American People*. Garden City, NY: Doubleday, 1974.

Meier, Matt S., and Feliciano Rivera. *Readings on La Raza: The Twentieth Century*. New York: Hill & Wang, 1974.

Samora, Julian (Ed.). *La Raza: Forgotten Americans*. Notre Dame, IN: University of Notre Dame Press, 1966.

Santillan, Richard A. "El Partido La Raza Unida: Chicanos in Politics." *Black Politician* (July), 1971.

———. "Third Party Politics: Old Story, New Faces." *Black Politician* (October), 1971.

Schapsmeier, Edward L., and Frederick H. Schapsmeier. *Political Parties and Civic Action Groups*. Westport, CT: Greenwood, 1981.

Steiner, Stan. *La Raza: The Mexican Americans*. New York: Harper & Row, 1970.

Liberal Party

Formed by a group of dissident members of the American Labor Party in New York City in 1944.

Generally a left-of-center but noncommunist group, the party hoped to promote and elect candidates to offices on the municipal, state, and national levels and to provide an alternative to the American Labor Party for liberals.

Instrumental in the establishment of the party were David Dubinsky, president of the International Ladies' Garment Workers'

Union; Alex Rose, affiliated with the United Hatters, Cap and Millinery Workers International Union; Professor George S. Counts of Columbia University, a past president of the American Federation of Teachers; theologian Reinhold Niebuhr; and Adolf Berle, a leading adviser to President Franklin D. Roosevelt.

The Liberal Party, although a New York state party, has been involved in national elections as well. In 1944, for example, its support of the candidacy of incumbent President Franklin D. Roosevelt was important in electing him to an unprecedented fourth term. In 1948, the Liberal Party's opposition to the Progressive candidacy of Henry Wallace helped to deflect support for his candidacy from many potential liberal Democratic voters. The party also endorsed Harry S Truman in 1948. The Liberal Party was the main source of electoral recruitment for Truman in both the city and the state of New York. The Democrats, probably assuming that New York Republican Thomas E. Dewey already had the presidential election well in hand, did very little to help the Truman cause. Truman delivered one of his famous "give 'em hell" speeches at a Liberal Party rally at Madison Square Garden. Seemingly amazingly, Truman a week later scored a dramatic upset victory in the presidential election, defeating Dewey in defiance of predictions, and doing it with the considerable help of the Liberal Party. A photo of Truman holding the *Chicago Tribune* bearing the headline "Dewey Defeats Truman" has since become a classic.

The party was also instrumental in electing Herbert Lehman to the U.S. Senate in 1950 and Averell Harriman to the New York governorship in 1954. John F. Kennedy's candidacy for the presidency benefited from Liberal Party support in 1960, as did the mayoral victories of John Lindsay in New York City in 1965 and 1969. The Liberal Party consistently supported Republican Senator Jacob Javits. The Liberal Party also supported the Independent candidacy of John Anderson of Minnesota for the presidency and Wisconsin Governor Patrick Lucey for the vice presidency in 1980.

Traditionally heavily supported by labor (especially the garment workers' unions) and intellectuals of the left, the Liberal Party has espoused such causes as collective bargaining, civil rights and social welfare programs, opposition to communism in its various forms, and continued U.S. participation in foreign affairs and the United Nations.

Sources/References

Danish, Max D. *The World of David Dubinsky*. Cleveland: World, 1957.

Dashwood, W. "Professor in Politics." *Christian Science Monitor Weekly Magazine* (July 22), 1944.

Dubinsky, David, and A. H. Raskin. *David Dubinsky: A Life with Labor*. New York: Simon & Schuster, 1977.
"New Liberal Party." *New Republic* (May 29), 1944.
Schapsmeier, Edward L., and Frederick H. Schapsmeier. *Political Parties and Civic Action Groups*. Westport, CT: Greenwood, 1981.

Liberal Republican Party

Created in 1872 in Cincinnati, Ohio, by a faction of dissatisfied members of the Republican Party.

Unhappy with the performance of President Ulysses S. Grant during his first term of office, this party, composed of reformers, newspaper editors, and others opposed to Grant, attacked the corruption that had been rampant during the Grant administration. The critics focused especially on the need for reforms in civil service administration and procedures and on Reconstruction policy in the South.

The Liberal Republican Party held its convention in Cincinnati, Ohio, in May of 1872. The impetus for the new party came from a coalition of Democrats and reform Republicans in Missouri.

The convention was spearheaded by anti-Grant forces and newspaper editors known as the Quadrilateral. The party influentials did not lack eminence. Indeed, among the particularly influential were Horace Greeley and Whitelaw Reid, editors of the *New York Tribune*; Carl Schurz, Lyman Trumbull, and editor Murat Halstead of the *Cincinnati Commercial*; and editors Horace White, Henry Watterson, and Samuel Boweles, of, respectively, the *Chicago Tribune, Louisville Courier-Journal*, and *Springfield Republican*. Other influentials included Salmon P. Chase and David Davis, justices of the U.S. Supreme Court.

On the sixth ballot, delegates nominated well-known and controversial *New York Tribune* editor Horace Greeley as their presidential nominee. Governor B. Gratz Brown of Missouri was nominated as their vice presidential candidate on the second ballot.

Greeley's career had been a tumultuous one. He was not particularly popular among either reformers in the Liberal Republican camp or Democrats. But anti-Grant forces gave him their strong support.

Among the major elements of the Liberal Republican platform were the following:

> We recognize the equality of all men before the law, and hold that it is the duty of Government in its dealings with the people to

mete out equal and exact justice to all of whatever nativity, race, color, or persuasion, religious or political.

We pledge ourselves to maintain the union of these States, emancipation, and enfranchisement. . . .

We demand the immediate and absolute removal of all disabilities imposed on account of the Rebellion . . . believing that universal amnesty will result in complete pacification in all sections of the country.

. . . We demand for the individual the largest liberty consistent with public order; for the State, self-government, and for the nation a return to the methods of peace and the constitutional limitations of power.

The Civil Service of the Government has become a mere instrument of partisan tyranny and personal ambition and an object of selfish greed. It is a scandal and reproach upon free institutions and breeds a demoralization dangerous to the perpetuity of republican government. We therefore regard such thorough reforms of the Civil Service as one of the most pressing necessities of the hour; that honesty, capacity, and fidelity constitute the only valid claim to public employment; that the offices of the Government cease to be a matter of arbitrary favoritism and patronage, and that public station become again a post of honor.

We demand a system of Federal taxation which shall not unnecessarily interfere with the industry of the people, and which shall provide the means necessary to pay the expenses of the Government economically administered, the pensions, the interest on the public debt, and a moderate reduction annually of the principal thereof. . . .

The public credit must be sacredly maintained.

The platform also contained planks dealing with "return to specie payment," the "heroism and sacrifices of the soldiers and sailors of the Republic," opposition to "further grants of lands to railroads or other corporations," "the duty of the Government, in its intercourse with foreign nations to cultivate the friendship of peace," and a welcome to "all patriotic citizens, without regard to previous affiliations," to support the candidates of the Liberal Republican Party.

The Democrats at their convention in July endorsed the candidates and the platform of the Liberal Republicans. Even though this was the case, the Democratic-Liberal Republican relationship proved unsuccessful, many of the disgruntled Democrats refusing to support Greeley. Thus, Greeley won only six states and received 43.8 percent of the popular vote. Grant won by more than 750,000 votes.

Greeley died soon after the election was held, and the Liberal Republican Party went out of existence.

Sources/References

Burdette, Franklin L. *The Republican Party: A Short History* (2nd ed.). New York: D. Van Nostrand, 1972.

Congressional Quarterly, Inc. *National Party Conventions, 1831–1984.* Washington, DC: Congressional Quarterly, Inc., 1987.

Downey, Matthew T. "Horace Greeley and the Politicians: Liberal Republican Convention in 1872." *Journal of American History,* 53, 1967.

Johnson, Donald Bruce (Comp.). *National Party Platforms: Vol. 1, 1840–1956.* Urbana: University of Illinois Press, 1978.

Julian, George W., *Political Recollections, 1840 to 1872.* Miami: Mnemosyne, 1960. (Original work published 1883.)

Mayer, George H. *The Republican Party, 1854–1964.* New York: Oxford University Press, 1964.

Ross, Earle D. *The Liberal Republican Movement.* New York: AMS Press, reprint of 1919 ed.

Schapsmeier, Edward L., and Frederick H. Schapsmeier. *Political Parties and Civic Action Groups.* Westport, CT: Greenwood, 1981.

Van Deusen, Glyndon G. *Horace Greeley: Nineteenth Century Crusader.* Philadelphia: University of Pennsylvania Press, 1953.

Libertarian Party

Established in 1971 by David Nolan and Susan Nolan in Westminster, Colorado.

Among the most important persons involved in the founding of this party were Dr. John Hospers, a philosophy professor at the University of Southern California; Edward H. Crane III, the party's first national chair; Manuel Klausner, editor of *Reason* magazine; Murray Rothbard, an economics professor at Brooklyn Polytechnic Institute, now at the University of Nevada, Las Vegas, and dean of the Von Mises Institute at Auburn University; R. A. Childs, a noted libertarian author; Theodore Nathan, an Oregon businessman; and Jim Dean of the *Santa Ana Register* newspaper.

The basic philosophy of the party emphasizes personal liberty and opposition to welfare state policies. But its philosophy is highly eclectic and combines many of the thoughts of social Darwinism as developed by Herbert Spencer, some of Thomas Jefferson's views of government, Friedrich A. von Hayek's notion of laissez-faire economics, and the objectivism of Ayn Rand, among others. The party opposes interference with personal liberty in almost any significant way, and actively seeks and argues for reduction of the size and involvement of government in human affairs. For example, one of the founders of the party has asserted:

> Everywhere that the free market has been permitted to flourish, prosperity for the masses of the people has followed. To the

extent that the government has interfered with the functioning of the free market, the economy is plagued with shortages, inefficiency, and a lower standard of living. (Hospers, 1971, p. 131)

The party membership is likewise eclectic and encompasses individuals from all walks of life and professions. Yet all seem united in their belief that the individual person should be left essentially to do what he or she desires without government restrictions. Libertarian philosophy thus appears anarchical, but the party does not advocate the total abolition of government.

Only four years after its establishment, the Libertarian Party had grown from a minuscule organization to what was essentially the third largest party in the United States. In 1972 it nominated Dr. John Hospers as its presidential candidate and Theodore Nathan of Oregon as his vice presidential running mate. An interesting development took place during this election—a Republican member of the electoral college from Virginia deviated from his party to cast his electoral vote for the Libertarian candidate. This elector, Roger Mac-Bride, soon became something of a celebrity among Libertarians. Indeed, so significant did they consider his vote that they made him their presidential candidate in 1976.

The 1972 platform of the Libertarian Party set the tone for the party's continuing objectives. In its "Statement of Principles," the party began by asserting:

> We, the members of the Libertarian Party, challenge the cult of the omnipotent state, and defend the rights of the individual.
>
> We hold that each individual has the right to exercise sole dominion over his own life, and has the right to live his life in whatever manner he chooses, so long as he does not forcibly interfere with the equal right of others to live their lives in whatever manner they choose.
>
> Governments throughout history have regularly operated on the opposite principle, that the State has the right to dispose of the lives of individuals and the fruits of their labor. Even within the United States, all political parties other than our own grant to government the right to regulate the life of the individual and seize the fruits of his labor without his consent.
>
> We, on the contrary, deny the right of any government to do these things, and hold that the sole function of government is the protection of the rights of each individual: namely (1) the right to life—and accordingly we support laws prohibiting the initiating of force against others; (2) the right to liberty of speech and action—and accordingly we oppose all attempts by government to abridge the freedom of speech and press, as well as government censorship in any form; and (3) the right to property—and accordingly we oppose all government interference with private property, such as confiscation, nationalization, and eminent

domain, and support laws which prohibit robbery, trespass, fraud, and misrepresentation.

Since government has only one legitimate function, the protection of individual rights, we oppose all interference by government in the areas of voluntary and contractual relations among individuals. Men should not be forced to sacrifice their lives and property for the benefit of others. They should be left free by government to deal with one another as free traders on a free market; and the resultant economic system, the only one compatible with the protection of man's rights, is laissez-faire capitalism.

Other planks in the platform addressed such ideas as the repeal of all victimless crime laws; the protection of due process for those accused of crime, and emphasis on the provisions of the Sixth Amendment regarding a speedy trial and restitution for losses incurred by those not convicted; broadening of the rights of speech and press; protection of privacy, including even the participation in the census on only a voluntary basis; the right to keep and bear arms; opposition to the selective service; the sanctity of property rights; the rights of unions and collective bargaining; and opposition to "all intervention by government into the area of economics." Reduction of taxes; elimination of budget deficits; enhancement of free trade; repeal of wage and price controls; opposition to subsidies, tariffs, and quotas; and specifics related to both domestic ills and foreign policy measures (such as comments on foreign aid, currency exchange, military alliances and capability, diplomatic relations, and the United Nations) were also included. This is only a partial list of the many planks included in the platform.

As stated earlier, because of Roger MacBride's bold electoral college vote deviation in the 1972 election, the Libertarian Party, at its convention in Washington, D.C., chose him as its presidential candidate. His vice presidential running mate was California lawyer David P. Bergland. MacBride's background is different from that of the "usual" presidential candidate: he was one of the creators of the television series *Little House on the Prairie,* and before that had been active in Vermont politics, both in the legislature and as a Republican candidate for governor. By 1976, the Libertarian Party had gained enough strength to appear on the ballot in 32 states. It had been increasingly successful in attracting voters from a wide spectrum of the population.

In his 1976 book, *A New Dawn for America: The Libertarian Challenge,* MacBride proclaimed: "There *is* a Libertarian political party. It seeks your vote, and more. It will grow as it has grown since 1971: from nothing to a fifty-state organization in four years. It will run some hundreds of persons for office devoted to its principles this year, and some thousands in election years to come" (pp. 109–110).

In that year its platform began with the statement: "No conflict exists between civil order and individual rights. Both concepts are based on the same fundamental principle: that no individual, group, or government may initiate force against any other individual, group, or government." The platform also contained provisions dealing with a variety of other subjects, ranging from victimless crime, the problems of government secrecy, freedom of religion, privacy, commercial trade, and the economy through such matters as air and water pollution, protection of the consumer, education problems, matters related to occupational health and safety, campaign finance laws, and general military policy, including presidential war powers, Middle East policy, independence for American colonial dependencies (as in the Pacific Ocean, for example), and foreign aid. Other issues were also touched upon. The platform concluded with the statement, "Our silence about any other particular government law, regulation, ordinance, directive, edict, control, regulatory agency, activity, or machination should not be construed to imply approval."

Although support for the Libertarian Party had increased significantly, MacBride received 173,011 votes, only some 0.2 percent of the vote total. He ran well in such states as Alaska, Hawaii, Arizona, Idaho, California, and Nevada.

But the party continued to seek support. It established an organization known as the Young Libertarian Alliance, the objective of which was to attract college and university students. The party also set up the Center for Libertarian Studies in New York City. The center has published various journals and occasional papers, and has emphasized free market—that is, Austrian—economics. A Libertarian Health Association was also established, with the objective of attracting medical doctors and dentists to the Libertarian cause.

By 1980, the Libertarian Party had acquired enough support to appear on the ballot in all 50 states and the District of Columbia. Thus, it had become *the* major third party, nominating hundreds of candidates throughout the country for a variety of offices on all levels of government.

Again, the party's platform enunciated such objectives as a tax cut for everyone; a gradual elimination of the social security system; doing away with military conscription and draft registration; elimination of welfare programs; reduction in military spending, and withdrawal of U.S. troops from foreign countries; freezing pay of government employees; support for the Equal Rights Amendment; legalization of marijuana; full rights for homosexuals; doing away with the Department of Education; withdrawal from NATO; withdrawal from the United Nations; and eliminating the Federal Reserve Board. And the list went on.

The party's presidential and vice presidential candidates that year, Edward E. Clark of California, a lawyer, and David Koch of New York, president of the Koch Engineering Company, received 1.1 percent of the vote, well over 900,000 votes. Because of its views of politics and government, the Libertarian Party accepts no federal funding for its campaigns, based on its belief that this is not a proper role for government to perform.

In 1984, the Libertarian Party appeared on the ballots of some 38 states and the District of Columbia. David P. Bergland was again the party's presidential candidate, and Jim Lewis, a Connecticut sales representative for a bookbinding company, became the vice presidential nominee. Interestingly, 24 of the delegates chose "none of the above." The party platform in 1984 called for the legalization of all drugs; bringing all American troops and weapons home from overseas; and doing away with such government agencies as the CIA, the IRS, national parks, and public schools. In an interview, Bergland also suggested that he would allow the private sector to build all roads, bridges, and dams, and that he would continue public police forces, but do away with municipal fire departments.

In 1988, Representative Ron Paul, a Texas Republican, defeated American Indian activist Russell Means by 76 votes to become the Libertarian Party's presidential candidate in a convention in Seattle. Paul, who has written for the John Birch Society, is a physician who represented part of Houston in Congress for six years. Although he was an early supporter of Ronald Reagan, he indicated that he was driven from the Republican Party by record budget deficits and because the promise to do away with the Departments of Education and Energy was not kept. Paul is a long-time supporter of the gold standard and a vehement opponent of the Federal Reserve Bank, social security programs, the income tax, compulsory health insurance, and farm supports.

The 1988 platform of the party espoused, among other things, the following:

Freedom, coupled with responsibility

Impartial law enforcement to suppress crime

Restitution for victims of crimes

Volunteer jury duty

The right to sue the state

The right to full use, control, and disposal of personal property

Privacy

Opposition to government subsidies

The right to keep and bear arms

The total separation of education from the state

Abolition of the Civil Service System

Many other points were also included in the platform, which stated as well, "Our silence about any other particular government law, regulation, ordinance, directive, edict, control, regulatory agency, activity, or machination should not be construed to imply approval."

The party qualified for the ballot in 40 states. The party received 431,499 votes, or 0.47 percent of the total.

Sources/References

Clark, Edward. *A New Beginning*. Ottawa, IL: Caroline House, 1980.

Collier, Peter. "The Next American Revolution: The Libertarian Party Wants to Set You Free." *New West* (August 27), 1979.

Congressional Quarterly, Inc. *National Party Conventions, 1831–1984*. Washington, DC: Congressional Quarterly, Inc., 1987.

Crane, Ed. "America's Third Largest Party Success!" *Reason*, 9 (August), 1977.

Day, Glenn. *Minor Presidential Candidates and Parties of 1988*. Jefferson, NC: McFarland, 1988.

de Rosa, Peter. "Where They Stand: The Libertarian Party and Its Competition." *Journal of Libertarian Studies*, 3 (4), 1979.

Frazier, Mark. "The Case for Libertarianism." *Ripon Forum* (March), 1973.

Hospers, John. *Libertarianism: A Political Philosophy for Tomorrow*. Los Angeles: Nash, 1971.

MacBride, Robert L. *A New Dawn for America: The Libertarian Challenge*. Ottawa, IL: Green Hill, 1977.

Nolan, David F. "The Road to Liberty: A Brief History of the Modern Libertarian Movement." *Reason*, 10 (May), 1978.

Peterson, Larry. "Here Come the Libertarians, but at the Expense of Which Party?" *California Journal* (June), 1980.

Rand, Ayn. *For the New Intellectual: The Philosophy of Ayn Rand*. New York: Random House, 1961.

Schapsmeier, Edward L., and Frederick H. Schapsmeier. *Political Parties and Civic Action Groups*. Westport, CT: Greenwood, 1981.

Liberty Party (1839)

Established in Warsaw, New York, to foster the abolition of slavery.

Heavy grass-roots support for a new antislavery party was evident in upstate New York, a location in which the great preacher Charles

Grandison Finney had undertaken a religious revival movement. Other influentials were such men as Beriah Green, Gerritt Smith, and William Goodell. Most antislavery men were Whigs.

The party nearly disappeared even before it began: some 500 delegates to its convention, although not formally initiating a new party, had nominated James G. Birney (himself a former slaveholder) and Francis Julius LeMoyne as presidential and vice presidential candidates. Both declined to accept their nominations.

Following this setback, another convention was called in 1840, this time at Albany, New York. This convention was called the National Convention of Friends of Immediate Emancipation. With only 121 delegates present, James G. Birney, who had by now split from the William Lloyd Garrison faction of the Anti-Slavery Society (a faction that opposed political means to achieve its ends) was again nominated. This time he accepted the nomination and the candidacy. Thomas Earle of Pennsylvania was chosen as the vice presidential nominee of the party.

The most important objective of the Liberty Party platform was the immediate abolition of slavery. The fact that it focused almost exclusively on this issue and paid little attention to others was noted by the voters: Birney received only 7,069 votes, some 0.29 percent of the votes cast.

But the Liberty Party had entered into the contest with the full realization that it could not win the election. Indeed, it had no real campaign organization, given the fact that the party's candidate was in England between May and late November.

In 1843, at an August convention held at Buffalo, New York, delegates nevertheless once again named Birney as their standard-bearer. Thomas Morris of Ohio was designated vice presidential candidate. This time the party platform was more eclectic, not only supporting the abolition of slavery by declaring that it was "against natural rights" and stating that the government had "no power to establish or continue slavery," but also advocating public education, freedom of speech and of the press, and the right to petition the government. The platform invited Negroes to join the party. It also called for Irish independence.

The platform ran to more than 3,000 words, making it the longest platform presented by any party fielding candidates in the nineteenth century. Among excerpts from the platform are the following:

> The Liberty party . . . will demand the absolute and unqualified divorce of the General Government from Slavery, and also the restoration of equality of rights, among men, in every State where the party exists, or may exist.
>   . . . we hereby give it to be distinctly understood . . . that, as abolitionists, considering that the strength of our cause lies in its

righteousness—and our hope for it in our conformity to the LAWS of GOD, and our respect for the RIGHTS OF MAN we owe it to the Sovereign Ruler of the Universe, as a proof of our allegiance to Him, in all our civil relations and offices, whether as private citizens, or as public functionaries sworn to support the Constitution of the United States, to regard and to treat the third clause of the second section of the fourth article of that instrument, whenever applied to the case of a fugitive slave, as utterly null and void, and consequently as forming no part of the Constitution of the United States, whenever we are called upon, or sworn, to support it.

But additional support for the Liberty Party ticket did not seem to be forthcoming. In 1844 Birney received 62,300 votes, running well behind James K. Polk, the Democratic winner, and Henry Clay, the Whig.

A convention of the Liberty Party met yet again in Buffalo in 1847. There delegates endorsed the idea that Congress could not intervene directly with slavery. They also nominated John P. Hale as their presidential candidate and Leicester King as vice presidential nominee. But Hale withdrew his candidacy, and in 1848 Gerritt Smith of New York and Charles Foote of Michigan were nominated. They also withdrew.

From its beginning, the party's primary objective was to focus attention on the slavery issue and its abolition. The party deemphasized or ignored other major issues facing the country. It was never able to acquire a broad enough power base to invite widespread support. Then the Liberty Party died; most of those who had been its advocates moved to the Free Soil Party (q.v.).

Sources/References

Bretz, Julian P. "The Economic Background of the Liberty Party." *American Historical Review*, 24 (January), 1929.

Congressional Quarterly, Inc. *National Party Conventions, 1831–1984*. Washington, DC: Congressional Quarterly, Inc., 1987.

Dumond, Dwight Lowell. *Antislavery Origins of the Civil War in the United States.* Ann Arbor: University of Michigan Press, 1959.

_____. *Antislavery: The Crusade for Freedom in America.* Ann Arbor: University of Michigan Press, 1961.

_____. *The Secession Movement 1860–1861.* New York: Octagon, 1963.

Filler, Louis. *The Crusade Against Slavery, 1830–1860.* New York: Harper & Brothers, 1960.

Fladeland, Betty. *James Gillespie Birney: Slaveholder to Abolitionist.* Ithaca, NY: Cornell University Press, 1955.

Schapsmeier, Edward L., and Frederick H. Schapsmeier. *Political Parties and Civic Action Groups.* Westport, CT: Greenwood, 1981.

Sewell, Richard H. *John P. Hale and the Politics of Abolition.* Cambridge, MA: Harvard University Press, 1965.
Smith, Theodore Clarke. *The Liberty and Free Soil Parties in the Northwest.* New York: Russell & Russell, 1967. (Original work published 1897.)

Liberty Party (1932)

Founded by socialist Frank E. Webb in St. Louis, Missouri, in 1932.

The Liberty Party was created to cope with what were felt to be the major ravages of the Great Depression. Its platform focused on such goals as the creation of additional public works projects, nationalization of basic industries, and the expansion of assorted relief projects to be undertaken by the federal government.

The party nominated William H. Harvey—an 81-year-old Populist and well-known author of *Coin's Financial School*—as its presidential candidate, and Frank F. Hemenway of Washington as its vice presidential contender.

As one journal observed, "The nomination was forced upon him [Harvey]—on a platform calling for monetary revision, public ownership of utilities and a five-year moratorium on all private debts" (*Outlook and Independent*, September 9, 1931).

Harvey attempted to merge the Liberty Party with the Jobless Party, but this effort failed largely as a consequence of a disagreement over who would become the presidential candidate of the merged group.

The Liberty Party ticket received a popular vote of only 0.13 percent, or 53,425. It received no electoral votes. Those who did vote for the party were probably persons who might otherwise have supported the Democrat, Franklin D. Roosevelt. But his overwhelming victory over Republican Herbert Hoover made virtually any defection from the Democratic ranks unimportant to the outcome of the 1932 election. Moreover, the party was on the ballot in only nine states— Arkansas, California, Michigan, Montana, New Mexico, North Dakota, South Dakota, Texas, and Washington. The party's poor showing was exacerbated by at least two other factors that seem endemic to the campaigns of third parties: its inability to raise funds and the fact that most voters viewed the party as excessively radical, even for the trying economic times of the 1930s.

The election of Franklin D. Roosevelt and the beginning of the implementation of the liberal left policies of the New Deal made the Liberty Party largely irrelevant.

Sources/References

"Coin Harvey Again." *Outlook and Independent* (September 9), 1931.

Congressional Quarterly, Inc. *National Party Conventions, 1831–1984.* Washington, DC: Congressional Quarterly, Inc., 1987.

"Father Cox Splits with Harvey Group." *New York Times* (August 17), 1932.

"Jobless Name Cox, End Convention." *New York Times* (August 18), 1932.

"Liberty Party Nominates." *New York Times* (July 5), 1932.

McCoy, Donald R. *Angry Voices: Left-of-Center Politics in the New Deal Era.* Port Washington, NY: Kennikat, 1971.

"Maps Presidential Race." *New York Times* (August 15), 1932.

"Repudiate Liberty Party." *New York Times* (July 9), 1932.

Schapsmeier, Edward L., and Frederick H. Schapsmeier. *Political Parties and Civic Action Groups.* Westport, CT: Greenwood, 1981.

Liberty Union Party

Created by former members of the New Party in West Rupert, Vermont, it has been on the ballot in Vermont primary elections since 1974.

This party's platform advocated "a materially secure life for all"; democratic procedures in all aspects of life; that individuals' life-styles be "totally free of government restriction"; that work be "personally satisfying," and that it create a condition of personal security; that males and females have equal rights; that seniors in society be given the respect and dignity they deserve; that nuclear energy programs and power plants be eliminated; and that utilities be made reasonable in terms of costs to consumers. Worldwide human love, solidarity, and the abolition of war were also promoted.

The Liberty Union Party served as a launching pad for the career of one of the most popular independent candidates of the 1980s, socialist Mayor Bernard Sanders, who came close to upsetting the Democratic candidate in the 1988 race for the governorship of Vermont. Dr. Lenora Fulani was its presidential candidate in 1988.

Source/Reference

Day, Glenn. *Minor Presidential Candidates and Parties of 1988.* Jefferson, NC: McFarland, 1988.

Locofoco (Equal Rights) Party

Created in 1836 in New York City by a number of dissident Democrats.

The Democratic Party of New York had historically been divided into at least two factions. The party's early factionalism revolved around personality politics—the names of such eminent personalities as Burr, Clinton, and Livingston figured strongly in the divisive equation. The division was particularly exacerbated during the second administration of Andrew Jackson, when a large dissident group was formed that advocated the radical view that Jackson's campaign against the national bank be extended to state banks and other monopolistic enterprises as well. The immediate objective of this movement was to defeat candidates supported by Tammany Hall.

Opponents of the dissident faction labeled them Locofocos. The appellation had its origin in an event that occurred at a meeting of Democrats at Tammany Hall. A large contingent of dissidents, opposing the Tammany nominations, appeared at a meeting held at the Wigwam on October 29, 1835. Because of the intensity of the factional fight, the Tammany supporters left the meeting, turning off the gaslights as they departed. The dissidents, however, had come "armed" with a new style of match called loco-focos, and they lit candles that they had also been carrying, thus relighting the hall and making it possible to continue the meeting. The label stuck, and, indeed, for a time thereafter, many Whigs referred to Democrats in general as Locofocos.

Among the basic provisions of the Locofoco platform were a call to end the chartering of state banks, direct presidential election, limitations on the power of the national government, a hard-money policy, doing away with monopolies, defending labor unions, and enhancing free trade.

The Locofocos were able to achieve political control over New York City largely through nomination of fusion candidates whom the Whig Party found acceptable. Especially influential in this effort was William Leggett, editor of the *New York Evening Post*. Former members of the Workingmen's Party (q.v.) were also among Locofoco membership.

The Locofocos gave their support to Martin Van Buren of the Democratic Party. Generally, the party supported Van Buren's policies, especially his ideas about an independent treasury. The Van Buren administration eventually adopted much of the Locofoco program. Ultimately, Tammany Hall did likewise.

By 1838 most of the Locofocos once again supported the Democratic Party, and by 1848 the Locofoco Party was defunct.

Sources/References

Byrdsall, Fitzwilliam. *The History of the Loco-Foco or Equal Rights Party.* New York: Burt Franklin, 1967. (Original work published 1842.)

Degler, Carl N. "Locofocos: Urban 'Agrarians.'" *Journal of Economic History,* 16 (1956).

Schapsmeier, Edward L., and Frederick H. Schapsmeier. *Political Parties and Civic Action Groups.* Westport, CT: Greenwood, 1981.

Stanwood, Edward. *History of the Presidency from 1788 to 1897.* Boston: Houghton Mifflin, 1924.

Lowndes County Freedom Organization

A local party established in 1966 in Haynesville, Alabama, by members of the Student Nonviolent Coordinating Committee (SNCC). It used the black panther as its emblem.

The objectives of the organization, according to Stokely Carmichael, leader of SNCC, were to advance the opportunities of blacks in Alabama by getting them involved in local politics and electing members of their ranks to local offices. Its leaders, given their experience with attempts to organize blacks in Mississippi, felt that by remaining a county-level organization the party's chances of success in Alabama would be increased.

It was the intention that the party serve somewhat as a "pilot project" confined only to one county—Lowndes County, Alabama—and only to blacks in an area in which the number of blacks exceeded the number of whites by approximately four to one. The hope was that if the Lowndes County effort proved successful, similar organizational efforts would be undertaken in other Alabama counties in which the black population exceeded the white. A state law permitted such independent county parties.

Black efforts were impeded, however, by the passage of a law that increased the lengths of office terms of incumbent local officers—a move that effectively removed such incumbents from having to compete in the 1966 election. Although that law specifically affected only Bullock County, Alabama, the Democratic Party of Lowndes County added to difficulties faced by blacks by raising the fee to qualify for the primary ballot. Blacks had less money to pay the higher fees and thus were seriously hampered in their running for office. Blacks were adamant, however. They countered by boycotting the Democratic Party's primary election, voting instead for their own candidates. Stokely Carmichael argued that holding their own primary and nominating their own candidates would raise dignity among blacks and would offer hope of their having at least a modicum of control over their own political future. The Lowndes County Freedom Organization thus came into existence. It was at the time the smallest political party in the United States.

Dr. Martin Luther King, Jr., the eminent black leader and clergyman, disagreed with the Carmichael strategy. He urged blacks to vote for all candidates who had been endorsed by black political organizations, regardless of their race. Even so, he did not interfere with the actions that blacks had undertaken in Lowndes County.

The Lowndes County Freedom Organization nominated seven candidates for county office, but election results were dismal: all of the Lowndes County black candidates were defeated. The party then attempted to gain more support by joining with the National Democratic Party of Alabama (q.v.), an organization also advocating black objectives. This merger proved relatively successful, and some black candidates were elected to state and national offices. Although the Lowndes County Freedom Organization was itself unsuccessful as a separate and distinct black party organization, it did offer blacks an opportunity to vote for "their own." It also lent dignity and prestige to the black movement and encouraged blacks to increase their participation in the political process generally. Not necessarily intended at its inception to be an exclusively black party, no southern whites seemed willing to join its ranks. Systematic fear and violence imposed by whites had so intimidated blacks that they felt it futile to brave various threats in order to vote. The Lowndes County Freedom Organization was thus founded as a democratic alternative to existing party structure and practice.

Sources/References

"Alabama Vote Test Voided by U.S. Court." *New York Times* (March 30), 1966.

Corry, John. "The Changing Times in Lowndes County: An All Negro Ticket." *New York Times* (October 31), 1966.

Grant, Joanne (Ed.). *Black Protest: History, Documents, and Analyses, 1619 to the Present*. Greenwich, CT: Fawcett, 1968.

Hulett, John, Stokely Carmichael, and J. Benson. *The Black Panther Party*. New York: Merit, 1966.

"Negroes Lose Fight To Oust All Officers in Lowndes County." *New York Times* (April 1), 1966.

Roberts, Gene. "Student Rights Group Lacks Money and Help but Not Projects." *New York Times* (December 10), 1965.

_____. "Dr. King Bids Alabama Negroes Conquer Fears and Vote as Bloc." *New York Times* (April 30), 1966.

Schapsmeier, Edward L., and Frederick H. Schapsmeier. *Political Parties and Civic Action Groups.* Westport, CT: Greenwood, 1981.

Walton, Hanes, Jr. *Black Political Parties: An Historical and Political Analysis.* New York: Free Press, 1972.

_____. *Black Politics: A Theoretical and Structural Analysis.* Philadelphia: J. B. Lippincott, 1972.

Loyal Democrats of Mississippi

Established in Jackson, Mississippi, in 1968.

Leaders of this movement came from the National Association for the Advancement of Colored People and from the Mississippi Freedom Democratic Party (q.v.), as well as the AFL-CIO of Mississippi, the Young Democrats, and other liberally oriented groups.

The aim of the Loyal Democrats of Mississippi was to challenge the regular Democratic Party of Mississippi to open its membership to blacks. The organization was itself an integrated one that included whites sympathetic to its cause. The regular Democratic Party was not integrated; it not only attempted to exclude blacks but refused even to recognize their political and voting importance in many counties in which they constituted a majority of voters. By forming this integrated group, the Loyal Democrats of Mississippi hoped to challenge the legitimacy of the dominant party and possibly even to elect some candidates in the black-dominated counties.

Challenging the regular Mississippi Democratic delegation (it originally had three black members, but two withdrew) at the national convention of the party in 1968, the Loyal Democrats of Mississippi attacked the regular party for having gerrymandered state districts to make impossible the fair representation of blacks. It also charged that blacks had not been allowed to participate in choosing the state delegates to the national convention. The regular party delegation attempted to defend itself before the national convention's Credentials Committee by arguing that significant progress had been made toward the inclusion of blacks in the politics of the party. After hearing the arguments, the Credentials Committee decided to seat the Loyal Democrats' delegation rather than the virtually all-white delegation sent by the regular party. This decision, which was endorsed by Hubert Humphrey, the ultimate 1968 nominee of the Democratic Party, and by the other leading candidates for the nomination, was important in that it displayed to other convention delegations—

particularly those from the South—that barring blacks from participation in party affairs would no longer be accepted as standard Democratic practice.

In 1969, candidates of the Loyal Democrats of Mississippi were elected to office in Fayette, Mississippi. Notable among these was Charles Evers, a former congressional candidate, who was elected mayor against a white who had held the office for nearly 20 years.

Sources/References

Schapsmeier, Edward L., and Frederick H. Schapsmeier. *Political Parties and Civic Action Groups*. Westport, CT: Greenwood, 1981.
Walton, Hanes, Jr. *Black Political Parties: An Historical and Political Analysis*. New York: Free Press, 1972.

Mississippi Freedom Democratic Party

Established in Jackson, Mississippi, in 1964.

Blacks had effectively been barred from participating in Mississippi politics in almost any capacity since 1876. Before that, during the so-called Reconstruction Period from 1871–1876, blacks had been quite active in state politics. Indeed, with the adoption of a new state constitution and the readmission of Mississippi into the Union in 1870, some 70 percent of the black voting-age population had registered to vote, and many blacks had assumed state office and some had even been elected to both houses of the national Congress. But white resistance, often taking the form of terror tactics and intimidation, subsequent amendments to the Mississippi constitution, and other both legal and illegal methods soon suppressed black participation in Mississippi state politics. Literacy tests, white primaries, so-called grandfather clauses, and other devices were used to reestablish and maintain white control after the election of 1876. In effect, blacks had been systematically barred from any type of significant political participation in that state.

The Mississippi Freedom Democratic Party (MFDP) thus represented an effort on the part of blacks to become involved once again in politics on a meaningful level. Difficulties in establishing the organization were great, and the main sources of support ultimately came from the national government itself (especially from such agencies as the Civil Rights Division of the Department of Justice) and from supporters outside of Mississippi.

The principal effort to exert its political influence was made by the MFDP when it attempted to send its own integrated delegation to the 1964 Democratic National Convention in Atlantic City in order to challenge the all-white regular delegation sent by the Mississippi Democratic Party. The MFDP argued that a bill passed by the Mississippi State Legislature establishing two slates of electors—one pledged and one unpledged—meant that the delegates pledged to the national candidate would not be seated because of the unpopularity of the national Democratic Party in Mississippi. It also argued that the regular delegates were not loyal Democrats because they had not vowed to support the party's nominees, and, especially, that the regular party had violated the Fourteenth Amendment to the Constitution by excluding blacks from the political apparatus in the state.

Minnesota Senator Hubert Humphrey negotiated a compromise at the convention. It involved seating of the regular Mississippi delegation if they pledged to support the national party nominees, treating the Freedom Democrats as honored guests of the convention, and allowing the chairman and the national committeeman of the MFDP to be seated as delegates-at-large. Other parts of the compromise involved provisions for nondiscriminatory delegate selection procedures in the future, and the establishment of a committee to assist in the implementation of these provisions in time for the 1968 convention. The compromise was not accepted.

The Mississippi Freedom Democratic Party, although unsuccessful in its 1964 challenge, did focus national attention on the racial difficulties faced by the Mississippi Democrats in particular, and it did lead to the efforts in 1968 that resulted in the seating of the delegation of the Loyal Democrats of Mississippi (q.v.) at the 1968 Democratic Convention in Chicago. Full participation of southern blacks in the politics of the Democratic Party thus seemed assured for the future. The Mississippi Freedom Democratic Party thus found its ultimate success in the delegation it was able to seat at the convention that nominated Hubert H. Humphrey for president.

Sources/References

Congressional Quarterly, Inc. *National Party Conventions, 1831–1984.* Washington, DC: Congressional Quarterly, Inc., 1987.

Grant, Joanne (Ed.). *Black Protest: History, Documents, and Analyses, 1619 to the Present.* Greenwich, CT: Fawcett, 1968.

Mabry, William Alexander. "Disfranchisement of the Negro in Mississippi." *Journal of Southern History* 4 (August), 1938.

Schapsmeier, Edward L., and Frederick H. Schapsmeier. *Political Parties and Civic Action Groups.* Westport, CT: Greenwood, 1981.

Walton, Hanes, Jr. *Black Political Parties: An Historical and Political Analysis.* New York: Free Press, 1972.

_____. *Black Politics: A Theoretical and Structural Analysis.* Philadelphia: J. B. Lippincott, 1972.

Watters, Pat, and Reese Cleghorn. *Climbing Jacob's Ladder: The Arrival of Negroes in Southern Politics.* New York: Harcourt, 1967.

National Democratic Party (1860)

Established in Baltimore, Maryland, in 1860 to create a proslavery party movement.

Delegates to the regular Democratic Party, at its *earlier* nominating convention in Charleston, had split on the slavery issue. Delegates from the South wished to include in the party's platform a specific statement declaring that no government on any level in the United States could make slave ownership illegal in the territories. Southern delegates were also in opposition to Stephen A. Douglas of Illinois and his position that the people of a given territory should be allowed to make the decision about slavery when statehood was being considered. Northern delegates adopted a plank arguing that the issue should be decided by the U.S. Supreme Court. Not being able to convince the convention of the righteousness of their cause, the southern and anti-Douglas dissidents walked out. The issue of slavery resulted in another bolt by southerners of the same persuasion at a convention held *six weeks later.*

Calling themselves the National Democratic Party, they nominated John C. Breckinridge of Kentucky, who was vice president of the United States, and who had taken the position that the national government should not attempt to keep slavery out of the territories if the Union was to be preserved. Joseph Lane of Oregon was chosen as the vice presidential nominee of the party.

The platform adopted by the National (Breckinridge) Democrats "affirmed" the platform that the Democratic Party had adopted in Cincinnati, but it added several "explanatory resolutions." Among these were the following:

> The Government of a Territory . . . is provisional and temporary and during its existence all citizens of the United States have an equal right to settle with their property in the Territory, without their rights, either of person or property, being destroyed or impaired by Congressional or Territorial legislation. . . .
>
> . . . it is the duty of the Federal Government . . . to protect, when necessary, the rights of persons and property in the Territories, and wherever else its constitutional authority extends.

... when the settlers in a Territory ... [adopt] a State Constitution, the right of sovereignty commences, and being consummated by admission into the Union, they stand on an equal footing with the people of other States, and the State thus organized ought to be admitted into the Federal Union, whether its Constitution prohibits or recognizes the institution of slavery.

... that the enactments of State Legislatures to defeat the faithful execution of the Fugitive Slave Law are hostile in character, subversive of the Constitution, and revolutionary in their effect.

In addition, the platform called for acquisition of Cuba as an American territory, urged that equal protection be given to naturalized citizens, and that a railroad be constructed from the Mississippi River to the Pacific Ocean.

John C. Breckinridge ran third in the presidential voting, receiving nearly 850,000 votes and 72 electoral votes, the latter from the 11 states of the South. Thus, the party had an almost exclusively southern constituency. By its entry into the campaign, it contributed to the defeat of Stephen A. Douglas.

The National Democratic Party went out of existence after the election of 1860. Breckinridge went back to finish his term as vice president. The split in the Democratic Party served as one of the factors contributing to the Civil War and the secession of the South from the Union. Breckinridge himself fought on the southern side when the Confederacy came into existence.

Sources/References

Craven, Avery. *The Coming of the Civil War*. Chicago: University of Chicago Press, 1957.

Crenshaw, Ollinger. *The Slave States in the Presidential Election of 1860*. Gloucester, MA: P. Smith, 1969.

Graebner, Norman A. (Ed.). *The Politics and Crisis of 1860*. Urbana: University of Illinois Press, 1961.

Johnson, Donald Bruce (Comp.). *National Party Platforms: Vol. 1, 1840–1956*. Urbana: University of Illinois Press, 1978.

Schapsmeier, Edward L., and Frederick H. Schapsmeier. *Political Parties and Civic Action Groups*. Westport, CT: Greenwood, 1981.

National Democratic Party (1896)

Established in Indianapolis, Indiana, in 1896.

Made up of conservative Democrats favoring the gold standard, this faction split from the Democratic Party when it nominated William

Jennings Bryan and adopted a platform that favored the free coinage of silver.

Largely because of a national economic depression, monetary reform had become the major issue of the campaign of 1896. The Republican Party favored a hard, noninflationary currency based on the gold standard. The Democratic Party, meanwhile, had come under the influence of midwestern and southern populist forces favoring the free coinage of silver—a policy that spelled inflation and therefore a policy that would benefit debtors, especially those in agriculture. The Democratic Party had been able to gain the support of some Republicans who had left their party over the hard-money/inflationary money, or gold versus silver, issue, but those Democrats who espoused the gold standard and who differed with the Republicans over their pronouncements on the tariff issue decided to found a new party.

In their Indianapolis convention (which was attended by delegates from 41 states and 3 territories), the dissidents named themselves the National Democratic Party and nominated John M. Palmer of Illinois as their presidential candidate and Simon P. Buckner of Kentucky as his vice presidential running mate. The convention also approved a platform urging the gold standard as the foundation of the monetary system. Among the platform's provisions were an introduction that proclaimed that the convention "has assembled to uphold the principles upon which depend the honor and welfare of the American people," and pledges to "equal and exact justice," "freedom of the individual consistent with good government," "preservation of the Federal government in its constitutional vigor," "support of the states in all their just rights," "economy in . . . public expenditures," "maintenance of the public faith and sound money," and opposition to "paternalism and all class legislation."

It went on to condemn the regular Democratic platform as contrary to those principles and declared that it proposed "a reckless attempt to increase the price of silver by legislation to the debasement of our monetary standard, and threaten unlimited issues of paper money by the government." The platform declared that because of these violations of Democratic principles, those there assembled could not "support the candidates of . . . [the Democratic] convention nor be bound by its acts." The National Democratic platform then declared a series of democratic principles in which it particularly believed, addressing such issues as taxation, the tariff (which delegates believed should be used for the raising of revenue only), and free coinage of silver leading to the depreciation of money. Its statement on a gold standard said in part:

> The experience of mankind has shown that by reason of their natural qualities gold is the necessary money of the large affairs

of commerce and business, while silver is conveniently adapted to minor transactions, and the most beneficial use of both together can be insured only by the adoption of the former as a standard of monetary measure, and the maintenance of silver at a parity with gold by its limited coinage under suitable safeguards of law. Thus the largest possible enjoyment of both metals is gained with a value universally accepted throughout the world, which constitutes the only practical bimetallic currency, assuring the most stable standard, and especially the best and safest money for all who earn their livelihood by labor or the produce of husbandry.

Realizing these truths, demonstrated by long public inconvenience and loss, the Democratic Party, in the interests of the masses and of equal justice to all, practically established by the legislation of 1834 and 1853 the gold standard of monetary measurement, and likewise entirely divorced the government from banking and currency issues. To this long-established Democratic policy we adhere, and insist upon the maintenance of the gold standard and of the parity therewith of every dollar issued by the government, and are firmly opposed to the free and unlimited coinage of silver and to the compulsory purchase of silver bullion.

The platform concluded with praise for the Cleveland administration, stating that the reforms initiated under his leadership be continued. It demanded "strict economy," arbitration in disputes arising internationally, "a liberal policy of pensions to deserving soldiers and sailors," continued independence for the Supreme Court, and the supremacy of the law, among other aims.

William McKinley, the Republican candidate, defeated William Jennings Bryan in the presidential election, in large part because of the splitting away from the Democrats of the National Democratic insurgents, even though Palmer received only 133,435 votes (less than 1 percent of the total cast).

William Jennings Bryan ran again for the presidency in 1900 as the candidate of both the Democratic and the Populist parties. He continued to support free coinage of silver. Although the gold Democrat faction did not nominate candidates in 1900, they nevertheless withheld support from Bryan and did not campaign in his behalf. Bryan was again defeated in the national election by McKinley.

The coming of the Spanish-American War and the return of prosperity to the nation's economy sublimated the gold-silver controversy and the factionalism that had plagued the Democratic Party. The National Democratic Party went out of existence soon thereafter.

Sources/References

Coletta, Paola E. *William Jennings Bryan: Political Evangelist, 1860–1908.* Lincoln: University of Nebraska Press, 1964.

Congressional Quarterly, Inc. *National Party Conventions, 1831–1984*. Washington, DC: Congressional Quarterly, Inc., 1987.

Jones, Stanley L. *The Presidential Election of 1896*. Madison: University of Wisconsin Press, 1964.

Johnson, Donald Bruce (Comp.). *National Party Platforms: Vol. 1, 1840–1956*. Urbana: University of Illinois Press, 1978.

Merrill, Horace S. *Bourbon Leader: Grover Cleveland and the Democratic Party*. Boston: Little, Brown, 1957.

Schapsmeier, Edward L., and Frederick H. Schapsmeier. *Political Parties and Civic Action Groups*. Westport, CT: Greenwood, 1981.

Stanwood, Edward. *A History of the Presidency from 1788 to 1897*. Boston: Houghton Mifflin, 1924.

National Democratic Party of Alabama

Established in Birmingham, Alabama, in 1968, by the Alabama Democratic Conference.

The party was led by Charles Morgan, Jr., a white American Civil Liberties Union lawyer, and Dr. John Cashin, a black dentist. As has been the case with many other black parties, the National Democratic Party of Alabama began as an organized reaction to the regular Democratic Party's restriction on rights of participation in party primaries or serving as delegates to the national party convention.

At the party's 1968 conventions, a constitution and a platform were written. A delegation was also chosen whose task it would be to challenge the seating of the regular Democratic delegation at the 1968 national nominating convention. The party's constitution contained a provision accepting the loyalty pledge adopted by the 1964 national convention—a provision that required all delegates to pledge their support to the national nominees, regardless of who they were or what their political philosophy might be. The platform also addressed such issues as the right of all voters in Alabama to vote for any candidate for the nation's highest offices, and attacked the racist nature of Alabama politics. Various other issues were dealt with, all ultimately aimed at the establishment of a party able to create meaningful campaigns for candidates at all levels of public office.

The party's platform included, among others, planks urging changes in the state's tax structure to ensure that the wealthy paid their fair share; developing the economies of the rural areas of the state; addressing the problems of water and air pollution; assuring equal protection of everyone under the law, especially in education, housing, and employment; ensuring the right of political protest; doing away with the draft and with capital punishment; providing free legal services and bail bond laws; and reorganizing the prison system. The platform also advocated granting full rights to students as citizens, free education, and aid to farmers. It also sought assurance that the teaching of history in the state's schools would be accurate, that a consolidated and single welfare program would be established, and that collective bargaining would be assured. The platform also opposed national government foreign and military policies and advocated withdrawal of troops from Vietnam. It further proposed the abolition of the state liquor monopoly in Alabama.

The National Democratic Party of Alabama attempted to challenge the regular Democratic delegation at the 1968 national convention in Chicago. The regular delegation was pledged to support Governor George C. Wallace and his American Independent Party. The National Democratic Party's delegation was unsuccessful in its bid to be seated, and its members therefore returned to Alabama to develop other strategies.

There the party made the decision to run candidates for the governorship, lieutenant governorship, and all local, county, state, and congressional positions. Of the candidates nominated by the party, only 21 were victorious. Nevertheless, the successes signaled the dominant regular Democratic Party that blacks were increasingly a force to be reckoned with, and that their full participation in the activities of the regular party was probably inevitable. The National Democratic Party of Alabama's activities thus served as one more of the many efforts to bring the influence of blacks to bear on the politics of the South and of the nation as a whole. Although not broadly successful at the polls, the National Democratic Party of Alabama accomplished a major objective in its efforts to bring reform to the regular Democratic Party.

Sources/References

Schapsmeier, Edward L., and Frederick H. Schapsmeier. *Political Parties and Civic Action Groups*. Westport, CT: Greenwood, 1981.
Walton, Hanes, Jr. *Black Political Parties: An Historical and Political Analysis*. New York: Free Press, 1972.

National Labor Reform Party

Established in 1872 in Columbus, Ohio.

A creation of the National Labor Union, this party sought to elect candidates whose views were favorable to labor and to labor union objectives.

The party selected Judge David Davis of Illinois as its presidential nominee and Joel Parker of New Jersey as its vice presidential nominee. Calling for the use of greenbacks to help stimulate inflation, its platform also sought other labor-oriented objectives, among them the eight-hour workday, eliminating contract labor of convicts, excluding Chinese from the United States, and federal regulation of railroads and the telegraph industry. It also sought to limit the term of any president to a single four-year term, and advocated reform in civil service procedures.

The party suffered a stillbirth in that its presidential nominee refused to run. He nevertheless did receive one electoral vote from a deviant elector pledged to Horace Greeley, who was running on the Democratic ticket that same year.

Sources/References

Schapsmeier, Edward L., and Frederick H. Schapsmeier. *Political Parties and Civic Action Groups*. Westport, CT: Greenwood, 1981.

Ware, Norman J. *The Labor Movement in the United States, 1860–1895: A Study in Democracy*. Gloucester, MA: Peter S. Smith, reprint of 1929 ed., 1959.

National Liberty Party

Established on July 7, 1904, in St. Louis, Missouri.

The party was made up of blacks and had as its objective the promotion of their civil rights. At their convention, the delegates nominated George E. Taylor, of Iowa, who was president of the Negro National Democratic League, as their presidential candidate, but no other candidates were nominated.

The party's platform began as follows:

> We, the delegates of the National Liberty party of the United States, in convention assembled, declare our unalterable faith in the essential doctrine of human liberty, the fatherhood of God and the brotherhood of man.

Other provisions of the platform continued on this theme. They included such concepts as: "Equal liberty is the first concession that a republican form of government concedes to its people, and universal brotherhood is the cementing tie which binds a people to respect the laws." The platform denounced the idea of caste and called for universal suffrage. "The application of the fundamental principles of the rights of men is always the paramount issue before a people, and when they are strictly adhered to there is no disturbing element to the peace, prosperity, or to the great industrial body politic of the country."

The platform also asserted its belief in civilian control over the military, but it also stated that "when the civil law has been outraged and wrested from the hands of authority it should be understood that military law may be temporarily instituted."

The platform called for doing away with lynching and mob violence. It called for the abolition of polygamy. It suggested that "the right of any American citizen to support any measure instead of party should not be questioned, and when men conform themselves to party instead of principles they become party slaves." Universal suffrage was declared as a major objective and emphasis was placed on a call for the federal government to guarantee physical protection to all citizens. Indeed, the government was asked to indemnify the relatives of those citizens whose life had been taken or injured by any means other than due process. An increase of Negro regiments in the army was requested, and a request for pensions for ex-slaves was included. Government ownership of common carriers was requested to assure equal accommodations for the races, and the right of citizens of the District of Columbia to vote for president and vice president and to have representation in the Congress as well as the right to vote for officers of district local government were sought.

The name of the candidate of the National Liberty Party did not appear on the ballot in any state; nevertheless, some write-in votes were received. But lack of money and general disinterest on the part of both white and black citizens doomed the movement from its inception. The importance of the party perhaps lies in the very effort of blacks to raise public consciousness about the race issue during a period when any involvement of blacks in politics was viewed as beyond political reality. By 1908 the party had died.

Sources/References

Schapsmeier, Edward L., and Frederick H. Schapsmeier. *Political Parties and Civic Action Groups*. Westport, CT: Greenwood, 1981.

Stanwood, Edward. *A History of the Presidency from 1897–1916*. Boston: Houghton Mifflin, 1916.

Walton, Hanes, Jr. *Black Political Parties: An Historical and Political Analysis*. New York: Free Press, 1972.

National Party

Established in 1896 in Pittsburgh, Pennsylvania.

Members of this party came from a faction known as the "broad gaugers" who had seceded from the Prohibition Party (q.v.). The

Prohibition Party had been divided into two factions—the "broad gaugers" and the "narrow gaugers." The broad gaugers wanted the Prohibition Party to include in its platform resolutions on a variety of topics to make it more broadly appealing, perhaps in the style and appeal of the Populist Party (q.v.). The narrow gaugers wanted the party to promote only one issue—the prohibition of the sale and manufacture of intoxicating liquors.

The Prohibition Party was thus in disarray even before the convention of the National Party was held. The platform of the National Party consisted of one resolution made up of a condensation of six Prohibition resolutions, a woman's suffrage resolution, and eleven other planks taken from the minority report of the platform committee of the Prohibition Party.

The National Party platform stated, in part, the desire for

> suppression of the manufacture and sale, importation, exportation, and transportation of intoxicating liquors for beverage purposes. . . . The sale of liquors for medicinal and other legitimate uses should be conducted by the State, without profit, and with such regulations as will prevent fraud or evasion.
>
> No citizens should be denied the right to vote on account of sex.
>
> . . . For the purpose of honestly liquidating our outstanding coin obligations, we favor the free and unlimited coinage of both silver and gold, at the ratio of 16 to 1, without consulting any other nation.
>
> Land is the common heritage of the people and should be preserved from monopoly and speculation. . . .
>
> Railroads, telegraphs, and other natural monopolies should be owned and operated by the government. . . .
>
> The American public schools, taught in the English language, should be maintained, and no public funds should be appropriated for sectarian institutions.
>
> The President, Vice President, and United States senators should be elected by direct vote of the people. . . .
>
> Our immigration laws should be so revised as to exclude paupers and criminals. None but citizens of the United States should be allowed to vote in any State, and naturalized citizens should not vote until one year after naturalization papers have been issued.

The platform also included planks related to income and property taxes, import duties, the contract convict labor system, pensions for ex-soldiers and sailors, the protection of one day of rest out of the seven-day week, and advocacy of the initiative, referendum, and recall.

Some 27 states were represented in the convention, which proceeded to nominate the Reverend Mr. Charles E. Bentley of Nebraska as the party's presidential candidate. James H. Southgate of North Carolina became the vice presidential nominee.

The candidates received 14,003 votes from eighteen states. The comparatively small support for the candidates was probably due to the fact that many National Party members decided to vote for William Jennings Bryan, the candidate of both the Populist and the Democratic parties, whose chances of winning were perceived as being better than those of the candidates of the National Party.

In 1900, the nominees of the National Party were Donelson Caffrey of Louisiana and Archibald M. Howe of Massachusetts, for president and vice president, respectively. But both refused to accept the nomination, and the National Party disintegrated.

Sources/References

Blocker, Jack S., Jr. *Retreat from Reform: The Prohibition Movement in the United States, 1890–1913.* Westport, CT: Greenwood, 1976.

Schapsmeier, Edward L., and Frederick H. Schapsmeier. *Political Parties and Civic Action Groups.* Westport, CT: Greenwood, 1981.

Stanwood, Edward. *A History of the Presidency from 1788 to 1897.* Boston: Houghton Mifflin, 1924.

National Progressives of America

Established in 1938 in Madison, Wisconsin, by Governor Philip La Follette and Senator Robert M. La Follette, Jr., both Republicans.

Trading on their famous name, the La Follettes presented ideas that they hoped would help to extricate the United States from the Great Depression. They hoped to bring together a number of persons from the broad spectrum of political views—radicals, left-wing liberals, and Progressives—in a movement that, when united, would go further than the Roosevelt administration had to enhance the course of economic reform. Actually, Franklin Roosevelt had cut back public works measures, and some of the advances made in economic recovery had been reduced. Roosevelt's interventionist foreign policy also became the target of attack by the La Follettes. The La Follettes were well-known isolationists.

The La Follettes advocated, among other proposals, extensive public works programs; "trust busting"; establishment of minimum wages; ending naval expansion; and, in general, reducing expenditures for the armed services.

Although the La Follette movement aroused interest on the part of a number of individuals—from Norman Thomas, the Socialist, and William Lemke, the previous candidate of the Union Party, for example—others who were more traditional New Dealers and leading liberals, such as Senator George Norris of Nebraska and Mayor Fiorello La Guardia of New York City, did not lend their support to the movement.

The National Progressives performed poorly. Roosevelt's policies, especially those elements that established the Agricultural Adjustment Act and the Fair Labor Standards Act, cut deeply into Progressive support, as did Roosevelt's efforts to place greater expenditures in the Works Progress Administration and other public works programs.

Philip La Follette was defeated for reelection in 1938. Candidates of the National Progressives on the local levels in other states also did poorly—for example, Raymond Haight, who ran for the governorship of California, received fewer than 65,000 votes. Losses in other states served only to undermine the party further. The coming of the war in Europe also contributed to an erosion of the La Follette movement. Finally, the renomination of Franklin Roosevelt and his reelection in 1940 resulted in the demise of the La Follette movement.

Sources/References

McCoy, Donald R. *Angry Voices: Left-of-Center Politics in the New Deal Era.* Port Washington, NY: Kennikat, 1958.
Schapsmeier, Edward L., and Frederick H. Schapsmeier. *Political Parties and Civic Action Groups.* Westport, CT: Greenwood, 1981.
Young, Donald. *Adventures in Politics: The Memoirs of Philip La Follette.* New York: Holt, Rinehart & Winston, 1970.

National Republican Party

Established in Washington, D.C., in 1824 by John Quincy Adams and Henry Clay.

After the 1824 election, the Democratic-Republican Party became split into two factions, the Democratic-Republicans (later the Democrats), led by Andrew Jackson, and the National Republicans, led by President John Quincy Adams.

The National Republican Party was composed of a diverse membership of owners of business and industry, farmers, and laborers. Its primary objective was to prevent Andrew Jackson from winning the presidency. The party also advocated a list of internal improvements for the country.

In the election of 1824, no single candidate for the presidency received a majority of the electoral votes. The election therefore went into the House of Representatives, as provided by the U.S. Constitution. There, Speaker of the House Henry Clay urged the election of John Quincy Adams instead of Andrew Jackson. Adams became president. Once in office, he appointed Clay secretary of state in his administration.

Although the Adams faction controlled Congress from 1825 to 1827, in the election of 1828, Adams and his running mate, Richard Rush of Pennsylvania, were defeated by Andrew Jackson and John C. Calhoun of South Carolina, candidates of the Democratic Republican Party. Jackson and Calhoun received 178 electoral votes to 83 for Adams and Rush.

The only convention ever held by the National Republican Party took place in Baltimore on December 12, 1831. Seventeen states sent delegates, but Alabama, Illinois, Georgia, Mississippi, Missouri, and South Carolina did not. A committee was appointed to determine the legitimacy of the attendees' credentials. When voting for a candidate, delegates rose in their places as their names were called and stated their choice for the nomination. Both nominees—Henry Clay for president and John Sergeant of Pennsylvania for vice president— received unanimous support from the delegates. A committee was appointed to inform Henry Clay of his nomination. This was a device that came to be used for many years thereafter. It involved making a trip to the nominee to inform him of the fact that he had been chosen.

No platform, as such, was adopted by this convention, but it did issue a statement that attacked the corruption, partisanship, and political abuses of the incumbent administration. It also criticized the administration for its opposition to a system of internal improvements, its stand on the tariff issue, its attacks on the national bank, and its policy on Cherokee Indians in Georgia.

In May 1832, upon the recommendation of the convention held in 1831, a national assembly of young men convened in Washington; at this meeting a slate of resolutions was adopted. This list of resolutions is generally considered the first platform ever written at a national convention.

In 10 resolutions, the platform called for unity in order to fulfill such objectives as the "principles adopted by our fathers," protecting American industry, adopting a "uniform system of internal improvements," recognizing that the Supreme Court is the final arbiter of problems arising under the Constitution, and urging the "fearless and independent exercise" of the powers of the U.S. Senate. The platform also denounced the executive for not carrying out the principles of the American Constitution, and attacked the idea that "to the victor belong the spoils." In addition, it denounced the actions of the administration, which considered transferring part of American territory to a foreign government, and criticized the "arrangement between the United States and Great Britain relative to the colonial trade." It closed with the following resolution:

> It is the duty of every citizen of this republic, who regards the honor, the prosperity, and the preservation of our Union, to oppose by every honorable measure the reelection of Andrew Jackson, and to promote the election of Henry Clay, of Kentucky, and John Sergeant of Pennsylvania, as President and Vice-President of the United States.

Election results showed that Andrew Jackson, the Democratic Party nominee, had won over Henry Clay by an electoral vote of 219 to 49.

By 1836, the National Republican Party had largely ceased to exist. Many of its members entered the new Whig Party.

Sources/References

Congressional Quarterly, Inc. *National Party Conventions, 1831–1984.* Washington, DC: Congressional Quarterly, Inc., 1987.

Gammon, Samuel Rhea. *The Presidential Campaign of 1832* (University Studies in Historical and Political Science, Series 40, No. 1). Baltimore: Johns Hopkins University Press, 1922.

Schapsmeier, Edward L., and Frederick H. Schapsmeier. *Political Parties and Civic Action Groups.* Westport, CT: Greenwood, 1981.

Stanwood, Edward. *A History of the Presidency from 1788 to 1897.* Boston: Houghton Mifflin, 1924.

Van Deusen, Glyndon G. *The Life of Henry Clay.* Boston: Little, Brown, 1937.

National Socialist White People's Party

Established by George Lincoln Rockwell in Arlington, Virginia, in 1959.

The objective of the party was mainly to serve the cause of the development of Nazism in the United States. George Lincoln Rockwell, a former naval officer and cartoonist, appointed himself leader of the party. Rockwell had read Adolf Hitler's *Mein Kampf* and had used it as the basis for his own beliefs. The National Socialist White People's Party (NSWPP) grew out of the Committee to Free America from Jewish Domination, an organization that Rockwell had formed earlier.

The NSWPP, modeled on the format used by Nazis in Germany during World War II, was a paramilitary group. Its members wore uniforms similar to those worn by Nazis in Germany during the height of their power there—brown or black, with an arm band displaying a swastika. The party engaged in many demonstrations opposing Jews, blacks, and others it identified as having Jewish, black, or communist leanings. The party's slogans often included such ideas as "Hitler Lives!" and "White Power!" and "Dump Israel Now!"

Rockwell himself was reputed to be something of a recluse. Nevertheless, he published pamphlets such as *The Rockwell Report* and put out a book entitled *This Time the World.* The NSWPP also issued a racially and ethnically slanderous comic book called the *Diary of Anne Fink.* (Anne *Frank* was the Jewish girl who left a diary that later became a book and a movie depicting her life as lived in a secret compartment in the attic of a house in Copenhagen during World War II.)

Rockwell attempted to create a relationship with the Nation of Islam, under the leadership of Elijah Muhammad, but nothing came of it. Rockwell took his racism to London, where, in 1962, he established an organization known as the World Union of National Socialists. He there proclaimed himself "feuhrer" of the movement and openly advocated violent racism. He proclaimed his ultimate objective as achieving power in the United States by running for the presidency and, once having achieved that office, establishing fascism there. His ultimate aspiration was to do away with "undesirables" as he defined the term. Rockwell never succeeded in acquiring much power, but the media gave him significant coverage. His organization probably never exceeded 50 members, although some estimates have placed it as high as 500 money-contributing individuals. The NSWPP had branches in Chicago, Cleveland, Los Angeles, Milwaukee, Minneapolis, San Francisco, and Tracy-Stockton, California.

Other neo-Nazi parties have come into existence from time to time. One—the American National Party—was established in 1962 by John Patler (Patsalos). It joined the National Socialist White People's Party in 1963. Patler later assassinated Rockwell in an Arlington, Virginia, supermarket parking lot in 1967 and was sentenced to 20 years in prison. Rockwell was succeeded by Matt Koehl, Jr. Koehl encouraged members of the organization to seek power through existing political machinery.

The so-called Nazi party in the United States is made up largely of racists and individuals outside of the politically accepted boundaries of American politics. Members have been variously described as hatemongers and malcontents with real or potential personality disorders. Nazi party membership is minuscule—perhaps never in excess of 1,000—and, were it not for the coverage extended by the media, it would probably be largely unheard of. The Federal Bureau of Investigation has suggested that it does not consider the Nazis a real threat to the national security or to the party system. Even the Anti-Defamation League of B'nai B'rith has described the group as politically impotent.

Still other neo-Nazi groups, such as the Aryan Nation, the National Socialist Party, and The Order, have been active, sometimes violently, in recent years. Some of their members have been charged with activities ranging from murder to attempts to violently overthrow the government to civil disturbances and other infractions of the law.

Sources/References

"The Deadly Friendship: George Lincoln Rockwell and John Patler." *New Republic* (September 23), 1967.

Ellerin, Milton. "American Nazis: Myth or Menace?" *Intellect* 106:2397 (June), 1978.

Kneeland, Douglas. "Those American Nazis: Noisy but 'Politically Impotent.'" *This World* (supplement to the *San Francisco Examiner & Chronicle*) (April 30), 1978.

"Nazi Vote-Getter Dismays Carolina GOP." *San Francisco Chronicle* (May 9), 1980.

Schapsmeier, Edward L., and Frederick H. Schapsmeier. *Political Parties and Civic Action Groups.* Westport, CT: Greenwood, 1981.

National States' Rights Party

Created from the factions of the United White Party in 1958 in Atlanta, Georgia.

The membership of the party was composed of white supremacists unalterably opposed to racial integration. It was also a vehemently anti-Semitic organization. It transmitted its antiblack, anti-Jewish ideas in various media ranging from speeches to the publication and distribution of racist and anti-Semitic tracts and newspapers. The party maintained organizational units in 31 states, including all of the southern states. Although small in membership, it received significant media coverage because of its ability to create interest through advocacy of extremist positions. Indeed, its racist and Jew-baiting polemics have been compared to the similarly vitriolic pronouncements made by Gerald L. K. Smith during the 1930s.

Most influential in the establishment of the National States' Rights Party (NSRP) were chiropractor Edward R. Fields and lawyer Jesse B. Stoner. It was Stoner who was later convicted of having planned the bombing of a black church in the 1960s. Fields, of Birmingham, edited the party's newspaper, the *Thunderbolt*, and had been active against Jews since his teenage years. Stoner had been involved in Ku Klux Klan activity since the 1940s and had also been involved in organizing anti-Semitic groups. Another organizer, Matt Koehl, Jr. (see the National Socialist White People's Party), was regarded by the House Un-American Activities Committee as a leading neofascist and hate-group leader.

Among the objectives of the National States' Rights Party were the complete segregation of blacks and their ultimate resettlement in Africa; preventing marriage between whites and members of "mongrel" races, which, in the NSRP view, included Asians, blacks, and Jews; allowing only Caucasians to immigrate into the United States; and the impeachment of all public officials who advocated racial integration. In addition, the party was vehemently anticommunist and opposed U.S. participation in the United Nations. The party supported such activities and programs as the Tennessee Valley Authority, Medicare, social security, and increased pensions for the elderly. The party engaged in picketing the activities and meetings of the Southern Christian Leadership Conference, and in boycotts against businesses serving an integrated clientele or that had themselves integrated their employees. The party promoted a policy of not employing blacks—through this tactic the party hoped to encourage blacks to leave the southern states.

The organization's newspaper proved reminiscent of such racist and anti-Semitic newspapers as *Common Sense* and *The Cross and the Flag*. The *Thunderbolt* attacked not only the usual scapegoats of the neofascists, but also the Federal Bureau of Investigation itself, which the party saw as being part of the so-called Jewish-Communist conspiracy that was allegedly determined to take over the country. Even Senator Herman Talmadge—long a staunch defender of segregation—was portrayed as part of some diabolical Jewish conspiracy. The newspaper advocated the impeachment of President John F. Kennedy and asked that all members of the U.S. Supreme Court be given the death penalty for having provided aid and comfort to America's enemies—acts that, in the party's opinion, made them guilty of treason under the Constitution. The paper repeatedly insisted that the reports that 6 million Jews had been killed by the Nazis during their reign of terror in Europe during World War II were nothing but a hoax.

Members of the party wore armbands picturing a bolt of lightning, and the party was represented by a flag with a white circle containing a red bolt of lightning (the lightning bolt was supposed to be an ancient symbol of the white race). The party's constitution proclaimed that its members were chosen by God to preserve the white race in order to in turn preserve civilization.

In the 1960 presidential election, the National States' Rights Party selected Governor Orval Faubus of Arkansas to run as its presidential nominee, and Admiral John G. Crommelin, an ex-naval officer, to run as vice presidential candidate. The candidates were on the ballot in six states and received 227,881 votes, the most from Louisiana. In 1962, Crommelin, former leader of the U.S. Navy's stunt-flying team, the Blue Angels, ran unsuccessfully against Senator Lister Hill of Alabama. In 1964, the party nominated John Kasper for president and Jesse B. Stoner for vice president. These candidates, on the ballot in three states—Arkansas, Kentucky, and Montana— received fewer than 7,000 votes. In 1972, the party chose not to nominate a candidate. It supported instead Governor George Wallace, who was attempting to gain the Democratic Party's nomination for the governorship of Alabama.

The NSRP was generally able to attract only a handful of racists and demagogues whose primary purpose seemed to be the spreading of hate and vengefulness against blacks and Jews. As the various civil rights laws took effect, the influence of the party waned. The party's ideas had virtually no impact on opinion in the North, and, indeed, ultimately very little on that in the South.

Sources/References

Cook, James Graham. *The Segregationists.* New York: Appleton-Century-Crofts, 1962.

Schapsmeier, Edward L., and Frederick H. Schapsmeier. *Political Parties and Civic Action Groups.* Westport, CT: Greenwood, 1981.

National Unity Campaign

An organization created by ex-Republican Congressman John B. Anderson in 1980.

Never an authentic or actual "third party," this campaign organization was built largely around the somewhat charismatic persona of Anderson himself.

Anderson had first entered politics as the state's attorney in Illinois after he had returned from an assignment as a U.S. foreign service officer in West Berlin. He was later elected to Congress from a traditionally Republican district in Illinois. He served in Congress for 20 years, and eventually became the third-ranking Republican in the House of Representatives.

Anderson had generally taken a traditional Republican—even conservative—approach to politics in the House of Representatives during his tenure there, but his political philosophy seemed to change as a result of American involvement in Vietnam and the civil rights movement, which had led to tumultuous confrontations throughout the country. In what was a significant departure from his generally conservative views, his positions on prayer in public schools, abortion, homosexual life-styles, and other controversial issues began to take on a liberal cast. His attention also focused on the wide economic gap between the nations of the Northern and Southern hemispheres. He sought to deal with the problem of stabilizing the political systems of Third World countries. He hoped thus to stave off direct political and possibly military confrontations between the United States and other countries having political interests in those areas.

In 1980, Anderson had unsuccessfully attempted to gain the Republican nomination for the presidency. Even though he had served in the House of Representatives for nearly 20 years, he had not acquired a distinguished and nationally known political reputation nor had he done anything in particular to identify himself with new or innovative proposals. In other words, he had not excited a great deal of national interest in his program and policy statements.

Yet his early efforts in the 1980 primary elections proved quite successful, and he impressed leaders and voters alike. In Massachusetts and Vermont, for example, he ran very well against both George Bush and Ronald Reagan. But in his home state of Illinois, Anderson lost to Republican Reagan, and in the Wisconsin primary in April, he ran third against both Reagan and Bush.

The National Unity Campaign held no convention. Instead, Anderson announced on April 24, 1980, that he was running for president as an independent. On August 25, 1980, he announced that Patrick J. Lucey, former Democratic governor of Wisconsin, had accepted his offer to become the vice presidential candidate for the movement. Recognizing his own political vulnerability among the voters, Anderson's selection of Lucey was clearly a move toward what he hoped would bring him the support of liberal Democrats.

By the time Anderson had made his decision to enter the presidential race, he faced one of the traditional difficulties of minor candidates in the presidential contest—it was already too late to get on the ballot through regular filings in many states because of the expiration of filing deadlines for third party candidacies. But running as an independent helped to circumvent this difficulty.

Aside from suffering difficulties in getting on the ballot, Anderson, from the outset of his entry into the campaign, had to confront at least two other major problems: raising sufficient funds to run a meaningful campaign, and getting necessary publicity to make people aware that he was there—and that he was a serious candidate. Moreover, although Anderson had run strongly in early public opinion polls, by August of 1980 his stature and support had begun to wane. However, because of efforts on the part of the League of Women Voters, Anderson was provided the opportunity to participate in the televised presidential debates for that year. Anderson did debate the Republican candidate, Ronald Reagan, but Jimmy Carter, the Democratic nominee, refused to debate him. Funding for Anderson's campaign was also approved by the Federal Election Commission, but only on a retroactive basis (thus making the money essentially useless in the immediate sense) and dependent upon whether he would receive at least 5 percent of the popular vote in the election. Thus, forced to borrow money, Anderson was never able to compete fully and effectively on a financial basis with the major Republican and Democratic contenders.

John Anderson's name ultimately did appear on the ballots of all 50 states, and he did receive more than 5 percent of the number required to receive federal funding. In fact, he received more than 5.7 million popular votes. This was the second-largest number of votes ever received by a third party or independent candidate in the nation's history.

In what will surely be documented as one of the lengthiest platforms in American political history (it runs to some 75 pages in Donald Bruce Johnson's compilation of American party platforms), Anderson first presented a litany of problems besetting the country, declaring that "to cure our nation's ills, we must begin by understanding them." Suggesting that "we are all liberals, we are all conservatives," Anderson stated that his campaign would be based on "clear and simple" principles, among which would be restoring the nation's "economic vitality" through use of the tax code, stimulation of increased savings, and increase in the formation of capital. In addition, it would be necessary to control inflation and to "move aggressively to keep American capital at home to be used for American purposes."

The platform continued with lengthy discussions of recession, inflation, and attempts to gain full employment and focused on technological research efforts, the use of regulations to "make . . . a safer and more prosperous economy," problems of energy, and industrial and business policy. Other sections of the platform dealt with transportation, agricultural problems, the space program, international economics, and the need to consult with "the working man and woman of America." Extensive treatment was given to the role of cities in the future of the country, housing and neighborhood problems, health care, reforms in the welfare system ("one of the great unfulfilled promises of government"), and the needs of senior citizens and the family. Problems of veterans and education were also examined. The arts and the environment were addressed, along with civil rights, immigration, "justice for American women," and help for the handicapped. National security and U.S. relations with various nations in various sections of the world were given extensive analysis, and the issues of human rights, foreign aid, intelligence, nuclear weapons proliferation, and the role of the United Nations were covered.

The platform concluded with a plea from Anderson for an "Independent President." Such a president was needed, he argued, because the two major parties had been inadequate to deal with the job of running the country and of forming policies relevant to the present age. Among other things, said the platform, the president must be a "problem-solver" and a "policy coordinator," and must exhibit leadership and resolve. In conclusion, the platform declared:

> We seek a workable synthesis of policy and program, for the next administration must blend new ideas with old, innovative concepts with traditional values, proven approaches with tentative ones. In responding to the challenges we face, government must be frankly experimental in some fields, conventional in others. It must also be utterly ruthless in judging its performance and pruning its failures. These convictions will animate our administration.

> We speak for a patriotism greater than party. And we invite patriots of all persuasions to join with us in shaping a government that can shape the future.

Anderson kept his options open for 1984, but because of the realities of the situation in 1984, his candidacy did not resume. Although he and some supporters attempted actually to establish a National Unity Party, those efforts failed and he did not run again. Anderson continued to feel, nevertheless, that neither Democrats nor Republicans offered viable alternatives to the problems that faced the country.

Sources/References

Congressional Quarterly, Inc. *National Party Conventions, 1831–1984.* Washington, DC: Congressional Quarterly, Inc., 1987.

Johnson, Donald Bruce (Comp.). *National Party Platforms of 1980: Supplement to National Party Platforms, 1840–1976.* Urbana: University of Illinois Press, 1982.
Smallwood, Frank. *The Other Candidates: Third Parties in Presidential Elections.* Hanover, NH: University Press of New England, 1983.

National Woman's Party

An organization formed by a merger of the Congressional Union for Woman Suffrage, the Congressional Committee of the National American Woman Suffrage Association, and contingents from the state level, in Washington, D.C., in 1916.

The roots of the National Woman's Party (NWP) can be traced to the work of Alice Paul and Crystal Eastman as early as 1912, although Alice Paul became its driving force. Paul was a Quaker (as was Susan B. Anthony) and, thus, "always believed in Woman Suffrage" (Irwin, 1971, p. 7). A woman of extraordinary achievement for her time, she held a B.A. from Swarthmore, and an M.A. and Ph.D. from the University of Pennsylvania. She had also graduated from the New York School of Philanthropy; had been a student at the Woodbrooke Settlement for Social Work at Woodbrooke, Birmingham, England; had attended the University of Birmingham; and had been a graduate student of sociology and economics in the University of London. Her involvement in social work was no less extraordinary. For example, she had been a resident worker of the New York College Settlement and a worker in the Summer Lane Settlement, and she had been involved with the Charity Organization Society in London and the Peel Institute for Social Work in Clerkenwell, London. She had also been a resident worker for the Christian Social Union Settlement of Oxton, in London, and had been active in the Pankhurst movement there.

Paul had once been a member of the National American Woman Suffrage Association, an organization that repudiated her militant tactics and with which she ultimately severed her relationship. Indeed, there was widespread disagreement over how to accomplish the objectives of women among such organizations as the NWP, the League of Women Voters, the Consumers' Union, the Business and Professional Women, and the U.S. Women's Bureau. NWP activists were generally of the upper middle class, with a number of wealthy and socially prominent women also involved. Many were related by birth or marriage, and virtually all of the influential members of the movement lived in the Northeast. Through its use of militant tactics, the National Woman's Party was instrumental in securing the adoption of the Nineteenth Amendment to the Constitution of the United States in 1920.

The National Woman's Party attacked in particular the Democratic Party (which, in the opinion of the feminists, had prevented women from achieving universal suffrage) and President Woodrow Wilson, who had originally openly opposed voting for women. NWP members thus resorted to demonstrations, marches, and virtually daily picketing outside the White House. The NWP argument was that Wilson's behavior was hypocritical: on the one hand he wished to make the world safe for democracy, yet, on the other, he opposed woman suffrage at home. The National Woman's Party itself became the object of counterdemonstrations and outright harassment; even the police were frequently hostile to the party's activities. The National American Woman Suffrage Association also opposed the NWP largely because of the latter's militant tactics.

The 1916 platform of the NWP read as follows:

> The National Woman's Party stands for the passage of the Amendment to the United States Constitution known as the Susan B. Anthony Amendment, proposing an Amendment to the Constitution of the United States extending the right of Suffrage to women:

> Resolved by the Senate and the House of Representatives of the United States in Congress assembled (two-thirds of each House concurring therein) that the following article be proposed in the legislatures of the several States as an Amendment to the Constitution of the United States, which, when ratified by three-fourths of the said legislatures, shall be valid as part of such Constitution, namely:

> Article 1, Section 1. The right of citizens of the United States to vote shall not be denied or abridged by the United States on account of sex.

> Section 2. Congress shall have power, by appropriate legislation, to enforce the provisions of this article.

> The National Woman's Party, convinced that the enfranchisement of women is the paramount issue, pledges itself to use its united vote to secure the passage of the Susan B. Anthony Amendment, irrespective of the interests of any national political Party, and pledges its unceasing opposition to all who oppose this Amendment.

The National Woman's Party was particularly influential in the 1918 election. Indeed, its intense efforts in opposition to the Democrats were in part responsible for the election of a majority of Republicans to the U.S. Senate. Congress soon endorsed a woman suffrage amendment that was ratified by the necessary number of states, thus enabling women to vote in the 1920 presidential election. Still, not having become habituated to voting, women did not participate in the numbers that might have been expected. Indeed, the actual percentage of Americans voting (given the fact that the number eligible had effectively doubled) dropped precipitously in the 1920 election.

It should be noted also that Alice Paul was able to exert sufficient influence in Congress to get the introduction of the first Equal Rights Amendment, known as the Lucretia Mott Amendment, in 1923. But it was not until the 1970s that the amendment was submitted to the states, and, once submitted, it was not approved, even after an extension of time beyond that allowed in the original submission to the states.

Never a political party in the sense in which we understand the term today (involving the nomination of candidates, for example), the NWP reached its zenith of power during the 1920s, when some 50,000 individuals were on its rolls. Since then, the party has declined steadily. It is currently involved in efforts to resuscitate the Equal Rights Amendment and to urge women to run for political office, and in attempts to exert its influence in the appointment of women to government positions. In short, the National Woman's Party has lost most of its effectiveness, and its militancy is now mainly of historical interest.

Sources/References

Becker, Susan D. *The Origins of the Equal Rights Amendment: American Feminism between the Wars.* Westport, CT: Greenwood, 1981.

Flexner, Eleanor. *Century of Struggle.* Cambridge, MA: Harvard University Press, 1959.

Irwin, Inez Haynes. *The Story of the Woman's Party.* New York: Kraus Reprint, 1971. (Original work published 1921.)

Irwin, Inez Haynes, and Florence Kelley. "Equal Rights Amendment." *Good Housekeeping,* 78 (March), 1924.

Kraditor, Aileen. *The Ideas of the Woman Suffrage Movement, 1890–1920.* Garden City, NY: Doubleday, 1971.

Parkhurst, Genevieve. "Is Feminism Dead?" *Harper's,* 170 (May), 1935.

Paul, Alice, et al. "Should Congress Approve the Proposed Equal Rights Amendment to the Constitution? PRO." *Congressional Digest,* 9 (November), 1930.

Schapsmeier, Edward L., and Frederick H. Schapsmeier. *Political Parties and Civic Action Groups.* Westport, CT: Greenwood, 1981.

New Alliance Party

Established in 1979 in New York City.

Beginning national organizational efforts in 1983, the group was composed mainly of persons advocating the interests of welfare labor, and community groups. Leonora Fulani was the presidential candidate of the party in 1988.

Among objectives of the party were the abolition of poverty, attainment of housing for all, raising taxes on landlords and corporations, the cessation of police violence, a livable wage, rights for homosexuals of both sexes, doing away with discrimination against AIDS victims, the right to trade unions for all, enhancing women's rights, doing away with U.S. intervention in various places, parity for farm production and an end to mortgage foreclosures on farms, and sovereignty for Native Americans.

Fulani received 218,159 votes in 1988, or 0.24 percent of votes cast.

Source/Reference

Day, Glenn. *Minor Presidential Candidates and Parties of 1988.* Jefferson, NC: McFarland, 1988.

Nonpartisan League

Established in Bismarck, North Dakota, in 1915.

Although by definition not a political party per se, the Nonpartisan League nevertheless was active in nominating and supporting various candidates and in attempting to elect them to office.

Led by Arthur C. Townley, a former Socialist, the Nonpartisan League was instrumental in efforts to organize farmers to vote in support of their own special interests. Especially influential in Minnesota and the Dakotas, the League's activities extended at one time or another through an area ranging from the states of Wisconsin to Washington and even into parts of the Southwest.

Its socialist-oriented ambitions involved primarily the fulfillment of the organization's perceptions of the needs of agriculture defined more or less as a cohesive bloc: crop insurance against the vicissitudes of the weather; farm credits and loans through state banks; agricultural tax exemptions; and state ownership of such facilities as grain elevators, storage sites, meat-packing firms, and processing companies. These goals were rejected as objectives of public policy by most Americans during the 1920s. Moreover, the antiwar and otherwise pacifist statements by some of the Nonpartisan League's prominent spokesmen—having to do especially with the U.S. role in World War I—tended to impede its expansion and, at the time, were interpreted as advocating a pro-German, anti-American, view.

Still, the Nonpartisan League was able to use its power to elect Lynn J. Frazier governor of North Dakota in 1916. Many of its candidates were also successful in their campaigns for state legislative offices. After a decline in its impact during the decade of the 1920s, the Nonpartisan League became more vocal once again during the Great Depression of the 1930s. It was influential in introducing the Farm Bankruptcy Act (which placed a moratorium on foreclosures on farm property) and became an especially vocal advocate of an isolationist foreign policy, vehemently opposing U.S. entry into World War II.

During its prime, the Nonpartisan League had been able to exercise its influence in the election of both Republican and Democratic politicians on the national and state levels. Perhaps one of its most important contributions during the earlier days of its existence was the influence it had on the origins of the Farmer-Labor Party in Minnesota (q.v.), and its influence on the election of North Dakota Senator Quentin Burdick in 1960.

Sources/References

Bruce, Andrew A. *Non-Partisan League.* New York: Macmillan, 1921.

Morlan, Robert. *Political Prairie Fire: Nonpartisan League, 1915–1922.* Minneapolis: University of Minnesota Press, 1955.

Russell, Charles E. *The Story of the Nonpartisan League: A Chapter in American Evolution.* New York: Harper & Brothers, 1920.

Saloutos, Theodore. "Rise of the Non-Partisan League in North Dakota." *Agricultural History,* 20 (January), 1946.

Schapsmeier, Edward L., and Frederick H. Schapsmeier. *Political Parties and Civic Action Groups.* Westport, CT: Greenwood, 1981.

Peace and Freedom Party

Established in Ann Arbor, Michigan, in 1967.

This party should not be confused with the Freedom and Peace Party, which nominated comedian Dick Gregory as its candidate in some states.

The objective of the party was to instigate revolutionary change in the United States. The party thus nominated Eldridge Cleaver, then minister of education for the Black Panther Party (q.v.), as its presidential candidate. A Cornell University economics professor, Douglas F. Dowd, was selected as the vice presidential candidate. The Peace and Freedom Party and the California Black Panther Party (the latter not to be confused with the Lowndes County Freedom Organization, q.v.) worked together to create a party with appeal to various groups of radical dissenters around the country.

Cleaver followed a radical line during his campaign for the presidency and formed a coalition with leaders of the so-called New Left movement of the 1960s, hoping that such a relationship would hasten the accomplishment of the Peace and Freedom Party's cause. In general, he called for "black liberation" from social, economic, and political oppression, and appealed to the cause of black nationalism. He attacked U.S. involvement in Vietnam. Calling the police "pigs," he urged that black people arm themselves for protection against alleged police brutality. He also insisted that the United Nations recognize the Black Panthers as legitimate representatives of an independent black minority nation.

Peace and Freedom activists were—and remain—mainly middle-class. Characteristics of income, occupation, and education data clearly point to this reality. Over 20 percent of the Peace and Freedom Party membership was made up of students.

> PFP evolved during a critical election year as a legitimate form of protest against the general inertia of established governmental institutions to deal radically with two crucial issues at the time: American commitment to the war in Vietnam and the question of black liberation. (Elden and Schweitzer, 1971, p. 764)

The Peace and Freedom candidates appeared on the ballot in 19 states, drawing 136,385 votes but no electoral votes in 1968.

A similar pattern of defeat followed in 1970 in California, where the Peace and Freedom candidates ran a long list of candidates for the state legislature and for the governorship. More recently, the Peace and Freedom Party has taken more "mainstream" positions; in California's First Congressional District its candidate received an unprecedented 14.7 percent of the vote in 1990, thereby spoiling the Democratic incumbent's chance for re-election and giving victory to a Republican.

To summarize, the Peace and Freedom Party policies reflected "an underlying sense of discontent and disenchantment with the general inefficacy of existing political institutions" (Elden and Schweitzer, 1971, p. 771). But the degree of support they received was always marginal.

In 1988, the party advocated, among other things, ending the arms race; withdrawing U.S. troops from foreign countries; doing away with the CIA and the NSC and other intelligence-gathering groups; establishing guaranteed income; ending discrimination;

guaranteeing equal pay for equal work; replacement of nuclear energy by such alternatives as wind, tidal, and solar energy; restoration of clean air and environment; and abolition of the death penalty. The party's candidate, Herbert Lewin, received only 10,312 votes, some 0.01 percent of the popular vote cast. The party continues to be active on feminist and socialist causes, especially in California.

Sources/References

Day, Glenn. *Minor Presidential Candidates and Parties of 1988*. Jefferson, NC: McFarland, 1988.

Elden, James M., and David R. Schweitzer. "New Third Party Radicalism: The Case of the California Peace and Freedom Party." *Western Political Quarterly*, 24 (December), 1971.

Romero, Patricia W. (Ed.). *In Black America*. New York: Publishers Co., Inc., 1969.

Schapsmeier, Edward L., and Frederick H. Schapsmeier. *Political Parties and Civic Action Groups*. Westport, CT: Greenwood, 1981.

Sheer, Robert (Ed.). *Eldridge Cleaver: Post-Prison Writings and Speeches*. New York: Random House, 1969.

Walton, Hanes, Jr. *The Negro in Third Party Politics*. Philadelphia: Dorrance, 1969.

_____. *Black Political Parties: An Historical and Political Analysis*. New York: Free Press, 1972.

_____. *Black Politics: A Theoretical and Structural Analysis*. Philadelphia: J. B. Lippincott, 1972.

People's Party (1823)

Established in Albany, New York.

This party's specific objective was to elect John Quincy Adams president of the United States. The party also wished to achieve various electoral reforms.

The party opposed the so-called Bucktail Republicans, members of the Democratic-Republican Party who favored the election of Andrew Jackson as president. Support for the People's Party came from such eminent figures as Henry Wheaton, Isaac Ogden, and Peter A. Jay.

The party held its convention in Utica, New York, in 1824, where it nominated DeWitt Clinton, the former governor, as its candidate for governor that year. General James Tallmadge was the party's candidate for lieutenant governor. One of the innovative planks in the party's platform was the call for direct popular election of presidential electors. The platform also advocated the election of John Quincy Adams to the presidency. The strategy of the party proved to be successful: not only did the People's Party win control of the government of the state of New York, but it was instrumental in gaining the support of New York for John Quincy Adams's candidacy for the presidency.

The People's Party expired in 1826 when its various elements were able to come together once again to unite behind the candidacy of Andrew Jackson and to coalesce into the Democratic Party.

Sources/References

Fox, Dixon Ryan. *The Decline of Aristocracy in the Politics of New York 1801–1840*. New York: Harper & Row, 1965.

Schapsmeier, Edward L., and Frederick H. Schapsmeier. *Political Parties and Civic Action Groups*. Westport, CT: Greenwood, 1981.

People's Party (1971)

Established in Dallas, Texas, by radical "antiwar" and "peace" groups.

Cochairs of the group were Dr. Benjamin Spock, the well-known pediatrician, and Gore Vidal, author of a number of best-selling books. Representatives from such groups as the National Conference for a New Politics and the Peace and Freedom Party (q.v.) were also involved in organizing the party.

In 1972, at St. Louis, the convention chose as its presidential candidate Dr. Spock himself, and as its vice presidential candidate Julius Hobson, a well-known black activist, of Washington, D.C. Spock had long since established for himself a reputation as an antiwar protester, having been chair of the National Conference for a New Politics and the National Committee for a Sane Nuclear Policy. A democratic socialist, he advocated such objectives as reducing the military budget by at least one-half, placing a $50,000 limit on personal income, doing away with property and sales taxes, and establishing a minimum income of $6,500 for every family.

The party's platform was a lengthy one. It devoted attention to such subjects as ageism, culture and the arts, the natural environment, business and economic conditions, education in general, the special problems of the farmer, the details of foreign policy, the lack of people's influence in the governing process, health care, the legal system and law enforcement, racism, sexism, and other matters. In the preamble to the platform, the party asserted, for example:

> We recognize that the fulfillment of the basic needs common to all
> of us is frustrated by the big-finance, big-corporation, big-military

> establishment which maintains its control through its servants in the Demo-republican Party and which constantly tightens its stranglehold over our foreign and domestic policies and our very lives. . . .
> Since we believe that the present political parties of the United States neither represent nor reflect the political, economic and social hopes of a large segment of people in this country, we shall unite into a new party for positive change which will ensure a creative future for our people.

On the subject of ageism, for example, the platform declared its support for, among other objectives, the right to vote and to hold office for young people, "beginning at whatever age an individual decides to accept those responsibilities." For the elderly it demanded "an end to mandatory retirement," assurance of good housing, doing away with the property tax, development of a good transportation system, and "the right to guaranteed annual income, providing supplementary income, if necessary." Other elements of the platform urged the establishment of a Department of Culture and the Arts, an effort to "de-professionalize the arts in order to encourage the creative potential in every individual," development of a Center for Ecological Research and Action, and voluntary population control through sex education and contraception. The platform declared that "the major economy of this country should become the property of the people collectively," and that schools no longer "serve the interests of the ruling class of the nation, the governing class of the rich and the powerful." It insisted that "our farmers need to be liberated from the cost-price squeeze resulting from the scuttling of the parity formula that makes farmers the main shock absorber of an inflation-ridden economy." Its foreign policy section was lengthy, and touched upon such topics as self-determination for all people in the world, ending military aid, withdrawing U.S. troops and supplies, giving "meaningful assistance to Third World people," and use of the World Court to solve international differences. It also declared that "health care is a right, not a privilege." It urged that "inequities in the American judicial system" be corrected through a seven-point program. It attacked racism and sexism, and demanded rights for homosexuals and other groups against whom alleged discrimination had been perpetrated by society.

The party's aspirations were significantly dashed that year, however, when its candidates—on the ballot in 10 states—received only 78,751 votes, only 0.1 percent of the total cast nationally. Of those, some 55,000 came from California. Critics of the People's Party effort suggested that the Spock-Hobson ticket took votes away from George

McGovern's campaign for the Democratic Party, thus giving Republican Richard M. Nixon a greater opportunity to win reelection.

After the 1972 election, the People's Party became a congeries of autonomous groups on the state level. These groups had different names—Country People's Caucus, New America Party, No Party, Commongood Party, and others.

As its 1976 candidates, the People's Party selected Margaret Wright of California, a black well known for her involvement in civil rights activities, as its presidential nominee, and Maggie Kuhn of Pennsylvania, a woman active in the Gray Panthers, a group of senior citizens involved in lobbying for causes for the elderly, as vice presidential nominee. Kuhn refused to run, however, and Dr. Spock, the former presidential candidate, replaced her as the nominee after a mail and telephone poll was taken of the delegates. Wright and Spock were officially endorsed at the 1976 convention of the party in San Francisco. The Wright-Spock ticket was also supported by the California-headquartered Peace and Freedom Party (q.v.), the Human Rights Party (Michigan), and the Bicentennial Reality Party (Washington).

The platform of the party that year declared:

> The People's Party is a national coalition of state and local organizations and individuals working together to build socialism. We struggle against the capitalist economic system, which puts power and wealth in the hands of a few. We work for a classless society. We work to abolish the employer-employee wage labor relationship. We work for production for people's needs rather than for private profit. At the same time, we struggle in our lives against oppressive power relationships: male domination, white skin privilege, privilege of adults over the young and elderly, and the privilege of heterosexuals over gay males and lesbians. To build this socialist system we recognize the long-term need for a united organization of all working class people. We seek cooperation, both for this organized class-wide unity and for ongoing struggles, with compatible groups and organizations.

The platform then addressed ageism, agricultural problems and programs designed to deal with them, ecological problems, the American economic condition, foreign policy goals (e.g., "dismantling of the Defense Department, CIA, DIA, U.S. participation in Interpol, and all other agencies which exist to destroy the struggles of working people around the world"), health care problems, changes in the legal system, the control of the media by the "economic rulers of the capitalist system," racism, and sexism.

In a conclusion expressing certain "organizational principles," the platform proclaimed:

> We are a socialist party, because in unity we believe that socialism
> is the answer to the decay and increasing barbarism of this society
> and that the working class, as opposed to the capitalist class, is the
> agent of revolutionary change, which can and will take power and
> run a new society on a collective democratic basis.

The party was again not very successful in exciting people's
support, notwithstanding its title. The national vote for Wright was
only 49,024, with 85 percent of that total coming from California.

The party has not run candidates since that time. The People's
Party, which is not to be confused with the old Populist Party (q.v.),
which was also known as the People's Party, never won wide support
mainly because of its radicalism.

Sources/References

Congressional Quarterly, Inc. *National Party Conventions, 1831–1984.* Washington, DC: Congressional Quarterly, Inc., 1987.

Johnson, Donald Bruce (Comp.). *National Party Platforms: Vol. 2, 1960–1976.* Urbana: University of Illinois Press, 1978.

Malcolm, Andrew H. "Spock Nominated by People's Party." *New York Times* (July 30), 1972.

Schapsmeier, Edward L., and Frederick H. Schapsmeier. *Political Parties and Civic Action Groups.* Westport, CT: Greenwood, 1981.

People's Peace Prosperity Party

An extremely short-lived party established by the Reverend Kirby
James Hensley in Modesto, California, in 1970.

This party's objective was to create a strong third party so that control
of the government could be returned to the people. Hensley considered himself to be the spokesman of the only party that could effectively bring this about.

Earlier the founder and presidential candidate of the Universal
Party (q.v.), Reverend Hensley was the bishop of the Universal Life
Church, Inc. He was particularly notorious for selling mail-order divinity degrees. Any man, woman, or child could, in fact, become a
minister of the Universal Life Church and, having the certificate from
Hensley, could perform marriages, officiate at funerals, perform baptisms, and fulfill a number of other functions usually reserved for
regularly ordained ministers and priests.

Reportedly, Hensley could neither read nor write, although he
possessed a Ph.D. from Hollywood University of Los Angeles,

another mail-order degree mill. A product of the North Carolina mountains and a one-room schoolhouse, he became a leader of young people for the Church of God in Oklahoma. He later moved to California, where he organized churches in Bakersfield, San Jose, and Sunnyvale, and became successful as a contractor as well. He organized the Universal Life Church in 1962 after allegedly memorizing the Bible by having it read to him. He believes that heaven is having what you want, and hell is not having it. He has "ordained" at least 65,000 "ministers" since 1962.

Running for the governorship of California in 1970, and as the presidential candidate of the People's Peace Prosperity Party in 1972, he received an insignificant number of votes. His support was so insignificant that the party ceased to exist almost immediately.

Sources/References

"Dispenser of Divinity." *Newsweek* (May 5), 1969.
"Mail Order Ministries." *Time* (February 21), 1969.
Schapsmeier, Edward L., and Frederick H. Schapsmeier. *Political Parties and Civic Action Groups.* Westport, CT: Greenwood, 1981.

Poor Man's Party

Established in Newark, New Jersey, by swine producer and saloon owner (the establishment was known as Tammany Hall Tavern) Henry Krajewski in 1952.

Putting himself forward as the Poor Man's Party candidate in 1952, Krajewski named Frank Jenkins, also of New Jersey, as vice presidential candidate of the party. Krajewski campaigned while holding a black-and-white pig under his arm. The pig, he said, symbolized the squealing of the American people as a result of government "hogging."

The "platform" of the Poor Man's Party included the following objectives, among others: lowering taxes, maintaining a strong defense posture, the achievement of total victory in the Korean War, refusal to recognize Communist China, the annexation of Canada, general opposition to communist movements throughout the world, that one year of work on a farm be required of every young person in the United States, and something Krajewski referred to as a "two-president system"—that both a Democrat and a Republican be elected to the presidency so that they could watch each other and thus prevent a dictatorship from being established.

The Krajewski-Jenkins team received only slightly more than 4,000 votes in 1952. Apparently undaunted, Krajewski ran for the Senate in 1956 and received more than 35,000 votes. Speculation was that the support given Krajewski may have contributed to the defeat of Democrat Charles Howell for that position.

The death of Krajewski in 1960 denied him the chance to run for the presidency, which he had planned to do. The party died almost immediately after his death.

Sources/References

"Poor Man's Candidate." *Time* (March 17), 1952.

Schapsmeier, Edward L., and Frederick H. Schapsmeier. *Political Parties and Civic Action Groups.* Westport, CT: Greenwood, 1981.

Populist Party

Established at a convention in Cincinnati, Ohio, in May 1891.

Membership in this party, known also as the People's Party, was composed primarily of farmers and former members of the Greenback Party (q.v.) who protested against existing poor agricultural conditions and the chronically depressed prices for farm commodities evolving out of the Panic of 1873. In the 1880s, loosely organized groups known as farmers' alliances were created; they agitated for various reforms they felt were needed to resolve their basic financial difficulties. Growth of these organizations was so rapid that talk of forming a third party soon arose, leading to the 1891 meeting of interested persons. In particular, Populists attacked high rail shipping costs and a decline in the currency supply, blaming the country's economic problems on eastern bankers and industrialists.

At its July 2, 1892, convention in Omaha, Nebraska, the party nominated James B. Weaver of Iowa (formerly the 1880 presidential candidate of the Greenback Party) as its presidential candidate. As his running mate, the party nominated James G. Field of Virginia. The party's objective was no less than to replace the Democratic Party by forming an unbreakable alliance between farmers and urban workers. But the Populists never succeeded in attracting many of the latter to their membership ranks; their aspirations were thus seriously impeded from the outset.

The 1892 Populist Party platform proclaimed that "we meet in the midst of a nation brought to the verge of moral, political, and material ruin." Citing corruption, demoralization, the muzzling of public opinion, high mortgages, business stagnation, impoverishment of workers, and a host of other problems, the platform declared that "from the . . . womb of governmental injustice we breed the two great classes—tramps and millionaires." Lamenting a series of other deficiencies in the public order of things, the platform declared for a number of specifics:

> That the union of the labor forces of the United States this day consummated shall be permanent and perpetual. . . .

> Wealth belongs to him who creates it, and every dollar taken from industry without an equivalent is robbery. . . .

> We believe that the time has come when the railroad corporations will either own the people or the people must own the railroads. . . .

> We demand a national currency, safe, sound, and flexible, issued by the general government only, a full legal tender for all debts, public and private. . . .

> We demand free and unlimited coinage of silver and gold. . . .

> We demand a graduated income tax. . . .

> . . . we demand that all State and national revenues shall be limited to the necessary expenses of the government, economically and honestly administered.

> We demand that postal savings banks be established. . . .

> . . . the government should own and operate the railroads in the interest of the people. The telegraph and telephone . . . should be owned and operated by the government in the interest of the people.

> The land . . . is the heritage of the people, and should not be monopolized for speculative purposes, and alien ownership of land should be prohibited.

Among other things proposed was a graduated income tax and the direct election of senators.

Weaver received 1,024,280 votes (8.5 percent of the popular vote), one of the larger percentages of support received by a minor party in the annals of American party history. The party received 22 electoral votes from four states.

Moreover, the party showed significant strength in midwestern and far western states, particularly in the 1894 congressional campaign. Polling nearly 1.5 million popular votes, the Populist Party managed to elect six members to the Senate and seven members to the House of Representatives.

But, in general, the party's proposals were perceived as being far too extreme for many members of the electorate of the time, and its appeal to rural interests tended to alienate urban voters in particular.

In 1896, the Populists supported Democratic Party nominee William Jennings Bryan, who espoused a free silver platform, a doctrine supported by the Populists. They did, however, nominate a vice presidential candidate of their own, Thomas E. Watson of Georgia, while the Democrats had nominated Arthur Seawall of Maine.

The platform called for similar demands made in its first campaign. Among them were direct election of the president, vice president, and U.S. senators; public jobs for unemployed workers; giving Cuba its independence; implementing the initiative and referendum; and the abolition of labor injunctions. It also called for "home rule in the Territories and the District of Columbia; pensions for disabled Union troops" and "a full, free and fair ballot and an honest count," and concluded with an admonition that underlying the entire 1896 campaign was "the financial question, and upon this great and specific issue between the parties we cordially invite the aid and co-operation of all organizations and citizens agreeing with us upon this vital question."

Although Bryan's defeat in 1896 meant in effect the demise of populism as a viable movement, the Democratic Party was able to retain the support of many Populists after that election. And, although the party also continued to run presidential candidates until 1908, it became an insignificant force on the American political scene.

In 1900, meeting in Cincinnati, the weak remaining vestiges of the party, known as the antifusion group, nominated Wharton Barker of Pennsylvania for the presidency and Ignatius Donnelly of Minnesota as their vice presidential nominee. A platform reiterating the demands of the past was adopted, and calls for direct election of judges and public ownership of public utilities were included. But the party's candidates won support of only slightly more than 50,000 persons.

A smaller group of Populists, known as the Fusion Party, supported Bryan in 1900 but nominated Charles A. Towne of Minnesota as their vice presidential candidate. This group added virtually nothing to Bryan's support; President McKinley won election once again.

In 1904, the party convened in Springfield, Illinois, and chose Thomas E. Watson of Georgia and Thomas H. Tibbles of Nebraska as nominees for president and vice president, respectively. The party's platform declared, "The People's party reaffirms its adherence to the basic truths of the Omaha platform of 1892, and of the subsequent platforms of 1896 and 1900." It then reiterated many of its former aspirations and called also for an eight-hour workday, abolition of child labor, abolition of the policy of using foreign paupers as laborers, and the right to recall government officials. But Watson and Tibbles received only 117,000 votes and no electoral votes.

Holding a convention in St. Louis in 1908, the party once again nominated Thomas E. Watson for the presidency, and this time Samuel W. Williams of Indiana for vice president. Running on a platform similar to those advocated in the past, the two candidates received only slightly more than 29,000 votes.

Although the party ran local candidates in 1912, it did so only unsuccessfully. In effect the party had ceased to exist, having been replaced by the forces of Progressivism. Outcroppings of populism have sometimes recurred, as in the case of the candidacy of former Senator Fred Harris for the Democratic nomination in 1972 under the banner of "neo-Populism."

And, in 1984, the party reappeared after a nearly three-quarter-century hiatus. For president, the party nominated Bob Richards of Texas and for vice president, Maureen Kennedy Salaman of California. Although it managed to appear on the ballot in 14 states, it received only a modicum of support.

And, in 1988, the party originally selected Congressman George Hansen as its candidate, but, because he declined, David Duke became the nominee. In the election, Duke received 48,267 votes, some .05 percent of the vote cast. The Populist platform advocated repealing the federal income tax, protecting American industry and American jobs, preventing national bankruptcy and inflation, protecting the right to keep and bear arms, revitalizing family farming, avoiding involvement in foreign affairs, equal rights, freedom of choice in matters related to health and education, and repudiation of the national debt.

Sources/References

Allen, Emory A. *Labor and Capital*. Chicago: Caxton, 1891.

Congressional Quarterly, Inc. *National Party Conventions, 1831–1984*. Washington, DC: Congressional Quarterly, Inc., 1987.

Day, Glenn. *Minor Presidential Candidates and Parties of 1988*. Jefferson, NC: McFarland, 1988.

Donnelly, Ignatius. *The American People's Money*. Chicago: Laird & Lee, 1896.

Durden, Robert F. *The Climax of Populism: The Election of 1896*. Lexington: University of Kentucky Press, 1965.

Goodwyn, Laurence. *Democratic Promise: The Populist Movement in America*. New York: Oxford University Press, 1976.

Harvey, William Hope. *Coin's Financial School*. Chicago: Coin, 1894.

Hicks, John D. *The Populist Revolt*. Lincoln: University of Nebraska Press, 1961.

Johnson, Donald Bruce (Comp.). *National Party Platforms: Vol. 1, 1840–1956.* Urbana: University of Illinois Press, 1978.

_____ (Comp.). *National Party Platforms: Vol. 2, 1960–1976.* Urbana: University of Illinois Press, 1978.

Schapsmeier, Edward L., and Frederick H. Schapsmeier. *Political Parties and Civic Action Groups.* Westport, CT: Greenwood, 1981.

Stanwood, Edward. *A History of the Presidency from 1897 to 1916.* Boston: Houghton Mifflin, 1916.

_____. *A History of the Presidency from 1788 to 1897.* Boston: Houghton Mifflin, 1924.

Tindall, George Brown. *A Populist Reader.* New York: Harper & Row, 1966.

Watson, Thomas E. *The People's Party Campaign Book.* Washington, DC: National Watchman, 1892.

Progressive Party (1912)

Established in Albany, New York, in 1912 as a result of a split in the Republican Party.

Personal and ideological differences between President William Howard Taft and ex-president Theodore Roosevelt caused the Roosevelt faction to leave the Republican Party after its June convention. Roosevelt had become disaffected because of Taft's conservative stance on issues Roosevelt thought fundamental in fulfilling the objectives of the Republican Party.

The bolting faction soon became known as the Bull Moose Party, the label resulting from a comment made by Roosevelt that he felt as fit as a bull moose. Although the ideological differences between the two leading Republican personalities were the immediate cause of the division of the party, the Roosevelt forces and their ideas had tapped the deep-rooted sense of progressivism that had become a significant movement within both major parties by 1912. The National Progressive Republican League headed by Wisconsin Senator Robert M. La Follette provided a significant foundation for the insurgents who supported Roosevelt.

Roosevelt had been able to defeat Taft in a number of Republican primaries, but the conservatives continued to control the party and enabled Taft to be renominated. This renomination infuriated Roosevelt and his supporters to the extent that they formed an insurgent movement and decided to leave the party.

The Roosevelt Progressives thus held their own convention in Chicago in August of 1912. Although most leaders of the Republican Party remained loyal to Taft, the mainly middle- and upper-class delegates at the convention were imbued with the spirit of reform.

Black delegates from the South were discouraged in the hopes that the Progressives would attract substantial Democratic support to their cause. The convention turned out to be a Roosevelt convention—Roosevelt's personality and proposals dominated throughout. He himself appeared on the second day of the proceedings to give his "confession of faith"—a speech that declared his principles and his hopes and aspirations for America. Roosevelt was nominated by acclamation.

Although La Follette had hoped to receive the Progressive nomination, delegates nevertheless had turned to Roosevelt as their presidential nominee and to Hiram Johnson—the well-known Progressive reformer of California—as their vice presidential candidate. Then it was La Follette's turn to become furious. He and his supporters withheld their support from the Roosevelt campaign.

Roosevelt's campaign was based on what he called the "New Nationalism," which rested on the ideas developed by Herbert Croly in his book *The Promise of American Life*. Croly had advocated following the Hamiltonian idea of using government to enhance society's ends—developing a strong central government—and to bring big business under control. This constituted a rejection of the Jeffersonian idea of limited government, states' rights, and laissez-faire economics. It also was an extension of the Square Deal philosophy that Roosevelt had enunciated while he was president before Taft.

The platform opened with appeals to the conscience of the American people and attacks on the existing major parties:

> The conscience of the people, in a time of grave national problems, has called into being a new party, born of the nation's sense of justice. We of the Progressive party here dedicate ourselves to the fulfillment of the duty laid upon us by our fathers to maintain the government of the people, by the people and for the people whose foundations they laid. . . .
> Political parties exist to secure responsible government and to execute the will of the people.
> From these great tasks both of the old parties have turned aside. Instead of instruments to promote the general welfare, they have become the tools of corrupt interests which use them impartially to serve their selfish purposes. Behind the ostensible governments sits enthroned an invisible government owing to allegiance and acknowledging no responsibility to the people.

The platform sought to make it easier to amend the Constitution, to extend national jurisdiction to deal with problems that had eluded solution by the states, and to seek equal suffrage. It pledged a quest for passage of corrupt practices legislation, publicity of government activities and registration of lobbyists, and greater restrictions on the courts and general reform of legal procedures in order to increase respect for the judicial system. It pledged support for the establishment of a department of labor and for an increase in prosperity and reduction in the high cost of living. It advocated that more powers be granted the Interstate Commerce Commission and it sought abolition of the Commerce Court. It advocated currency reforms, conservation, the building of improved roads, and the development of Alaskan resources. It argued that the Panama Canal was to be used for the benefit of the American people and that America's waterways be developed as the "natural arteries of this continent." It advocated a protective tariff, a graduated income tax, and an inheritance tax. It pledged attempts to seek "judicial and other peaceful means" to resolve international disputes, proclaiming:

> The Progressive Party deplores the survival in our civilization of the barbaric system of warfare among nations with its enormous waste of resources even in time of peace, and the consequent impoverishment of the life of the toiling masses. We pledge the party to use its best endeavors to substitute judicial and other peaceful means of settling international differences.

It also sought such objectives as the direct primary nominating election; the short ballot; the initiative, referendum, and recall; and ways to deal with foreign immigration. In a sweeping appeal, the platform concluded:

> On these principles and on the recognized desirability of uniting the Progressive forces of the Nation into an organization which shall unequivocally represent the Progressive spirit and policy we appeal for the support of all American citizens, without regard to previous political affiliations.

The campaign in 1912 saw four widely known and dynamic contenders competing for the presidency: Democrat Woodrow Wilson, Socialist Eugene V. Debs, Republican William Howard Taft, and Roosevelt. During a campaign visit to Milwaukee, Wisconsin, in October, Roosevelt was wounded in an assassination attempt. He was able to complete the campaign, nevertheless, and he received over 4 million votes, some 27.4 percent, the largest proportion of the vote ever tallied by a third party candidate. His own success, however, seriously undercut the chances of success for the Republican Party. Taft received 3,485,000 votes and Wilson over 6,000,000. Thus, Woodrow Wilson, the Democratic nominee, went on to win the election largely as a result of Roosevelt's depriving Taft of the votes the latter needed to win, entering the White House with slightly less than 42 percent of the popular vote.

Bull Moose success at the national level did not carry much influence at the state and local levels, however. There the Progressives were able to win only a small number of seats in the House of Representatives, and were unsuccessful in putting into office any senators or governors.

Although the conservatives of the Republican Party never again fully accepted the progressive wing of the party, by 1916 Roosevelt had returned to the Republican fold, supporting the party's nomination of Charles Evans Hughes and declining attempts by the Progressives to nominate him a second time. With his withdrawal from the party, the Bull Moose Progressive Party came to an end. It would not be until 1924, when Senator Robert La Follette would attempt a re-creation of the movement, that the Progressives would be born again.

Sources/References

Congressional Quarterly, Inc. *National Party Conventions, 1831–1984.* Washington, DC: Congressional Quarterly, Inc., 1987.

Croly, Herbert. *The Promise of American Life.* New York: Macmillan, 1912.

DeWitt, Benjamin P. *The Progressive Movement: A Non-partisan, Comprehensive Discussion of Current Tendencies in American Politics.* New York: Macmillan, 1915.

Gable, John Allen. *The Bull Moose Years: Theodore Roosevelt and the Progressive Party.* Port Washington, NY: Kennikat, 1978.

Johnson, Donald Bruce (Comp.). *National Party Platforms: Vol. 1, 1840–1956.* Urbana: University of Illinois Press, 1978.

Mowry, George E. *Theodore Roosevelt and the Progressive Movement.* Madison: University of Wisconsin Press, 1946.

Olin, Spencer C., Jr. *California's Prodigal Sons: Hiram Johnson and the Progressives, 1911–1917.* Berkeley: University of California Press, 1968.

Pinchot, Amos Richards Eno. *History of the Progressive Party, 1912–1916.* New York: New York University Press, 1958.

Schapsmeier, Edward L., and Frederick H. Schapsmeier. *Political Parties and Civic Action Groups.* Westport, CT: Greenwood, 1981.

Progressive Party (1924)

Launched in Cleveland, Ohio, on July 4, 1924.

Sponsored by the Conference for Progressive Political Action (an organization originally created in Chicago in 1922 by William H.

Johnston, president of the International Association of Machinists, and also by presidents of five railway unions) and now including hangers-on from Roosevelt's old Bull Moose campaign, the delegates were made up of farm, labor, and various liberal and left-of-center groups.

In February of 1924, the Conference for Progressive Political Action called for a July 4 convention to act on nominating presidential and vice presidential candidates. Dominated by the railroad brotherhoods, and under pressure from the socialist delegates to establish a permanent third party, the group decided to strike out on an independent course. Even before the convention met, the Conference for Progressive Political Action had given U.S. Senator Robert M. La Follette of Wisconsin its endorsement for the presidential nomination, and had also given him the right to name his own vice presidential choice. Thus Republican La Follette chose Democrat Burton K. Wheeler of Montana as his running mate. When La Follette, in his speech to the convention, predicted that a new party after the election was inevitable because of the demands that would be heard from the people, the socialists gave La Follette their support. Not unlike Theodore Roosevelt's Progressive Party in 1912, the La Follette Progressive Party of 1924 was thus a Republican-stimulated undertaking. Unlike the Roosevelt Progressives, however, the La Follette Progressives were drawn in large part from farmers, laborers, and socialists who for the first time did not nominate a candidate of their own, and from such additional organizations as the Nonpartisan League (q.v.) and the Minnesota Farmer-Labor Party (q.v.). The La Follette Progressives chose not to enter candidates on the state and local levels.

The Progressive Platform called for the destruction of monopolies, increased taxes on the rich, national control over natural resources, and the right of collective bargaining. It emphasized expansion of public works activities to help do away with unemployment, doing away with child labor, eliminating appellate jurisdiction of the Supreme Court, and the outlawing of labor injunctions. It sought direct election of judges to the federal courts, protection for women workers, heavy reduction in armaments, and, simply, outlawing warfare and, before any war could be entered into, a public referendum on the issue.

In 1924, the Conference for Progressive Political Action adopted a platform of its own; later, Senator La Follette published his own platform. Excerpts from both are included below.

From the Conference for Progressive Political Action:

For 148 years the American people have been seeking to establish a government for the service of all and to prevent the establishment of a government for the mastery of the few. Free men of every generation must combat renewed efforts of organized force and greed to destroy liberty. Every generation must wage a new war for freedom against new forces that seek through new devices to enslave mankind.

. . . The test of public officials and public polities alike must be: Will they serve or will they exploit the common good?

The platform of the Conference for Progressive Political Action then went on to assert the following goals: destruction of monopolies, public ownership of water power and natural resources, a surtax on large incomes, equal lending practices for all, the right to organize on the part of labor and farmers, "creation of a government marketing corporation," public ownership of railroads, ratification of the child labor amendment, and other similar aspirations. The platform concluded with the assertion: "The nation may grow rich in the vision of greed. The nation will grow great in the vision of service."

The La Follette platform began with the assertion that "the great issue before the American people today is the control of government and industry by private monopoly." Continuing its attack upon monopoly and its evils, the platform asserted: "The equality of opportunity proclaimed by the Declaration of Independence and asserted and defended by Jefferson and Lincoln as the heritage of every American citizen has been displaced by special privilege for the few, wrested from the government of the many."

The platform thus pledged "a complete housecleaning in the Department of Justice, the Department of the Interior, and the other executive departments." It pledged protection of natural resources, especially oil. It called for the public ownership of railroads and the correction of abuses connected with them. It called for a reduction in the federal income tax. It demanded a legislative veto over judicial opinions, and election of federal judges. It called for drastic protection of farmers and their financial operations, the abolition of injunctions in labor disputes, the fixing of wage standards and the establishment of a "prompt and dependable" postal service, "compensation for the veterans of the late war," and a "deep waterway from the Great Lakes to the sea." It insisted on the "supreme sovereignty of the people," and it denounced current American foreign policy.

The 1924 movement met stiff opposition from the Republican Party, from which La Follette had defected. His radicalism created vituperative attacks on his platform proposals. Likewise, the American Federation of Labor gave the Progressives only lukewarm assistance. La Follette was also considered by some to be pro-German, and his isolationist policy did not endear him to the vast majority of

Americans. President Calvin Coolidge was thus reelected with some 54 percent of the popular vote. Most of the real support for the La Follette movement came from farm interests west of the Mississippi and from La Follette's home state of Wisconsin—the only state he carried in the election. He received 4,822,856 votes, or 16.6 percent of the popular vote.

La Follette's death in 1925 effectively ended the party's national influence. His two sons, Robert M. La Follette, Jr., who became a U.S. senator, and Philip La Follette, who became governor of Wisconsin, attempted to keep the movement alive, but without success.

Sources/References

Congressional Quarterly, Inc. *National Party Conventions, 1831–1984.* Washington, DC: Congressional Quarterly, Inc., 1987.

Johnson, Donald Bruce (Comp.). *National Party Platforms: Vol. 1, 1840–1956.* Urbana: University of Illinois Press, 1978.

La Follette, Belle Case, and Fola La Follette. *Robert M. La Follette, June 14, 1855–June 18, 1925* (2 vols.). New York: Macmillan, 1953.

Mackay, Kenneth C. *The Progressive Movement of 1924.* New York: Octagon, 1947.

Schapsmeier, Edward L., and Frederick H. Schapsmeier. *Political Parties and Civic Action Groups.* Westport, CT: Greenwood, 1981.

Progressive Party (1948)

Established in Philadelphia, Pennsylvania, in 1948.

This party was started by one of two groups that bolted from the Democratic Party, this one led by Henry A. Wallace, former secretary of commerce under the Roosevelt administration, former secretary of agriculture, and eventually the vice president. At the same 1948 convention, Senator Glen H. Taylor of Idaho, a Democrat, was declared Wallace's running mate.

A visionary idealistic liberal, Wallace—who called his group Gideon's Army—was ultimately removed from the Truman administration as secretary of commerce because of his willingness to accommodate the policy positions of the Soviet Union, as well as for other more pragmatic reasons that had arisen within the politics of the Democratic Party. According to some scholars, Wallace felt that Truman's "get tough" policy with the Soviet Union would lead only to disaster. Peaceful coexistence with the Soviet Union should be the goal. This presumably led to "red baiting" on the part of Wallace's opponents, and Wallace received only a few over a million votes although the campaign was well financed.

Wallace is said to have regarded the world as a political unity, and he was a self-expressed internationalist. Indeed, although he was distressed by what he called greedy capitalism, and although he expressed a degree of admiration for the Soviet Union, his criticisms of that country were frequently overlooked. Wallace, originally a Republican, and a devout Christian, expressed particular concern over the atheistic programs of the Russians. Still, he was removed by Truman from the cabinet, in the words of President Truman himself, because "it had become clear that between his views on foreign policy and those of the administration . . . there was a fundamental conflict" (quoted in Walton, 1976, p. 115).

The party's platform was heavily focused on criticizing American foreign policy—especially to oppose the icy cold-war opposition of the Truman administration toward the Soviet Union and, indeed, voicing the desire to do away with the Marshall Plan and the Truman Doctrine, which focused on aid to Greece and the countries in the southern European region. Emphasizing the need to increase the rights of women and minority races, and equal rights in general, the Progressive Party platform dealt with a number of issues, of which the following are representative: it attacked the Marshall Plan, the Truman Doctrine, and the development of military installations in various parts of the globe; it advocated an end to universal military training and military aid, recognition of Israel, and discussions with the Soviet Union to find bases of common ground. It urged measures to find basic grounds for disarmament, means to seek arrangements to free Puerto Rico, and ways to assist the United Nations in becoming a world government. The platform also attacked discrimination against blacks and women, urged a minimum wage, and advocated price supports and minimum old-age pensions. It indicated that if its candidates were elected they would create a cabinet department dealing with culture and with education. The platform also advocated the repeal of the Taft-Hartley Act, the National Security Act, and the House Committee on Un-American Activities—the latter a body that had been particularly a burr under the saddles of liberals, left-wingers, and radicals throughout the period of the 1950s. It also stated that efforts should be undertaken to bring an end to outlawing the Communist Party in the United States. It stated:

> Three years after the end of the second world war, the drums are beating for a third. Civil liberties are being destroyed. Millions cry out for relief from unbearably high prices. The American way of life is in danger.

The root cause of this crisis is Big Business control of our economy and government.

... For generations the common man of America has resisted this concentration of economic and political power in the hands of a few. The greatest of America's political leaders have led the people into battle against the money power, the railroads, the trusts, the economic royalists.

We of the Progressive Party are the present day descendants of these people's movements and fighting leaders. We are the political heirs of Jefferson, Jackson and Lincoln—of Frederick Douglass, Altgeld and Debs—of "Fighting Bob" La Follette, George Norris, and Franklin Roosevelt.

The platform then went on to discuss the allegation that the major parties had not fulfilled the peace objectives of the American people but that they had instead brought the country only closer to war, and that their record was one "profaning the ideal of freedom." On the other hand, said the platform,

the Progressive Party is born in the deep conviction that the national wealth and natural resources of our country belong to the people who inhabit it and must be employed in their behalf; that freedom and opportunity must be secured equally to all; that the brotherhood of man can be achieved and the scourge of war ended.

The platform then invoked the name of Franklin Roosevelt to secure a just end for all peoples in America and to procure an abundant life for all American citizens. Speaking of American-Soviet relations, the drafting of young men, the hope of the United Nations, the goal of disarmament, cooperation with our ex-enemies, recognition of Israel, attempts on the part of Asians to acquire independence, the plight of colonial and dependent peoples, the problems of displaced persons, and an end to discrimination, the platform urged that there be recognition for "the varied contributions of all nationality groups to American cultural, economic, and social life" and stated that the party "considers them a source of strength for the democratic development of our country." The platform contained other sections on "Jim Crow in the armed forces," the separation of church and state, the problem of "uncontrolled inflation," "democratic economic planning," "public ownership of key areas of the economy," the importance of organized labor, the importance of the "family-type farm as the basic unit of American agriculture," the safeguarding of independent business, the necessity that government "guarantee the right of every family to a decent home at a price it can afford to pay," the "extension of social security," and the right to vote at the age of 18. The platform also advocated increased veterans' benefits; an "overhaul of the tax structure"; "the inalienable right to a good education to every man, woman, and child in America"; the importance of culture; and "legislation to promote science, including human and social sciences, so that scientific knowledge may be enlarged and used for the benefit of all people."

Perhaps a key difficulty faced by the 1948 Progressives from the outset was their image as being procommunist. Although neither Wallace nor Taylor were in fact communists, their political image was clearly tainted and their degree of support undermined when they supported communist causes and proposals. The defeat at the convention of the so-called Vermont Resolution—which declared, "Although we are critical of the present foreign policy of the United States, it is not our intention to give blanket endorsement to the foreign policy of any other nation"—only lent additional credence to the notion that the party was pro-Soviet. The fact that Wallace himself never specifically denounced communist support for his candidacy and his failure to realize that communist influence was in fact significant in his party caused him no small amount of difficulty and embarrassment. As a former New Deal Democrat under Roosevelt (and, as has been mentioned, former secretary of agriculture, vice president, and secretary of commerce), and, further, an editor of the left-wing *New Republic* magazine, he had in fact been on the "right side" for years in espousing the appropriate liberal causes. Still, his campaign rhetoric caused him to sound pro-Soviet—he had advocated cooperation with the Soviet Union, he had sought disarmament policies, and he had espoused working through the United Nations for settlement of disputes. His speeches ranged from outright apologies for Soviet policies to more idealistic solutions to problems that simply could not be so resolved.

Wallace's campaign was attacked by the press. His speeches often sounded as if they verged on treason—for example, his defenses of the Soviet Union in blockading Berlin and the Soviet Czechoslovakian takeover made him especially suspect. These and other events led some to conclude that Wallace was in the pocket of the communists during a time when the communists were in fact doing all they could to undermine American policy and the policy of the Western allies as well. His candidacy's endorsement by the Communist Party of the United States of America (q.v.) thus proved to be an especially damaging blow. Wallace, perhaps naively assuming that the endorsement of the CPUSA would enhance his own cause, accepted the support. He attempted to put distance between his own philosophy and that of the Communists, however, by suggesting that he supported a kind of "progressive capitalism."

Wallace eventually appeared on the ballot in 45 states. But, largely because of the Communist endorsement, he received only 1,157,057 votes, well over one-half of those coming from the state of New York alone. The Progressives under Wallace did not carry any single state; indeed, Truman won reelection even with their dissidence. Progressives also did very poorly with respect to congressional election efforts: they did not win one office on that level. Progressive opposition to the war in Korea also led to significant voter defection from their cause; in 1952, with candidates Vincent Hallinan and Charlotte Bass, they were able to attract the support of only 0.2 percent of the vote, slightly over 140,000 in total. After that election, the Progressive Party, as led by Wallace, was, essentially, dead.

Sources/References

Congressional Quarterly, Inc. *National Party Conventions, 1831–1984.* Washington, DC: Congressional Quarterly, Inc., 1987.

Johnson, Donald Bruce (Comp.). *National Party Platforms: Vol. 1, 1840–1956.* Urbana: University of Illinois Press, 1978.

Link, Arthur S. *Woodrow Wilson and the Progressive Era 1910–1917.* New York: Harper, 1954.

MacDougall, Curtis D. *Gideon's Army* (3 vols.). New York: Manzani & Munsell, 1965.

Schapsmeier, Edward L., and Frederick H. Schapsmeier. *Political Parties and Civic Action Groups.* Westport, CT: Greenwood, 1981.

Schapsmeier, Edward L., and Frederick H. Schapsmeier. *Prophet in Politics: Henry A. Wallace and the War Years, 1940–1965.* Ames: Iowa State University Press, 1970.

Schmidt, K. M. *Henry A. Wallace: Quixotic Crusade 1948.* Syracuse, NY: Syracuse University Press, 1961.

Walton, Richard J. *Henry Wallace, Harry Truman, and the Cold War.* New York: Viking, 1976.

Yarnell, Allen. *Democrats and Progressives: The 1948 Election as a Test of Postwar Liberalism.* Berkeley: University of California Press, 1974.

Prohibition Party

Established in Chicago in September 1869, at a convention called by the Independent Order of Good Templars.

The Prohibition Party, which ultimately became the longest-surviving American minor party, was created in part in response to the movement toward legalization and taxation of liquor by the federal government during the Civil War period. Those supporting the Prohibition Party viewed the federal government's action as a specific policy that singled out a particular industry for its protection from regulation by state laws. Other factors influential in the establishment of the party were a more widespread and general support of the temperance movement, which had been in existence since 1800, and the general drive for reform that had been begun before the Civil War by the abolitionists. Other factors contributing to the creation of the party included the fact that the major parties had given the temperance movement only little or modest support, failure of government to enforce local prohibition laws, and the establishment of the United States Brewers' Association.

Delegates to the convention represented 20 states. Women delegates were represented equally with men. The various platforms developed by the party—which did not run its first candidates until 1872—emphasized its support for the prohibition of the manufacture, transportation, and sale of alcoholic beverages.

It should be noted, too, that before nominating its first presidential candidate, the Prohibition Party had entered candidates in the elections of nine states between the years 1869 and 1871.

As noted above, the first presidential nominating convention of the Prohibition Party was held in Columbus, Ohio, in 1872. The platform opened with the reaffirmation of resolutions that had been adopted at the party's convention in Chicago in 1869, among them that "the traffic in intoxicating drinks greatly impairs the personal security and personal liberty of a large mass of citizens, and renders private property insecure," and

> that the traffic in intoxicating beverages is a dishonor to Christian civilization, inimical to the best interests of society, a political wrong of unequalled enormity, subversive of the ordinary objects of government, not capable of being regulated or restrained by any system of license whatever, but imperatively demanding for its suppression effective legal Prohibition by both State and National legislation.

It also declared:

> That there can be no greater peril to the nation than the existing party competition for the liquor vote; that any party not openly opposed to the traffic, experience shows, will engage in this competition, will court the favor of the criminal classes, will barter away the public morals, the purity of the ballot, and every object of good government, for party success.

> That while adopting national political measures for the Prohibition of the liquor traffic, we will continue the use of all moral

means in our power to persuade men away from the injurious practice of using intoxicating beverages.

That we invite all persons, whether total abstainers or not, who recognize the terrible injuries inflicted by the liquor traffic, to unite with us for its overthrow, and to secure thereby peace, order and the protection of persons and property.

Although focusing on the traffic in liquor, other planks included a call for "fixed and moderate salaries" for officeholders; direct election of the president, vice president, and U.S. senators; "a sound national currency"; the reduction of rates for postage and the costs of inland communication and transportation; equitable taxes on business and property; state-supported education; equal suffrage regardless of race or sex; and a "just policy . . . to promote foreign immigration."

The convention nominated James Black for president and the Reverend John Russell for vice president. But these candidates of the party in its first election drew only 5,588 votes from the electorate in only six states.

The Prohibition Party received only limited support during 1872, 1876, and 1880 as well, never receiving more than .1 percent of the popular vote. Then, between 1884 and 1920, support for the party grew, its vote totals ranging from slightly over 131,000 in 1896 to a high of approximately 271,000 in 1892. In that year the party, meeting in Cincinnati, nominated John Bidwell of California for its presidential candidate and J. B. Cranfill of Texas as his vice presidential running mate. In a two-day session, the convention adopted a platform that again emphasized the dangers of liquor. Declared the platform:

> The liquor traffic is a foe to civilization, the arch enemy of popular government, and a public nuisance. It is the citadel of the forces that corrupt politics, promote poverty and crime, degrade the nation's home life, thwart the will of the people, and deliver our country into the hands of rapacious class interests. All laws that under the guise of regulation legalize and protect this traffic or make the Government share its ill-gotten gains, are 'vicious in principle and powerless as a remedy.' We declare anew for the entire suppression of the manufacture, sale, importation, exportation and transportation of alcoholic liquors as a beverage by Federal and State legislation, and the full powers of Government should be exerted to secure the result. Any party that fails to recognize the dominant nature of this issue in American politics is undeserving of the support of the people.

The platform then went on to call for equal suffrage and equal wages regardless of sex, and took the following stands: that the country's money "should consist of gold, silver, and paper"; that tariffs should be used only in defense against other nations who levy them and with the specific objective of discriminating against American products; that the government should exercise control over rail and telegraph operations; and that immigration laws should be revised. The platform also called for protection of everyone under the law, for one day of rest per week, for arbitration in the settlement of international disputes, and for the suppression of speculation in grain and financial markets generally. It pledged itself to the granting of pensions for Union veterans and to support for the American public school system. It attacked the Republican and Democratic parties for being "faithless to the principles of the illustrious leaders of the past to whom they do homage with the lips." The platform's concluding paragraphs once again returned to the alleged evils of liquor:

> Recognizing and declaring that prohibition of the liquor traffic has become the dominant issue in national politics, we invite to full party fellowship all those who on this one dominant issue are with us agreed, in the full belief that this party can and will remove sectional differences, promote national unity, and insure the best welfare of our entire land.

> Resolved, That we favor a liberal appropriation by the Federal Government for the World's Columbian Exposition, but only on the condition that the sale of intoxicating drinks upon the Exposition grounds is prohibited, and that the Exposition be kept closed on Sunday.

After 1920, the fortunes of the party at the polls declined once again. Support for Prohibition Party candidates dipped to 189,467 in 1920, and then fluctuated between a low of 7,149 in 1980 and a high of 103,343 in 1948.

The Progressive movement had a substantial influence on the nature of the Prohibition Party during the first two decades of the twentieth century. Its impact is visible in the content of the party platforms during that period. Points emphasized included direct election of senators, the initiative and referendum, a single presidential term of office consisting of six years, conservation of resources, nationalization of public utilities, pensions for the aged, the item veto for the president, reform of divorce laws, and other progressively oriented proposals that departed from its single-issue concern with prohibition.

The Prohibition Party also became vocally antiwar during the period before World War I. It attacked the "wasteful military programme of the Democratic and Republican Parties," declaring that "militarism protects no worthy institution" but "endangers them all."

It then declared its support of the dismantling of the armed services, its opposition to "universal military service," and the making of "private profit" from the "manufacture of war munitions and all war equipment." It favored instead the use of the army in conservation programs and highway building, for example, which would make "soldiers constructive builders of peace." It also, in its 1916 platform, reaffirmed its continuing attachment to the concepts embodied in the Monroe Doctrine, and endorsed the use of force to protect American interests.

But its two candidates—James F. Hanly of Indiana and Ira Landrith of Tennessee—even though on the ballot in 42 states, drew only some 221,000 votes, just over 1 percent.

The ratification of the Eighteenth Amendment to the Constitution of the United States in 1919 brought a sense of elation to the members of the Prohibition Party. That amendment prohibited "the manufacture, sale, or transportation of intoxicating liquors within, the importation thereof into, or the exportation thereof from the United States and all territory subject to the Jurisdiction thereof for beverage purposes." It also granted to both Congress and the states "concurrent power to enforce this article by appropriate legislation."

The 1920 convention of the party, which took place in Lincoln, Nebraska, was thus a happy spectacle indeed. Its platform expressed the party's

> thanks to Almighty God for the victory over the beverage liquor traffic which crowns fifty years of consecrated effort. The principles which we have advocated throughout our history have been so far recognized that the manufacture and traffic in intoxicating drink have been forever prohibited in the fundamental law of the land; Congress has rightly interpreted the Eighteenth Amendment in laws enacted for its enforcement; and the Supreme Court has upheld both the Amendment and the law.

But the elation of the Prohibition Party over the adoption of the Eighteenth Amendment was to be relatively short-lived. Indeed, the ratification of the amendment itself seemed to suggest that the Prohibition Party had become a superfluous entity, no longer necessary given the apparent fact that its major mission had been accomplished. Perhaps more important, however, was the widespread violation of the provisions of the amendment and of the Volstead Act by the American people themselves. An increase in violent crime resulted from the illegal bootlegging of alcohol, gang violence epitomized by such notorious criminals as Al Capone became common in the streets of America's major cities, and the rise of the so-called speakeasies and the illegal distillation of liquor in virtually every remote hamlet of the country soon made enforcement of both the amendment and the Volstead Act impossible.

So widespread had the violation of the law become that by December 1933, the Twenty-first Amendment—which repealed the Eighteenth—went into effect. The amendment in this instance had been ratified by use of state conventions (the only time in American history that ratification of an amendment was accomplished by this means); supporters of repeal feared that use of state legislatures—still dominated by "dry" forces—would not succeed in doing away with prohibition. These state conventions quickly ratified the amendment, however. Thus, Americans by their behavioral norms alone had dealt a severe blow to the very substance of the raison d'être of the Prohibition Party. And so came to an end the national effort to implement an unpopular—and essentially unenforceable—law. And perhaps, thus, too, there came to an end the Prohibition movement.

In any event, the fortunes of the Prohibition Party continued to decline. The coming of the Great Depression, American entry into World War II, the events attendant upon resolving the problems after the war, and general attempts by Americans to bring their lives back into some semblance of normality all served to undermine the electoral potential of the Prohibition Party. Thus, from the 1930s on, the Prohibition Party has been a largely impotent force on the American political scene. In the 1960s and 1970s, for example, the party advocated such causes as "loyalty to the Constitution of the United States," "governmental restraints on our free enterprise system," opposition to communism as a "menace to civilization," national sovereignty, religious liberty, the home as a "sacred institution" whose "sanctity must be protected and preserved," and "the rendering of help to the handicapped, the aged, the chronically ill and those families without a breadwinner." It also continued to insist that

> the liquor traffic is linked with and supports a nationwide network of gambling, vice and crime. It also dominates the Republican and Democratic parties and, thru them, much of the governmental and political life of our nation. This is one of the major reasons for the inability of either party to operate on a morally sound basis.

But turnout in support of the party was minimal. Even a change in the party's name—to that of the National Statesman Party in 1980—did nothing to attract additional support. Indeed, only 7,212 votes were received by its candidates, Benjamin Bubar of Maine and Earl F. Dodge of Colorado. In 1988, Earl Dodge was the presidential candidate of the party; he received a total of only 7,984 votes.

The evolution of the Prohibition Party may be summarized in the context of a model presented by historian Roger C. Storms, who has divided the activity of the Prohibition Party into three periods. The first of these—from 1869 to 1896—he labels the "Prophetic Period." During this period, the party advocated a wide range of social reforms. During the second period—from 1896 to 1932—which Storms calls the "Pragmatic Period," the party focused its attention on the achievement of prohibition. The third period of the party's development, from 1932 to the present, Storms calls the "Fundamental Period"; the issues have emphasized returning to the basic moral values of an earlier America. Regardless of the matters emphasized, however, the party was never able to carry a single state in a presidential election throughout its lengthy history.

Currently, the Prohibition Party, although not dead, has become largely a shadow force. The attempt to attract more support by changing its name in 1980 only served to confuse matters. In 1984, the party decided to resume use of its old name because of the continued alcohol-related problems in the United States, although it expanded its efforts to appeal to those emphasizing religious freedom and opposing abortion. It is no longer significant on the American political party scene.

Yet, in 1988, the party nominated Earl Dodge for the presidency and George Ormsby for the vice presidency. Among the planks endorsed in its platform was, obviously, opposition to alcohol, but there were also such elements as opposition to communism and totalitarianism, a constitutional limitation on taxation and the spending powers of Congress, balancing the federal budget, prohibiting abortion, giving welfare only to the needy, permitting prayer in public schools, and creating a free market.

Sources/References

Blocker, Jack S. *Retreat from Reform: The Prohibition Movement in the United States, 1890–1913.* Westport, CT: Greenwood, 1976.

Clark, Norman H. *Deliver Us from Evil: An Interpretation of American Prohibition.* New York: Norton, 1976.

Colvin, David Leigh. *Prohibition in the United States.* New York: George H. Doran, 1926.

Congressional Quarterly, Inc. *National Party Conventions, 1831–1984.* Washington, DC: Congressional Quarterly, Inc., 1987.

Day, Glenn. *Minor Presidential Candidates and Parties of 1988.* Jefferson, NC: McFarland, 1988.

Hesseltine, William B. *The Rise and Fall of Third Parties.* Princeton, NJ: D. Van Nostrand, 1948.

Johnson, Donald Bruce (Comp.). *National Party Platforms: Vol. 1, 1840–1956.* Urbana: University of Illinois Press, 1978.

_____ (Comp.). *National Party Platforms: Vol. 2, 1960–1976.* Urbana: University of Illinois Press, 1978.

_____ (Comp.). *National Party Platforms of 1980: Supplement to National Party Platforms, 1840–1976.* Urbana: University of Illinois Press, 1982.

Nash, Howard P. *Third Parties in American Politics.* Washington, DC: Public Affairs, 1959.

Schapsmeier, Edward L., and Frederick H. Schapsmeier. *Political Parties and Civic Action Groups.* Westport, CT: Greenwood, 1981.

Smallwood, Frank. *The Other Candidates: Third Parties in Presidential Elections.* Hanover, NH: University Press of New England, 1983.

Stanwood, Edward. *A History of the Presidency from 1897 to 1916.* Boston: Houghton Mifflin, 1916.

_____. *A History of the Presidency from 1788 to 1897.* Boston: Houghton Mifflin, 1924.

Storms, Roger C. *Partisan Profits: A History of the Prohibition Party.* Denver, CO: National Prohibition Foundation, 1972. Cited in Smallwood.

Silver Republican Party

Established in St. Louis, Missouri, in 1896, by Republican Senator Henry M. Teller of Colorado.

Teller led an insurgency movement out of the national convention of the Republican Party because of its refusal to adopt a policy demanding free coinage of silver. The Republican Party had adopted a platform that declared, in part:

> The Republican party is unreservedly for sound money. It caused the enactment of the law providing for the resumption of specie payments in 1879; since then every dollar has been as good as gold.
>
> We are unalterably opposed to every measure calculated to debase our currency or impair the credit of our country. We are, therefore, opposed to the free coinage of silver, except by international agreement with the leading commercial nations of the world, which we pledge ourselves to promote, and until such agreement can be obtained the existing gold standard must be preserved. All our silver and paper currency must be maintained at parity with gold, and we favor all measures designated to maintain inviolable the obligations of the United States and all our money, whether coin or paper, at the present standard, the standard of the most enlightened nations of the earth.

Senator Teller took the floor after the reading of the platform and offered a substitute for this platform plank. His substitute read:

The Republican party favors the use of both gold and silver as
equal standard money, and pledges its power to secure the free,
unrestricted, and independent coinage of gold and silver at our
mints at the ratio of sixteen parts of silver to one of gold.

Teller's speech reflected a realization that his substitute would
not be successful; and he left no doubt that its defeat would result in
his—and his supporters'—bolt from the party. It was moved to lay his
substitute on the table—a move that was the same as defeating it.
When this occurred, Teller and some 33 others left the convention.

Members of the bolting group were composed primarily of individuals who represented western silver interests, especially the
American Bimetallic League, whose interests included the owners of
silver mines and who supported the Silver Republican Party with
campaign contributions.

The platform of the Silver Republican Party attacked the gold
standard and demanded the free coinage of silver. The party nominated William Jennings Bryan, who had been nominated by the Populist Party at a convention held simultaneously with that of the Silver
Republicans. This nomination resulted in an aberrant ticket—a fusion
of Populist-, Democratic-, and Silver Republicans who had as their
mutual objective the enhancement of the cause of silver remonetiza-
tion. But the party was without real power. Senator Henry Teller
went over to the Democrats and was active in support of Bryan for the
presidency in 1900.

The Silver Republicans again held a convention in 1900, this
time at Kansas City on July 4. Teller was chair of the convention, and
it once again endorsed Bryan for the presidency and Adlai E.
Stevenson of Illinois as vice president. The platform proclaimed, in
part:

> We declare our adherence to the principles of bimetallism as the
> right basis of a monetary system under our National Constitution,
> a principle that found place repeatedly in Republican platforms
> from the demonetization of silver in 1873 to the St. Louis Repub-
> lican Convention in 1896. Since that convention a Republican
> Congress and a Republican President, at the dictation of the
> trusts and money power, have passed and approved a currency
> bill which in itself is a repudiation of the doctrine of bimetallism
> advocated theretofore by the President and every great leader of
> his party. . . . We declare it to be our intention to lend our efforts
> to the repeal of this currency law, which not only repudiates
> ancient and time-honored principles of the American people be-
> fore the Constitution was adopted, but is violative of the principles
> of the Constitution itself, and we shall not cease our efforts until
> there has been established in its place a monetary system based
> upon the free and unlimited coinage of silver and gold into

money at the present legal ratio of 16 to 1, by the independent action of the United States, under which system all money shall be issued by the Government, and all money coined and issued shall be a full legal tender in payment of all debts, public and private, without exception.

The Silver Republicans—or the National Silver Party, as the organization was also referred to—were never in the mainstream of American political campaigns of the time. Senator Teller, given the fact that he seemed a good man around whom a coalition could be formed, was recognized as an unimpeachable supporter of the silver cause. He was able to identify his efforts with agrarian reform and his Republicanism made him appealing to Populists as well. His stand on the silver question had also made him attractive to Democrats. He was viewed as a man who, like the people at large, was opposed to domination by the plutocrats of society.

Generally, however, those who had been members of the Silver Republicans returned to the Republican Party after the election of 1900, and the 1900 campaign was largely an exercise in futility.

Sources/References

Ellis, Elmer. "The Silver Republicans in the Election of 1896." *Mississippi Valley Historical Review*, 18 (June 1921–March 1932).

_____. *Henry Moore Teller: Defender of the West*. Chicago: Caxton, 1941.

Goodwyn, Lawrence. *Democratic Promise: The Populist Movement in America*. New York: Oxford University Press, 1976.

Johnson, Donald Bruce (Comp.). *National Party Platforms: Vol. 1, 1840–1956*. Urbana: University of Illinois Press, 1978.

Jones, Stanley L. *The Presidential Election of 1896*. Madison: University of Wisconsin Press, 1964.

Schapsmeier, Edward L., and Frederick H. Schapsmeier. *Political Parties and Civic Action Groups*. Westport, CT: Greenwood, 1981.

Stanwood, Edward. *A History of the Presidency from 1788 to 1897*. Boston: Houghton Mifflin, 1924.

Social Democratic Party of America

Established by Eugene V. Debs in Chicago in 1897.

Debs was president of the American Railway Union at the time of the formation of the party. The party was originally named the Social Democracy of America. It was renamed when it was reorganized by Debs and Victor L. Berger, a well-known Wisconsin socialist.

Debs, of Illinois, was nominated as the presidential candidate of the party in 1900 at a convention in Indianapolis. His running mate was Job Harriman of California.

Debs was born in 1855 in Terre Haute, Indiana. He left high school to begin work on the railroads, and eventually organized a local union of the Brotherhood of Locomotive Firemen. By 1893 he had launched an industrial union that included all rail workers. He called it the American Railway Union, and he became its president. Before that, Debs had served in the Indiana State Legislature.

Debs became widely known as a strike leader, especially in the Pullman strike, which was broken by President Grover Cleveland by use of both troops and injunctions. Debs himself was sentenced to jail for violating the injunction. While in jail, Debs read widely in socialist literature and later himself became a socialist.

In its platform the Social Democratic Party reaffirmed its

> allegiance to the revolutionary principles of International Socialism and declare[d] the supreme political issue in America . . . to the contest between the working class and the capitalist class for the possession of the powers of government. The party affirms its steadfast purpose to use those powers, once achieved, to destroy wage slavery, abolish the institution of private property in the means of production, and establish the Co-operative Commonwealth.

The platform then made 12 "demands":

1. Revising the Constitution to make it possible to turn over control of the government to the people, "irrespective of sex"
2. "Public ownership of all industries"
3. Public ownership of communications and transportation
4. "Public ownership of all gold, silver, copper, lead, iron, coal, and other mines, and all oil and gas wells"
5. Reduction of the hours of labor
6. Introduction of public works projects for hiring the unemployed
7. Freedom of invention, with "inventors to be remunerated by the public"
8. Introduction of national and international labor legislation
9. National insurance for workers
10. Equal rights for women
11. Introduction of the initiative and referendum, use of proportional representation, and the recall

12. "Abolition of war and the introduction of international arbitration"

The Social Democratic candidates received only about 88,000 votes and no electoral votes. Debs later merged the Social Democratic Party of America with the Socialist Labor Party faction led by Morris Hillquit. This combination ultimately came to be known as the Socialist Party of America (q.v.).

Debs later became the candidate of the Socialist Party and editor of the Socialist weekly known as *Appeal to Reason*. He also lectured widely. In 1918, Debs was sentenced to a 10-year jail term on a sedition charge under the Espionage Act of 1917. Even from jail, his voice could not be stilled; he ran for president from his cell and received almost 920,000 votes!

Sources/References

Ginger, Ray. *The Bending Cross: A Biography of Eugene Victor Debs*. New Brunswick, NJ: Rutgers University Press, 1949.

Kipnis, Ira. *The American Socialist Movement, 1897–1912*. New York: Columbia University Press, 1952.

Morgan, H. Wayne. *Eugene V. Debs: Socialist for President*. Syracuse, NY: Syracuse University Press, 1962.

Schapsmeier, Edward L., and Frederick H. Schapsmeier. *Political Parties and Civic Action Groups*. Westport, CT: Greenwood, 1981.

Socialist Labor Party

Established in Newark, New Jersey, in 1877.

At first calling itself the Socialist Democratic Workingman's Party, the Socialist Labor Party—also sometimes referred to as the Workingman's Party of America—was founded in Newark by disparate elements of the Socialist International. It was the first national Marxist party established in the United States. Its first national secretary was Philip Van Patten, a leading figure in the Knights of Labor organization.

The Socialist Labor Party presented presidential candidates in every national election between 1892 and 1976. Its birth in the 1870s and its perennial running of candidates for the presidential office caused it to earn the distinction of being the second most enduring (after the Prohibition Party) third party in the history of the United States.

Under the leadership of Daniel DeLeon, a widely known Marxist revolutionary, one-time lecturer on the Columbia University law faculty, and editor of the *Daily People*, the party worked during its early years with members of other left-wing minor parties. It became increasingly militant in its demands and its tactics. DeLeon demanded strict party discipline from the membership. His authoritarian style and increasing opposition to the regular labor organizations served to alienate many of his supporters. He expounded his theories in such books as *Socialist Reconstruction of Society* and *As to Politics*. Among other things, DeLeon attempted to make the philosophy of Karl Marx applicable to the American political and economic system and attempted to integrate the ideas of syndicalism and anarchism into his approach to changing society. His ultimate objective was to create a classless society in the United States through worker revolution.

Always a small party, the apogee of support for the Socialist Labor Party on the national level never went much above 50,000 votes; its greatest success on the local level was reached in 1898. The party continued as a rigid far-left organization under the dominance of DeLeon, who continued to believe in revolution. Many more moderate members of the party left to join forces with the Socialist Party (q.v.) under the leadership of Eugene V. Debs. Even during the decline of the party during the 1970s, the platform continued to advocate worker action to take over control of industrial production.

The Socialist Labor Party ran its first national ticket in 1892. Its candidates were Simon Wing of Massachusetts as presidential nominee and Charles H. Matchett of New York as his vice presidential running mate. The party's platform of that year is instructive of the party's general point of view. Asserting that all men have inalienable rights to life, liberty, and the pursuit of happiness, it declared that the fulfillment of such rights was impossible under the present American economic system. The platform declared that "we hold that the true theory of politics is that the machinery of government must be owned and controlled by the whole people," and that "the true theory of economics is that the machinery of production must likewise belong to the people in common." The platform adopted the following resolution:

> RESOLVED, That we call upon the people to organize with a view to the substitution of the co-operative commonwealth for the present state of planless production, industrial war, and social disorder—a commonwealth in which every worker shall have the free exercise and full benefit of his faculties, multiplied by all the modern factors of civilization. We call upon them to unite with us in a mighty effort to gain by all practicable means the political power.

The platform then went on to discuss various "social demands" and "political demands." Among the former were a call to reduce hours of labor; nationalization of transportation and communications processes; municipal control of transportation and utilities; that "public lands be declared inalienable"; the exclusive right of the national government to issue money; and clauses dealing with natural resources, inventions, taxes, education, "repeal of all pauper, tramp, conspiracy, and sumptuary laws," the collection of labor statistics, equalization of wages for men and women, and "laws for the protection of life and limb in all occupations." Among the last were demands for a public referendum, doing away with the "Presidency, Vice Presidency, and Senate" and the establishment of an elected "Executive Board," the members of which "may at any time be recalled by the House of Representatives," self-government for municipalities, direct and secret ballots, the possibility of recall of all public officers, and a "uniform civil and criminal law throughout the United States."

In 1892, the Wing-Matchett ticket received 21,173 votes.

In 1896, the Socialist Labor Party nominated Charles H. Matchett for president and Matthew Maguire of New Jersey for vice president. The platform called for doing away with the class system, advocated a progressive income tax, sought compulsory education for those under 14, urged doing away with the executive veto power, and called for universal suffrage. In that year, the Socialist Labor Party candidates received 36,356 votes.

Running candidates Joseph F. Malloney of Massachusetts and Valentine Remmel of Pennsylvania in 1900, the party increased its vote total to nearly 41,000, again on a platform advocating the abolition of capitalism and the replacement of it by a government owned and operated by the people.

Between 1900 and 1952, the vote for the party's presidential candidates ranged from a high of 45,336 in 1944, when its candidates were Edward A. Teichert of Pennsylvania and Arla A. Albaugh of Ohio, to a low of 12,790 in 1936, when the party ran John W. Aiken (a previous vice presidential candidate for the party) for president and Emil F. Teichert for the vice presidency. Throughout the first 50 years of party activity, the platforms generally continued to emphasize the same themes. Urging the working class to organize itself so that a "cooperative commonwealth" could be established, it continued to advocate the destruction of the capitalist economic system. During World War I, the Socialist Labor Party largely ignored the military action itself and focused again on the need to replace capitalism. It called later for the establishment of a "Socialist Industrial Republic" and adherence to "sociologic laws" toward the eventual establishment of a socialist society run by the workers.

Even during the depths of the Depression of the 1930s, the Socialist Labor Party did not excite the minds of the American electorate—and especially those of the American worker. In 1936, for example, its candidates received only 12,790 votes—an astounding defeat during a period the party's leaders assumed would be a highly propitious one for the adoption of its policies. But Franklin D. Roosevelt's progressive policies did much to undercut the appeals of the Socialist Labor Party. Even when the party suggested that "a period of social dissolution" was facing the American society, and that the existing economic system was destroying the American worker, the party could not attract significant support.

Throughout the last 30 years the party has hardly fared much better. In 1952, for example, the party ran Eric Hass and Stephen Emery of New York as its candidates. The platform attacked U.S. involvement in the Korean War, militarism, U.S. efforts to prosecute communists, the Soviet Union's government as one "masquerading as 'Marxist,'" and the British Labour Party, which it regarded as merely "reformist." But the party's candidates gathered only .05 percent of the votes—some 30,250.

Between that election and the one held in 1976, when it ran its last slate of candidates, the Socialist Labor Party attacked such policy issues as the development of the hydrogen bomb and efforts leading to detente between the United States and the Soviet Union. It declared repeatedly that the type of socialism advocated by the Socialist Labor Party was the only true solution to the plethora of problems facing the nation. The party continued to blame the existing system for the problems of economic depression, unemployment, racism, crime, juvenile delinquency, mental illness, alcoholism, and other ills as more evidence of "capitalist decadence." But even during this period of intense radicalism focusing especially on opposition to American involvement in the Vietnam War, the Socialist Labor candidates did not win much support.

By 1976, the Socialist Labor Party, having nominated Jules Levin of New Jersey and Connie Blomen of Massachusetts as its candidates, seemed to have reached its nadir, the party receiving only about 9,600 votes. Its platform that year began with a question:

> What is socialism and how can it be established in the United States?
> While Americans will be swamped in this bicentennial year with an endless stream of empty debate "on the issues," the national candidates of the Socialist Labor Party will be putting this question before as many workers as possible. Even more importantly, they'll be answering it.

The candidates themselves "answered" the question by what they referred to in their platform as speaking "to the needs and problems of the American people in a way no other political platform can." Harking back to a theme that had consistently permeated its platforms down through time, the platform asserted that "it ties all the many and varied problems confronting workers today, from economic crises to racism, from eroding democratic rights to environmental suicide, back to their common origins in the system of capitalism." Asserting that most people did not have control over their lives and that most of them have been unable to provide for even the basic necessities of their existence, the platform suggested that

> the socialist program cuts through superficial excuses for this unequal status quo and gets to its roots. . . .
> The platform of the SLP is neither a bundle of promises nor a package of slogans. It's a plan for mobilizing the working people of the nation into organizations that will enable them to resist and overturn the rule of the capitalist class, and to build a better society, more democratic, more open and more free than any that has ever existed.

The platform called for nothing short of revolutionary change and for doing away with the ruling minority. It argued:

> Socialism does not mean control by the state, or domination by a party, or the regulation of capitalist rule, or more reforms and bureaucracy. It means the transfer of power over all social institutions and operations to the rank-and-file workers themselves.

Such an end could be accomplished, according to the platform, "only . . . through the direct activity of the workers themselves." This is unusual in the sense that although that year's platform was devoid of a long list of calls for specific policies and programs, it remains one of the more interesting statements of general socialistic aspirations. Yet it seemed something of a far cry from the early, more anarchical and syndicalist arguments raised by DeLeon. The platform concluded with the suggestion that its proposals were, nevertheless, "revolutionary," and that this "revolutionary alternative" would be put "before the workers of the country." It implored Americans to "find out more about it and join us in the effort."

But, as before, the party did not appeal significantly to the American electorate. The reasons for the party's withdrawal from presidential politics are unclear. Among suggestions that have been put forth is the death of Arnold Petersen, the person who had served as the general secretary of the party and who had commanded it with autocratic style; another suggestion is that the party had never been sufficiently aggressive, that party members had never aggressively asserted themselves by participating in demonstrations or parades but had confined themselves mainly to handing out flyers on street corners and participating in similar innocuous and unchallenging activities. Membership figures had reportedly by then dwindled to only a few hundred, and most of these members were in their 60s or 70s. Whatever the cause, the Socialist Workers Party seems less likely than ever to be attractive to the American voter in general and to the American worker in particular.

Sources/References

Congressional Quarterly, Inc. *National Party Conventions, 1831–1984.* Washington, DC: Congressional Quarterly, Inc., 1987.

Johnson, Donald Bruce (Comp.). *National Party Platforms: Vol. 1, 1840–1956.* Urbana: University of Illinois Press, 1978.

_____ (Comp.). *National Party Platforms: Vol. 2, 1960–1976.* Urbana: University of Illinois Press, 1978.

McKee, Don K. "Daniel DeLeon: A Reappraisal" *Labor History*, 1 (Fall), 1960.

Petersen, Arnold. *Daniel DeLeon: Socialist Architect* (2 vols.). New York: New York Labor News, 1941.

Reeve, Carl. *The Life and Times of Daniel DeLeon.* New York: Humanities, 1972.

Schapsmeier, Edward L., and Frederick H. Schapsmeier. *Political Parties and Civic Action Groups.* Westport, CT: Greenwood, 1981.

Seretan, L. Glen. *Daniel DeLeon: The Odyssey of an American Marxist.* Cambridge, MA: Harvard University Press.

Smallwood, Frank. *The Other Candidates: Third Parties in Presidential Elections.* Hanover, NH: University Press of New England, 1988.

Stanwood, Edward. *A History of the Presidency from 1897 to 1916.* Boston: Houghton Mifflin, 1916.

_____. *A History of the Presidency from 1788 to 1897.* Boston: Houghton Mifflin, 1924.

Socialist Party of America

Established in July of 1901 in Indianapolis, Indiana.

Key elements in formation of the party were delegates of the Social Democratic Party (q.v.) led and formed by Eugene V. Debs in 1898 and a moderate, anti-DeLeon group of the Socialist Labor Party (q.v.). The Socialist Labor Party had been the first significant socialist party in the United States. In the 1890s, it had been captured by Daniel

DeLeon—an autocratic and militant syndicalist—and his supporters. But Morris Hillquit and other members of the more moderate element of the party split from the DeLeon party and assisted in the formation of the new Socialist Party in 1901. Debs had been president of the American Railway Union and had for many years been a major labor activist and had a long reputation as a dedicated pacifist. He was totally dedicated to the socialist cause, which sought fundamental changes in the politicoeconomic system as it then prevailed in the United States.

Negotiations between these two factions had led to support in the 1900 presidential campaign for a presidential ticket led by Eugene V. Debs and Job Harriman of California. In that campaign, the Social Democratic Party reaffirmed its

> allegiance to the revolutionary principles of International Socialism and . . . [declared] the supreme political issue in America . . . to be the contest between the working class and the capitalist class for the possession of the powers of government. The party affirms its steadfast purpose to use those powers . . . to destroy wage slavery, abolish the institution of private property in the means of production, and establish the Co-operative Commonwealth.

But their initial effort netted only 0.6 percent of the popular vote, some 86,935.

The growth and support of the new party appeared to be rapid. In 1904, the Socialist Party ran Eugene V. Debs and New Yorker Benjamin Hanford as its presidential and vice presidential candidates. Attacking the capitalist system as the basic cause of oppression in American society, the platform declared:

> Socialism comes so to organize industry and society that every individual shall be secure in that private property is the means of life upon which his liberty of being, thought and action depend. It comes to rescue the people from the fast increasing and successful assault of capitalism upon the liberty of the individual.

Asserting that the "class struggle is due to the private ownership of the means of employment, or the tools of production," the platform stated that the Socialist Party was pledged "to use all political power, as fast as it shall be entrusted to us by our fellow-workers, both for their immediate interests and for their ultimate and complete emancipation." The Socialist Party candidates polled over 402,000 votes during that election year.

In 1908, the party once again nominated Debs and Hanford. Among an extensive list of platform demands were calls for employment relief through construction of public works projects; nationalization of industries, transportation, and communication networks; complete freedom of press, speech, and assembly; and the drastic improvement of working conditions. The platform also advocated adoption of a graduated income tax, equal suffrage, doing away with the U.S. Senate, "abolition of the power usurped by the Supreme Court of the United States to pass upon the constitutionality of legislation enacted by Congress," popular election of judges, and other objectives. "Such measures of relief," concluded the platform, "are but a preparation of the workers to seize the whole power of government, in order that they may thereby lay hold of the whole system of industry and thus come to their rightful inheritance."

The 1908 election netted the Socialist candidates 420,390 votes, nearly 3 percent of the total votes cast, but no electoral votes.

In 1912 membership in the Socialist Party reached about 118,000. In 1912, also, the Socialist Party achieved a high turnout in the election—when Debs, this time running with Emil Seidel of Milwaukee, received nearly 6 percent of the popular vote (some 900,369). That election year proved also to be very successful for the Socialist Party at the local level: it ran some 79 mayoral candidates across the country and was able to elect some 1,200 candidates to various offices.

The platform that year continued to call for the "collective ownership and democratic management" of communication and transportation systems. It also demanded a reduction in the cost of living; increased efforts toward the conservation of resources; reducing unemployment through expansion of public works; improving working conditions by shortening the workday and forbidding the employment of children; a graduated income tax; implementation of the initiative, referendum, and recall; adoption of a proportional representation system; doing away with the Senate and the president's veto power; direct popular election of the president and vice president; suffrage for residents of the District of Columbia and representation of the District's population in Congress; abolishing federal district courts and courts of appeal; and a number of other, for the time, relatively radical proposals. The platform concluded once more with the suggestion that such efforts would constitute "a preparation of the workers to seize the whole powers of government, in order that they may thereby lay hold of the whole system of socialized industry and thus come to their rightful inheritance."

The 1916 election focused on the imminence of American entry into the First World War. Taking a largely antiwar stance, the party's candidates—this time Allan L. Benson of New York and George R. Kirkpatrick of New Jersey—and platform called for a national referendum on the question of a war declaration, urged that the United States organize a "congress of all neutral nations to mediate between the belligerent powers in an effort to establish an immediate and lasting peace without indemnities or forcible annexation of territory and based on a binding and enforcible international treaty." It also called for the repeal of "all laws and appropriations" for the military, and taking from the president the power "to lead the nation into a position which leaves no escape from war." It also called for independence for the Philippines, and stated that the Monroe Doctrine "shall be immediately abandoned." Thus, taking its cue from Debs, the Socialist Party became a major source of anti–World War I protest. But support at the polls for the party dropped in that election. Benson and Kirkpatrick received 589,924 (just slightly over 3 percent) of the votes cast.

In 1918, Eugene V. Debs was convicted of sedition under the Espionage Act for having made an antiwar speech in Canton, Ohio. Sentenced to a federal penitentiary in Atlanta for a term of 10 years, he nevertheless ran for president in 1920 from his prison cell. His running mate was Seymour Stedman of Illinois. The Socialist platform that year strongly attacked the administration of Woodrow Wilson for its undercutting of civil liberties, the deporting of political radicals, and press censorship. The so-called Palmer raids were also singled out as worthy of the scorn of all of those who valued civil liberties. Reiterating many of the points in previous platforms, the 1920 platform also called for repeal of the Espionage Act, doing away with the writ of injunction by which courts could "restrain workers in their struggles against employers," dissolution of the League of Nations and in its place the establishment of an "international parliament," immediate peace with the Central Powers, and the payment in full of all war debts, along with other demands. In short, the platform proclaimed, "The outgoing administration, like Democratic and Republican administrations of the past, leaves behind it a disgraceful record of solemn pledges unscrupulously broken and public confidence ruthlessly betrayed."

After the Bolshevik Revolution in Russia, one element in the party advocated that the Socialists drop their advocacy of mere evolutionary change and adopt a policy that would be aimed at immediate overthrow of the American capitalistic system. This faction withdrew from the party in 1919, and the party was to that extent severely weakened.

Even though he was in prison during this campaign, Debs was able to capture well over 900,000 votes—but this total was still only some 3.4 percent of the popular vote. Debs was pardoned by President Harding in 1921.

In 1924, the Socialists supported the presidential candidacy of Robert M. La Follette of Wisconsin (who ran with Senator Burton K. Wheeler of Montana). Their endorsement of this ticket did not prove advantageous; La Follette and Wheeler lost.

In 1928 the Socialists again ran their own candidates, this time Norman Thomas (Debs had died in 1926), who had been a minister and a social worker, as their presidential nominee, and James H. Maurer, president of the Pennsylvania Federation of Labor, as vice presidential nominee. Thomas had also been one of the moving forces in the establishment of the American Civil Liberties Union and several other significant liberal organizations, and was probably a profound influence in getting the Democratic Party to include in its list of programmatic objectives many of his own aims as the Socialist leader. In its platform the Socialist Party indicated that it "offers itself as the political party of the producing classes, the workers in farm, factory, mine or office. It is our political weapon in the class struggle and in its triumph lies our hope of ending that struggle." It sought public ownership of natural resources and establishment of conservation measures, relief for the unemployed, enhanced labor legislation, changes in the tax structure, expanded civil liberties, an antilynching bill, "a modernized constitution," "nationalization of the banking and currency system," greater farm relief, opposition to "imperialism and militarism," and diplomatic recognition of the Soviet Union.

The party's candidates received 266,453 votes. As if to denounce and renounce the socialist program completely, the American people elected Herbert Hoover, the Republican, over Democratic Governor Al Smith of New York.

Thomas became the party's quadrennial candidate for a quarter century. In 1932, given the depths of the Depression, the Socialists campaigned on the theme that the country's economic collapse was clearly a manifestation of the full failure of capitalism. The party's platform once again called for more federal programs for relief and general economic assistance, insurance programs for the unemployed and for the elderly, protection of workers' rights, collective bargaining, the repeal of Prohibition, and American entry into the World Court and the League of Nations, among other things.

In 1932, Thomas and James Maurer were able to attract some 883,990 votes—2.2 percent of the popular vote. It thus seemed evident that if the Socialist Party was unable to attract a significant vote during the very depths of the Depression, it was likely that it would never be able to muster enough support to become a real force in American politics.

In succeeding elections, the Socialist Party continued to perform quite poorly indeed. Beset with internal difficulties, the death of

Morris Hillquit, and the party's special appeal to left-wing radicals, including communists (even though, as some scholars argue, many communists never thought much of the Socialists, often branding them "social fascists" and "misleaders of the working class"), the party never achieved the success it had sought. Hillquit, born in Riga, Latvia, came to the United States in 1886, and became the leader of the right-wing or constitutional socialists in opposition to Daniel DeLeon. He was from the outset the leading theoretician and tactician of the Socialist Party, opposed U.S. entry into World War I, and was a defense lawyer in many cases against U.S. socialists. He was the party's candidate for mayor of New York twice and for Congress five times. He eventually took his Socialists into La Follette's Progressive Party in 1924.

Although Thomas ran in 1934 as a candidate for the U.S. Senate (he lost), he did again run for the presidency under the Socialist banner in 1936, this time with George A. Nelson, who was leader of the Wisconsin Farmers Union. Declaring in its platform, "Not a penny, not a man to the military arms of the government," it continued its antimilitaristic stance of the past and urged the continuation of public works and other social programs aimed at the elevation and advancement of the workers. Thomas and Nelson received only 187,785 votes (0.41 percent of the vote) in 1936. The Socialists had been severely undercut by Franklin Roosevelt's New Deal policies.

Nominating Thomas and Maynard C. Krueger, a University of Chicago economics professor, as its candidates in 1940, the party's platform proclaimed:

> Every American knows that we have the resources and the machinery, the workers and the skill to conquer poverty. . . .
> That the situation has not already led to worse suffering and graver menace to our imperfect democracy is due to social legislation originating in socialist immediate demands. The best of what goes by the New Deal name; social insurance, minimum wage laws, guarantees of the right to collective bargaining, public power projects were first demanded by the Socialist Party.
> But these things, for reasons that Socialists have always proclaimed, have not averted the multiplying ills of a dying private capitalism.

Still, the Socialists received only 116,827 votes (.23 percent of those cast). Franklin Delano Roosevelt, in the meantime, went on to win an unprecedented third term.

In 1944, Thomas ran yet again, this time with Darlington Hoopes, who had served in the Pennsylvania legislature. The usual socialist appeals were again found in the platform for that year, and, seemingly also as usual, they had little impact on the American electorate. Thomas and Hoopes received only 80,518 votes. Franklin Delano Roosevelt—still embraced by the American people—was re-elected for yet a fourth term, although he would not survive its duration.

In 1948, Norman Thomas ran again as the Socialist Party presidential candidate, this time with Tucker P. Smith, an economics professor in Michigan's Olivet College. Its platform attacked capitalism in the usual ways. It urged vast increases in unemployment insurance programs, social security benefits, and aid to education. It opposed racial segregation and advocated public housing programs and repeal of the Taft-Hartley Act. It sought international regulation of atomic energy, doing away with trade restrictions, and continuing the Marshall Plan for aid to Europe. It advocated Palestinian self-government.

But the Democrat Harry Truman won the presidency, to the surprise of even the pollsters that year, and the Socialist ticket received only 138,973 votes.

In 1952, the Socialist Party nominated Darlington Hoopes, the party's former vice presidential nominee, and Samuel H. Friedman of New York as its candidates. Norman Thomas meanwhile had advocated that the party turn away from running candidates in elections and that it become, instead, mainly an educational group. In a seemingly utopian platform, the Socialists proclaimed:

> Socialism has been catapulted into a major political issue in the United States today by the action of its enemies. The press, the radio, the halls of Congress, are filled with the hate and hysteria of the diehards of American capitalism who fear they may no longer be able to dictate the economic life of the country for private profit. All the propaganda that their great fortunes can buy is unleashed in a vicious anti-socialist campaign.
>
> What is this Socialism that the American people are asked to fear and to reject? It is any form of enterprise where public service cuts out private profit.

The party did exceptionally poorly in 1952, receiving only 20,065 votes.

The plight of the Socialists became manifest in the debate among party members over whether even to run a candidate in the 1956 presidential election. Nevertheless, the Hoopes-Friedman duo was again selected as the party's candidates. Once again asserting that "the Socialist Party is pledged to building a new, more democratic society in the United States; a society in which human rights come before property rights; a nation which can take its place in a World

Federation of Cooperative Commonwealths which will eliminate war, racial antagonism, hunger, disease, poverty and oppression," the platform stated that "the Socialist Party . . . is dedicated to building socialism in this stronghold of capitalism because, even at its greatest, capitalism fails to satisfy the finest aspirations of its people." It argued that "the development of the highest living standard in the world cannot excuse the inequality in division of wealth, which means that one family in ten receives an annual income of less than $1,000 and more than two families in ten have less than $2,000 per year." The platform went on to discuss the usual Socialist goals, among them "full equality for all Americans," the "protection and improvement of the American standard of living," the revision of taxation programs, protection of minor parties and trade unions, and the repeal of the Smith Act. The platform concluded with the assertion: "This program is based on the highest ideals of human brotherhood. It will bring peace instead of war. It will replace fear and hate with goodwill and love. Death and despair will give way to life and hope."

But even these appeals once again did little if anything to attract support to the Socialists. Indeed, the party's showing at the polls was little short of disastrous—the party's national slate received only 2,044 votes in 1956.

After this defeat, the Socialist Party turned toward becoming an educational movement, rather than one that would focus on the running of candidates, even with the remote expectation of victory, a course long advocated by Norman Thomas. Moreover, in 1957, the Socialist Party of America joined with the Social Democratic Federation, and later took in the Independent Socialist League, composed of Trotskyites. The death of Norman Thomas in 1968 and the rise of younger, newer spokespersons for the Socialist idea, such as Michael Harrington, served also to change the course of the party. Harrington and others became influential in forming social programs that Presidents John F. Kennedy and Lyndon B. Johnson later implemented during their administrations.

But dissension continued to manifest itself within the party. Some Socialists continued to disagree with the notion that efforts to work with the Democratic Party should be continued; thus, some supported Benjamin Spock, the People's Party candidate, in 1972. Thus, too, a so-called Debs Caucus proposed former mayor of Milwaukee Frank Zeidler as its candidate for the presidency in 1976. Zeidler received slightly more than 6,000 votes.

In 1980, the party was renamed the Socialist Party USA, and its official headquarters were established in Milwaukee, Wisconsin. That year, David McReynolds, a member of the Debs Caucus and a recognized pacifist and member of the War Resisters' League, was nominated as its presidential candidate, and Sister Diane Drufen-brock, a Milwaukee school teacher, as its vice presidential nominee. The 1980 platform began with the following statement:

> Our focus in the 80s is the immediate halt in preparation for war; disarmament for survival; the development of safe energy programs; and a full-employment economy.
> We emphasize an immediate increase in the use of technical assistance, food and other resources, to the developing nations.
> Americans can take back the power to solve our problems by beginning the transfer of power from a small handful of inter-locking corporations back to our neighborhoods and democratic unions.
> More decentralized functions of government are essential to democratic socialism. . . .
> Our aim is the social ownership and democratic control of the major means of production and distribution. Democratic social-ism is the extension of democracy from the ballot box to the workplace and the community, the eradication of race and sex discrimination, and the recognition of the right of every individ-ual to maximum personal development, health care, economic security, and the humane use of science and technology.

Other planks in the platform called for reducing military ex-penditures; controls on rents, prices, transportation, and health care; nationalization of natural energy; affirmative action; the approval of the Equal Rights Amendment; doing away with NATO and other military agreements; and a number of other items related to assis-tance to veterans of the Vietnam War, opposition to the draft, and other foreign policy objectives.

On the ballot in 11 states, the party's candidates received only 6,898 votes.

Since that time, the party has been essentially engaged in edu-cational activities. The likelihood that it will ever be successful at the national level is increasingly unlikely; in 1988, for example, its can-didates—Willa Kenoyer and Ron Ehrenreich—received only 3,800 votes. Its platform contained planks dealing with personal and polit-ical freedoms; education emphasizing critical thinking as opposed to mere obedience; massive changes in health care programs, including research; housing for those who need it; peace in the world by way of nuclear disarmament, withdrawal of troops from around the world, abiding by World Court decisions, and related matters; an increased concern with ecological matters; and a change in the economy through turning away from the profit system. Other concerns were also addressed.

Sources/References

Congressional Quarterly, Inc. *National Party Conventions, 1831–1984*. Washington, DC: Congressional Quarterly, Inc., 1987.

Day, Glenn. *Minor Presidential Candidates and Parties of 1988*. Jefferson, NC: McFarland, 1988.

Ginger, Ray. *The Bending Cross: A Biography of Eugene Victor Debs*. New Brunswick, NJ: Rutgers University Press, 1949.

Hesseltine, William B. *The Rise and Fall of Third Parties*. Princeton, NJ: D. Van Nostrand, 1962.

Hillquit, Morris. *History of Socialism in the United States* (5th rev. ed.). New York: Russell & Russell, 1965.

Johnpoll, Bernard. *Pacifist's Progress*. Chicago: Triangle, 1970.

Kipnis, Ira. *The American Socialist Movement, 1897–1912*. New York: Columbia University Press, 1952.

Nash, Howard, Jr. *Third Parties in American Politics*. Washington, DC: Public Affairs Press, 1959.

Schapsmeier, Edward L., and Frederick H. Schapsmeier. *Political Parties and Civic Action Groups*. Westport, CT: Greenwood, 1981.

Seidler, Murray B. *Norman Thomas, Respectable Rebel*. Syracuse, NY: Syracuse University Press, 1961.

Shannon, David. *The Socialist Party of America: A History*. New York: Macmillan, 1955.

Smallwood, Frank. *The Other Candidates: Third Parties in Presidential Elections*. Hanover, NH: University Press of New England, 1983.

Weinstein, James. *The Decline of Socialism in America, 1912–1925*. New York: Monthly Review Press, 1967.

Socialist Workers Party

Established in Chicago in 1938 by James P. Cannon, Max Schactman, James Burnham, and other anti-Stalinist socialists who supported Leon Trotsky, who had been exiled from the Soviet Union and was living in Mexico.

The Trotskyites were originally an element of the Communist Party of the United States (q.v.), but upon the direct order of Joseph Stalin, they were expelled from the party in 1936. The expulsion of the Trotskyites from the Communist Party revolved around an ideological issue: Trotsky advocated "world revolution" through the implementation of the ideas of Marx, Lenin, and Trotsky himself, while dictator Joseph Stalin demanded "socialism for one country" (the Soviet Union). The Trotskyites briefly cooperated with the Socialist Party, but decided to become an independent group in 1938, largely as a result of their rigid and doctrinaire interpretation of Communist ideology. Internal controversy became typical of the organization's activities, and actual party membership was always small, perhaps never exceeding several hundred. It appealed especially to radical members of the intelligentsia, such persons as Edmund Wilson, Sidney Hook, Dwight MacDonald, Mary McCarthy, and others of similar intellectual bent.

Even though it had been listed as a subversive organization by the U.S. attorney general, the Socialist Workers Party nominated its first presidential ticket in 1948, when it put forth the candidacies of Farrell Dobbs of New York for president and Grace Carlson of Minnesota for vice president. In its platform, the party referred to the "ruinous condition" to which the country had been brought by its rulers and, more precisely, by the capitalist class, and that the system had at the same time "brought into being the working class comprising tens of millions of people, with a high standard of education, great technical skills and long traditions of democracy and social equality." And it was the workers, the middle classes, agricultural workers, and small farmers who were being "ravaged by the anarchy of the profit system."

Citing the oppression of youth, women, and blacks, the platform asserted that the "oppressed classes and groups are looking for a way out." But the capitalists were reacting to put down the struggles of the working class by enactment of the "Taft-Hartley Act, the Mundt Bill, the Committee on un-American Activities, the preparation for transforming the FBI into a Gestapo, militarization of the country, [and] the strangling of liberties traditional in the United States since the beginning of the Republic." Warning that the existing condition "must end either in the complete destruction of civilization or in the socialist reconstruction of society under the leadership of the working class," the Socialist Workers Party put itself forth "under the banner of Marx and Engels, Lenin and Trotsky, Debs and Haywood." Attacking the Democratic and Republican parties, Henry Wallace, the Stalinist-oriented Communist Party, and Norman Thomas's Socialist Party, the platform then asserted that "the Socialist Workers Party alone consistently and unconditionally champions the interest of the workers in their struggles against capitalism, and works to organize them for its abolition" and "the mobilization of the masses for a Workers and Farmers Government." Its 10-point platform then dealt with giving the people the power to decide questions of war or peace and matters of foreign policy ranging from withdrawal of all troops from foreign soil to an attack on the United Nations; placing an "escalator clause" in all labor contracts so that wages could reflect the rising cost of living; repealing the Taft-Hartley Act and doing away with "red-baiting, witch hunts and political persecution"; extending full rights to minorities; a farm program to be operated by farmers themselves; doing away with military conscription; declaring a national housing emergency; the repeal of all payroll taxes; nationalization of basic industries; and the breaking by labor of "all ties with the capitalist parties."

But Dobbs and Carlson received 13,614 votes in 1948, only .03 percent of the votes cast.

The Socialist Workers Party nominated Farrell Dobbs and Myra Tanner Weiss of New York as its candidates in 1952. Its platform stated, "We are told every day that Americans live in a special 'paradise-on-earth,' the richest, the most peaceful, the most stable country in the world. But the truth is we face disaster." Suggesting that it alone was the only true opponent to Stalinism and that it was not "'communism' which threatens America," the Socialist Workers Party urged the American people to "reorganize the wealth of our country on a socialist basis, to rid ourselves of minority government of the parasites and plutocrats and to establish genuine democracy—the rule of the workers and poor farmers. That is the only road to lasting peace." Its platform then touched upon matters of foreign policy, equal rights, women's rights, inflation, labor, taxes, welfare, militarism, farm policy, and nationalization of industry, and closed with the appeal that "only a Workers and Farmers Government can reorganize our society on a rational basis, and utilize the tremendous potential wealth and strength of our country for the benefit of humanity."

But this time Dobbs and his running mate Weiss polled even fewer votes than before—only 10,312, or only .02 percent of the popular vote.

The Socialist Workers Party continued to nominate candidates. In 1956, Dobbs and Tanner were again nominated, but in this election they received fewer than 8,000 votes. During their campaign, Dobbs and Weiss opposed the "peaceful coexistence" policy of the Soviet Union that had emerged under Khruschev and looked forward to increasing activity in the drive toward world socialism. Attacking the same problems that were denounced in preceding platforms, the party proclaimed, "only the Socialist Workers Party presents a principle[d], realistic vehicle for anti-capitalist political action through support of its national ticket." But in 1956 the ticket received only 7,797 votes, or .01 percent.

Dobbs and Weiss were again nominated in 1960. This time they cited the virtues of the Soviet Union and put forth a foreign policy goal that included recognizing Red China and lauding Castro's revolution in Cuba. Among other things, the platform declared:

At one time America was regarded as the hope of the oppressed everywhere. This is no longer true. The majority of the human race have turned toward the Soviet Union and China as representing the road of progress. Whether we like it or not, this happens to be today's outstanding fact. It is high time to ask ourselves, why has America become so feared and hated?

Notwithstanding these rhetorical flourishes, the party's candidates received only 40,165 votes.

Between 1964 and 1980, support for the party did not fall below 32,000. In 1964, the party nominated Clifton DeBerry, a black militant, and Edward Shaw, both from New York. Their candidacy netted some 32,327 votes. In 1968, candidates Fred Halstead and Paul Boutelle drew 41,390 votes, running on a platform that included vehement opposition to American participation in the Vietnam War. In 1972, the party opted for a feminist presidential candidate, Linda Jenness, who ran with Andrew Pulley, a steelworker, as the vice presidential nominee. But their support dropped to 37,423 votes. In 1976, despite previous investigation and infiltration of the party by the CIA and FBI and party-initiated litigation growing out of the party's discovery of that fact, the Socialist Workers ran Peter Camejo and Willie Mae Reid, both from California. The party was able to garner 91,310 votes in that election.

The 1980 election year saw the nomination of Andrew Pulley, this time for president, and Matilde Zimmerman, an activist opposed to the Vietnam War, as vice presidential candidate. Pulley, whose origins were in rural Mississippi, was ineligible to serve as president, however, because of the constitutional requirement that presidential candidates must be at least 35 years old (he was only 29). His name therefore appeared on the ballot in only six states. Thus, in the majority of states in which the party had qualified for the ballot, Clifton DeBerry became the party's candidate, while in Ohio, Rick Congress was their choice.

The platform opened with the following salvo:

> Every day Washington drags us closer to war. Closer to sending American youth to fight and die in a foreign land.
> From the Iran crisis to threats against Cuba, from support to racist regimes in southern Africa to secretly sending U.S. "advisers" to Thailand—the Carter administration is aggressively pushing to reassert the U.S. "right" to police the world.

Pulley asserted that banks, industry, and commerce had to be nationalized completely in order to protect the working class. During the campaign, the platform declared that the Socialist Workers Party would seek "full employment"; the protection of wages "against inflation with cost-of-living escalator clauses, so that wages go up . . .

with each rise in living costs"; the right to free education, medical care, and benefits for the retired and the disabled; opposition to nuclear power; support of vigorous affirmative action programs and opposition to right- and left-wing terrorists; equality for women; elimination of government involvement in repressive measures of all kinds, and "full democratic and human rights" for homosexuals, the handicapped, prisoners, and others; support for "a right to know the full truth about the decisions that affect our lives"; and policies that would require corporations to "open their books" and "show their records" to unions in order to determine "their real profits, production statistics, political payoffs, and tax swindles." Other proposals were also put forth.

But, even with the aid of the Young Socialist Alliance and active appeals in the *Militant,* the party's publication, the candidates received little support. Together, they received only a total of about 51,000 votes, DeBerry receiving the most, and Pulley and Congress a distant second and third, respectively. The candidates knew they could not possibly win the election, given the small number of their membership and voting support and the debilitating effects of the confusion surrounding the fact that several candidates were in contention for the same office. Their main objective was to seek exposure for the party's views. But the party's doctrinaire interpretation of Marxism had little appeal, and continues to have little appeal, to Americans. In 1988, for example, Socialist Worker candidate James Warren received only 13,338 votes, .01 percent of the total cast.

Sources/References

Cannon, James P. *The History of American Trotskyism: Report of a Participant.* New York: Pioneer, 1944.

Congressional Quarterly, Inc. *National Party Conventions, 1831–1984.* Washington, DC: Congressional Quarterly, Inc., 1987.

Deutscher, Isaac. *The Prophet Outcast, Trotsky: 1929–1940.* New York: Vintage, 1944.

Johnson, Donald Bruce (Comp.). *National Party Platforms: Vol. 1, 1840–1956.* Urbana: University of Illinois Press, 1978.

——— (Comp.). *National Party Platforms: Vol. 2, 1960–1976.* Urbana: University of Illinois Press, 1978.

——— (Comp.). *National Party Platforms of 1980: Supplement to National Party Platforms, 1840–1976.* Urbana: University of Illinois Press, 1982.

Myers, Constance Ashton. *The Prophet's Army: Trotskyists in America, 1928–1941.* Westport, CT: Greenwood, 1977.

Schapsmeier, Edward L., and Frederick H. Schapsmeier. *Political Parties and Civic Action Groups.* Westport, CT: Greenwood, 1981.

Smallwood, Frank. *The Other Candidates: Third Parties in Presidential Elections.* Hanover, NH: University Press of New England, 1983.

South Carolina Progressive Democratic Party

Established in Columbia, South Carolina, in May 1944.

This party's objective was to develop civil rights for blacks. It became the forerunner of the Mississippi Freedom Democratic Party (q.v.).

Originally known as the South Carolina Colored Democratic Party, the new party grew out of efforts to elect President Franklin Delano Roosevelt to a fourth term (his New Deal policies proved to be particularly appealing to blacks, inasmuch as those policies provided jobs at pay levels equal to those of whites and provided other opportunities for advancement) and to do away with South Carolina's white primary law, which prevented blacks from voting in primary elections. Thus, blacks in effect had no choice whatsoever when they voted in general elections—the candidates had already been chosen by whites.

A convention was called at Columbia, South Carolina; some 172 delegates were present. Interested persons from Alabama, Georgia, Mississippi, North Carolina, and Virginia also attended. The name of the party had been changed to South Carolina Progressive Democratic Party largely upon the suggestion of a retired white woman who contributed her pension check to the group. The convention organized three committee levels that made up the foundation of the new party's structural organization. The convention also called for the implementation of the decision reached by the Supreme Court in *Smith v. Allright,* in which the Court ruled that exclusively white primaries violated the Constitution of the United States. In addition, the convention endorsed a resolution insisting that blacks receive representation in the regular Democratic party proportional to their numbers in the population. The keynote speaker at the convention called for righting the wrongs that had denied both blacks and whites "some voice in their government, some control over their destinies."

Meeting with Democratic Party chairman Robert Hannagan and other Democratic leaders in Washington after their convention, South Carolina Progressive Democratic Party representatives were told that discriminatory procedures would be eliminated from the party's rules. Nevertheless, blacks were not ultimately included in the South Carolina delegation to the Democratic National Convention, and the South Carolina Progressive Democratic Party sent its own delegation to challenge the legitimacy of the all-white group. Indeed, the Democratic Convention's Credentials Committee never even officially received their challenge. Given this rebuff by the regular Democratic Party, members of the South Carolina Progressive Democratic Party returned to South Carolina, where they nominated Osceola McKaine as their own candidate to challenge Governor Olin D. Johnston for a seat in the U.S. Senate. McKaine was defeated, receiving only 4,500 votes.

The South Carolina Progressive Democratic Party then turned toward emphasizing registration-to-vote drives among blacks. Their success was noted in the increase of black registrations between 1944 and 1947—from some 3,500 to 50,000. Sympathetic white candidates were also supported by the party.

In 1946, at its annual convention, the South Carolina Progressive Democratic Party disbanded. The suggestion to disband had come from then National Association for the Advancement of Colored People lawyer Thurgood Marshall (who later was appointed to the U.S. Supreme Court), U.S. District Judge J. Waties Waring, and the Reverend James Hinton, who was the leader of the NAACP statewide conference. The rationale for disbanding the party rested on the idea that the party's continued existence would only excite the anger of the regular Democrats and work to the disadvantage of the black population in general. Moreover, the lack of financial and other resources on the part of the South Carolina Progressive Democratic Party made it generally impossible for it to challenge the Democratic Party itself effectively.

Continuing its registration drive, however, the South Carolina Progressive Democratic Party challenged the all-white delegation at the Democratic Party's national convention in 1948. Progress was made at this convention in that although the regular Democratic delegation was seated, a minority report was presented in behalf of the South Carolina Progressive Democratic Party's position and a strong civil rights plank was adopted by the national Democratic Party itself. So infuriated by this were the delegates of the South Carolina regular Democratic Party that they walked out of the convention. Members of this dissident faction went over to the States' Rights (Dixiecrat) Party (q.v.).

In 1956, the South Carolina Progressive Democratic Party again contested the delegation of the regular Democratic Party at the party's national convention. Here they received a pledge that the Democratic Party's rules would be revised in such a way that they would prevent efforts to engage in discrimination against blacks with respect to representation in future party conventions. The blacks who had led the challenge movement were slowly absorbed back into the regular South Carolina Democratic Party and the South Carolina Progressive

Democratic Party came to an end, although unhappiness and suspicion continued to linger and some continued to urge a renewal of their efforts.

Sources/References

Hoffman, E. "The Genesis of the Modern Movement for Equal Rights in South Carolina, 1930–1939." *Journal of Negro History* (October), 1959.

Schapsmeier, Edward L., and Frederick H. Schapsmeier. *Political Parties and Civic Action Groups*. Westport, CT: Greenwood, 1981.

"South Carolina Blacks Plan New Party." *New York Times* (November 24), 1969.

Walton, Hanes, Jr. *Black Political Parties: An Historical and Political Analysis*. New York: Free Press, 1972.

Southern Democrats

Established as a result of a split in the Democratic Party, which was meeting in Charleston, South Carolina, in 1860.

In 1860, Southern Democrats demanded that the Democratic Party include in its platform a plank that stated specifically that the institution of slavery would be protected in the territories. Before this, the party had been able to retain most of its membership by approving of legislation that protected southern slavery while at the same time permitting self-determination in the territories. The slavery protection proposal of the Southern Democrats was defeated at the convention. As a result, the delegates of most of the southern states walked off the convention floor.

The bolters from the Charleston convention, after that meeting had stalemated over a nomination for president, reconvened in Baltimore with other southern delegates. There, Stephen A. Douglas, the senator from Illinois, was nominated as the presidential candidate. Upon the choice of Douglas, southern delegates, as well as those from Oregon and California, left the convention.

These dissidents—numbering some 200—held their own convention and nominated Vice President John C. Breckinridge of Kentucky as their presidential candidate, and Senator Joseph Lane, a well-known states' rights supporter from Oregon, as their vice presidential candidate. Breckinridge argued that neither the federal nor local governments had any power to restrict slavery in any area of the country while that area was still a territory. And, although he believed that secession was a right, he did disapprove of such action in 1860.

Thus, the platform adopted by this rump convention specifically recognized the right of slavery in the territories.

The platform adopted by that convention, although similar to the one that the regular Democratic convention had approved in Charleston, included the specific provisions that

> the platform adopted by the Democratic Party at Cincinnati be affirmed, with the following resolutions:
>
> . . . the Government of a Territory organized by an act of Congress is provisional and temporary, and during its existence all citizens of the United States have an equal right to settle with their property in the Territory, without their rights, either of person or property, being destroyed or impaired by Congressional or Territorial legislation.
>
> . . . it is the duty of the Federal Government, in all its departments, to protect, when necessary, the rights of persons and property in the Territories, and wherever else its constitutional authority extends.
>
> . . . when the settlers in a Territory, having an adequate population, form a state constitution, the right of sovereignty commences, and, being consummated by admission into the Union, they stand on an equal footing with the people of other States; and the State thus organized ought to be admitted into the federal Union, whether its Constitution prohibits or recognizes the institution of slavery.

Thus the Democratic Party found itself with two sets of candidates, neither set of which could ultimately claim victory in the election. It also had two platforms that included different positions on the issue of the role of slavery in the territories. Unless the rift caused by these two factions could somehow be healed, it was certain that a Republican victory in the 1860 election would be achieved—as, of course, it was. And the split in the Democratic Party that so eloquently elucidated the division over slavery also presaged the coming of the Civil War.

Given the Democratic schism, Abraham Lincoln, the Republican, won the election with a plurality of the votes cast. Breckinridge and Lane received some 848,019 votes (18.1 percent of the popular vote). They carried nine southern and border states, and received 72 electoral votes.

The Southern Democrats were influential in providing many of the stimuli for the government of the Confederate States of America. Jefferson Davis himself was among those. But when the Civil War ended, the Southern Democrats no longer continued on their separate course. They rejoined the Democratic Party, and the Southern Democratic faction came to an end. Breckinridge, after his defeat, opposed the war efforts of the administration. When Kentucky declared in favor of the Union in September of 1861, Breckinridge offered his services to the Confederacy. He served with great distinction throughout the Civil War, and when the South finally capitulated, Breckinridge went to Cuba and then to Europe. After an amnesty proclamation in 1868, he was permitted to return to the United States.

Sources/References

Congressional Quarterly, Inc. *National Party Conventions, 1831–1984*. Washington, DC: Congressional Quarterly, Inc., 1987.

Johnson, Donald Bruce (Comp.). *National Party Platforms: Vol. 1, 1840–1956*. Urbana: University of Illinois Press, 1978.

Stanwood, Edward. *A History of the Presidency from 1788 to 1897*. Boston: Houghton Mifflin, 1924.

States' Rights Party

Established by dissident Southern Democrats in Birmingham, Alabama, in 1948.

Popularly known as Dixiecrats, this party's members were primarily conservative (some might say "racist") Democrats who bolted from the Democratic Party especially as a reaction to President Harry S Truman's civil rights policy and the planks on civil rights contained in the 1948 Democratic Party platform. The primary objective of the Dixiecrats was to maintain segregation between blacks and whites.

In response to the adoption by the Democratic convention of a strongly supportive civil rights position, all of the delegates from Mississippi and half of the delegates from Alabama walked out of the convention. Only three days after the conclusion of the Democratic convention, Governor Fielding Wright of Mississippi invited the anti-civil rights Democrats to Birmingham in order to choose a slate of their own candidates.

Major supporters of the new Dixiecrat movement were drawn from conservative southern governors and similarly oriented southern state and local leaders. Although the new party did not actually organize a fully independent party apparatus, it did attempt to use what it could of the existing Democratic Party organization, and it did adopt a platform. At its Birmingham convention, the party's delegates nominated J. Strom Thurmond, governor of South Carolina, as their presidential candidate (after Senator Richard Russell of Georgia had declined to be the nominee) and Fielding Wright, governor of Mississippi, as vice presidential candidate.

The Dixiecrat platform opened with an affirmation, as follows:

> We affirm that a political party is an instrumentality for effec-
> tuating the principles upon which the party is founded; that a
> platform of principles is a solemn covenant with the people and
> with the members of the party; that no leader of the party, in
> temporary power, has the right or privilege to proceed contrary
> to the fundamental principles of the party, or the letter or spirit
> of the Constitution of the United States; that to act contrary to
> these principles is a breach of faith, a usurpation of power, and a
> forfeiture of the party name and party leadership.
>
> We believe that the protection of the American people against
> the onward march of totalitarian government requires a faithful
> observance of Article X of the American Bill of Rights which
> provides that: "The powers not delegated to the United States by
> the Constitution, nor prohibited by it to the states, are reserved to
> the states respectively, or to the people."

It then referred to a clause in the first platform of the Democratic party drafted in 1840, in which it was resolved that "Congress has no power under the Constitution to interfere with or control the domestic institutions of the several states, and that such states are the sole and proper judges of everything appertaining to their own affairs not prohibited by the Constitution."

The platform also suggested that "abuses and usurpations" of this principle by "unfaithful leaders" of the party had become intolerable, and that the policies of the executive branch of government in particular and especially its control of the Supreme Court were leading to a totalitarian state and to threats to "the integrity of the states and the basic rights of their citizens." Charging that the Democratic convention had been "rigged to embarrass and humiliate the South," and that it had adopted a call for eliminating segregation and discrimination in all walks of life, both public and private, the Dixiecrat platform asserted that the "convention hypocritically denounced totalitarianism abroad but unblushingly proposed and approved it at home." Indeed, the platform proclaimed that "if a foreign power undertook to force upon the people of the United States the measures advocated by the Democratic convention . . . with respect to civil rights, it would mean war and the entire nation would resist such an effort."

The platform referred to the undeviating historic loyalty of the South to the support of the Democratic Party, but that the party had now allowed states dominated by Republicans to determine its policies. The platform therefore declared its support for the Constitution of the United States; opposition to attempts to destroy the rights of states and citizens guaranteed by the American Constitution; opposition to totalitarianism, centralization, and bureaucratization of government; and support of "segregation of the races and the racial integrity of each race" and "the constitutional right to choose one's associates." It was opposed to the government's civil rights program and to the Democratic Party's civil rights program; it advocated checks and balances in government; and it argued for a return to the people of "those powers needed for the preservation of human rights and the discharge of our responsibility as Democrats for human welfare." The platform concluded with an appeal to all Americans to support the program and platform of the States' Rights Party.

The majority of Southern Democrats who were influential in the party did not support the Dixiecrat bolters. Nor did its candidates receive widespread support—particularly in the effort to stop President Truman's reelection. The party's presidential vote total reached only 1,169,134, or 2.4 percent of the popular vote, from, mainly, Alabama, Louisiana, Mississippi, and South Carolina, bringing it 39 electoral votes. It did not nominate candidates for other offices. Indeed, many Dixiecrats later supported Dwight D. Eisenhower for president.

The party faltered immediately after the election, and most of its members returned to the Democratic Party. It is perhaps ironic that J. Strom Thurmond himself became a Republican while serving in the U.S. Senate.

The party ran no candidates in 1952. But, to a considerable degree in response to *Brown v. Board of Education of Topeka* (the 1954 Supreme Court decision concerning school segregation), in 1956 the States' Rights Party was rejuvenated with the nomination of Virginian T. Coleman Andrews and Californian Thomas H. Werdel. Still, these candidates received only 107,929 votes and no electoral votes. The party also had a rival in Kentucky. There, a party also calling itself the States' Rights Party nominated Harry Byrd, a Virginia Democrat, as presidential nominee, and Will E. Jeure, a conservative Republican senator from Indiana, as its vice presidential candidate. But their campaign netted only some 2,657 votes.

The party became extinct after 1956.

Sources/References

Ader, Amile B. "Why the Dixiecrats Failed." *Journal of Politics*, 15 (August), 1953.

_____. *The Dixiecrat Movement: Its Role in Third Party Politics.* Washington, DC: Public Affairs Press, 1955.

Carleton, William G. "The Dilemma of the Democrats." *Virginia Quarterly Review,* 24 (Summer), 1948.

_____. "The Fate of Our Fourth Party." *Yale Review,* 37 (December), 1948.

Congressional Quarterly, Inc. *National Party Conventions, 1831–1984.* Washington, DC: Congressional Quarterly, Inc., 1987.

Hofstadter, Richard. "From Calhoun to the Dixiecrats." *Social Research,* 16 (June), 1949.

Johnson, Donald Bruce (Comp.). *National Party Platforms: Vol. 1, 1840–1956.* Urbana: University of Illinois Press, 1978.

Lemmon, Sarah McCulloh. "The Ideology of the 'Dixiecrat' Movement." *Social Forces,* 30 (December), 1951.

Schapsmeier, Edward L., and Frederick H. Schapsmeier. *Political Parties and Civic Action Groups.* Westport, CT: Greenwood, 1981.

Straight-Out Democratic Party

Established by Democratic dissidents in Louisville, Kentucky, in 1872.

The party was formed to protest the regular Democratic Party's nomination of Horace Greeley. His nomination had been widely expected, and he won nomination with well over the two-thirds of the vote needed at the convention. Yet many Democrats remained dissatisfied with what had happened. Many objected to what they saw as a surrender of their own principles when those of the Liberal Republicans became part of the Democratic program in what seemed to be an obvious ploy made simply to win the election. They thus called for a "straight Democratic" convention and adopted a series of resolutions. Among these were the following:

> The people of each State voluntarily created their State, and the States voluntarily formed the Union; and each State has provided, by its written Constitution, for everything a State should do for the protection of life, liberty, and property within it; and each State, jointly with the others, provided a Federal Union for foreign and inter-state relations.
>
> . . . That all government powers, whether state or federal, are trust powers coming from the people of each State; and that they are limited to the written letter of the Constitution and the laws passed in pursuance of it. . . .
>
> . . . That the interests of labor and capital should not be permitted to conflict. . . .
>
> . . . That we proclaim to the world that principle is to be preferred to power. . . .

. . . That, having been betrayed at Baltimore into a false creed and a false leadership by the convention, we repudiate both, and appeal to the people to approve our platform and to rally to the polls and support the true platform, and the candidates who embody it.

. . . That we are opposed to giving public lands to corporations, and favor their disposal to actual settlers only.

. . . That we favor a judicious tariff for revenue purposes only, and that we are unalterably opposed to class legislation which enriches a few at the expense of the many under the plea of protection.

The Straight-Out Democrats nominated Charles O'Conor of New York for president and John Quincy Adams II of Massachusetts as vice presidential candidate. When O'Conor was notified of his nomination, he declined. The convention then attempted to get James Lyon of Virginia to accept the nomination, but he, too, declined. Adams refused any nomination except that for the vice presidency, and then only if O'Conor in fact accepted the presidential nomination. The party ultimately proposed a ticket composed of O'Conor and Adams, even though both had declined! Ironically, the nominees nevertheless received 29,464 votes.

The party disbanded after the election.

Sources/References

Haynes, Fred E. *Third Party Movements Since the Civil War.* New York: Russell & Russell, 1916.

Schapsmeier, Edward L., and Frederick H. Schapsmeier. *Political Parties and Civic Action Groups.* Westport, CT: Greenwood, 1981.

Stanwood, Edward. *A History of the Presidency from 1788 to 1897.* Boston: Houghton Mifflin, 1924.

Tax Cut Party

Established by Lar Daly in Chicago in 1960.

The party was formed primarily to advance the candidacy of Lar Daly himself, whose main platform demand was the reduction of taxes on all levels. His vice presidential running mate was Merrit B. Curtis of the District of Columbia.

Unique in his campaign techniques, Daly would travel from place to place dressed in a red, white, and blue Uncle Sam costume. His campaign never excited many people, but because of his insistence that he was a bona fide candidate for the nation's highest office, and therefore entitled to equal time for his messages on radio and television, Congress felt compelled to repeal the equal-time provision in the national broadcasting law in order to permit the Kennedy-Nixon television debates to proceed as planned.

Never considered as a serious candidate by the media, or, indeed, by virtually anyone else, Daly did occasionally appear on television shows as something of a curiosity. His run for office drew only 1,761 votes. The party died after the election.

Sources/References

Costello, W. "That Ridiculous Lar Daly FCC Ruling." *New Republic* (March 30), 1959.
"Free, Equal and Ridiculous." *Time* (March 30), 1959.
Schapsmeier, Edward L., and Frederick H. Schapsmeier. *Political Parties and Civic Action Groups.* Westport, CT: Greenwood, 1981.
Seldes, G. "TV and Radio: NBC-Chet Huntley Affair." *Saturday Review* (April 11), 1959.

Union Labor Party

Established at Cincinnati, Ohio, in 1887.

The formation of the party was spearheaded by some former Greenback Party (q.v.) members, debtors, and farmers; it sought a merger between farmers and members of trade unions.

The 1888 nominating convention of the party was also held in Cincinnati. Approximately 200 delegates from 20 states were present. The party chose Alson J. Streeter of Illinois as its presidential candidate by acclamation. Samuel Evans of Texas was the party's vice presidential nominee.

The party's platform was relatively brief. The tenor of the party's program was set in the preamble:

> General discontent prevails on the part of the wealth-producer. Farmers are suffering from a poverty which has forced most of them to mortgage their estates, and the prices of products are so low as to offer no relief except through bankruptcy. Laborers are sinking into greater dependence. Strikes are resorted to without bringing relief. . . . Business men find collections almost impossible, and meantime hundreds of millions of idle public money which is needed for relief is locked up in the United States Treasury or placed without interest in favored banks, in grim mockery of distress. . . . Under these and other alarming conditions, we

appeal to the people of our country to come out of old party organizations, whose indifference to the public welfare is responsible for this distress, and aid the Union Labor Party to repeal existing class legislation and relieve the distress of our industries.

The platform then went on to oppose monopoly in land and to advocate limitations on land ownership:

> We believe the earth was made for the people and not . . . [for] an idle aristocracy to subsist through rents upon the toils of the industrious, and that corners in land are as bad as corners in food, and that those who are not residents or citizens should not be allowed to own lands in the United States.

It called for public ownership of communication and transportation systems and the "establishment of a national monetary system in the interest of the producer, instead of the speculator and usurer." It called for the establishment of postal savings banks, arbitration in labor disputes, pensions for soldiers and sailors of the United States who were honorably discharged, a graduated income tax, and direct election of senators. It demanded Chinese exclusion and "strict enforcement of laws prohibiting the importation of subjects of foreign countries under contract." It called for the right to vote for women, and concluded with the statement:

> The paramount issues to be solved in the interests of humanity are the abolition of usury, monopoly, and trusts, and we denounce the Democratic and Republican parties for creating and perpetuating these monstrous evils.

Campaigning on this platform drew the candidates only slightly more than 1 percent of the popular votes cast, and no electoral votes. The party disbanded, most of its followers joining the Populist Party (q.v.).

Sources/References

Johnson, Donald Bruce. *National Party Platforms: Vol. 1, 1840–1956*. Urbana: University of Illinois Press, 1978.

Schapsmeier, Edward L., and Frederick H. Schapsmeier. *Political Parties and Civic Action Groups*. Westport, CT: Greenwood, 1981.

Stanwood, Edward. *A History of the Presidency from 1788 to 1897*. Boston: Houghton Mifflin, 1924.

Union Party

Established in 1936 at Royal Oak, Michigan.

The Union Party was an agglomeration of forces put together by a rather forceful number of uniquely radical individuals—Father

Charles Coughlin, William Lemke, and Thomas O'Brien. The intention of the party was to challenge the Democratic and Republican parties in the national election of that year. Although an extension of Father Coughlin's so-called National Union for Social Justice, the party also received the support of such radicals as Dr. Francis E. Townsend and Gerald L. K. Smith. Senator Huey Long's ideas were also significant in providing a foundation for the movement. The prime movers of the party were thus men oriented toward arousing political emotions, rather than toward rationality.

Although the party did not hold a convention, Father Coughlin was largely responsible for bestowing on William "Liberty Bell" Lemke the presidential nomination of the party; he was also a prime mover of the Nonpartisan League (q.v.) and a member of the U.S. House of Representatives. Thomas O'Brien, a Boston union lawyer, was nominated as the party's vice presidential candidate.

Lemke, of the four major organizers of the party, was its only significant politician holding office as a member of Congress. His experience and ability to win public office thus made him most "available" of the candidates under consideration. Manifestations of support for his candidacy had come from various parts of the country; he felt he could run a strong race, using especially the proposals that had been made by Coughlin, Smith, and Townsend.

The Union Party platform, written by Coughlin, Lemke, and O'Brien themselves, contained 15 planks. The platform emphasized the following points:

1. That "America shall be self-contained and self-sustained."
2. That "Congress . . . alone shall coin, issue and regulate all the money and credit in the United States through a central bank of issue."
3. That "Congress shall provide for the retirement of all tax-exempt, interest-bearing bonds and certifications of indebtedness of the Federal Government . . . [and] shall refinance all the present agricultural mortgage indebtedness for the farmer and all the home mortgage indebtedness for the city owner."
4. That "Congress shall legislate . . . an assurance of a living annual wage for all laborers capable . . . and willing to work."
5. "That there will be assurance of production at a profit for the farmer."
6. "That there will be an assurance of reasonable and decent security for the aged."
7. "That American agricultural, industrial, and commercial markets will be protected from manipulation of foreign

moneys and from all raw material and processed good
produced abroad at less than a willing wage."

8. That "Congress shall establish an adequate and perfect
defense for our country . . . with the understanding that
our naval, air and military forces must not be used under
any consideration in foreign fields or in foreign waters
either alone or in conjunction with any foreign power. If
there must be conscription, there shall be conscription of
wealth as well as a conscription of men."

9. That "Congress shall . . . legislate that all federal offices
and positions of every nature shall be distributed through
civil service qualifications."

10. That "Congress shall restore representative government
to the people of the United States."

11. That "Congress shall organize and institute federal works
for the conservation of public lands, waters and forests."

12. That "Congress shall protect small industry and private
enterprise by controlling and decentralizing the economic
domination of monopolies."

13. That "Congress shall protect private property from
confiscation through unnecessary taxation."

14. That "Congress shall set a limitation upon the net income
of any individual in any one year and a limitation on the
amount that such an individual may receive as a gift or . . .
inheritance."

15. That "Congress shall re-establish conditions so that . . .
youths of the nation . . . may have the opportunity to earn
a decent living while in the process of perfecting
themselves in a trade or profession."

The Union Party thus made its appeal to the debtors in society,
but because of its support from such anti-Semitic personalities as
Father Coughlin and Gerald L. K. Smith, many voters refused to be
convinced of its objectives. Lemke himself did not add to the support
of the party because of his inability to reach into the minds of the
increasingly sophisticated urban voters.

Franklin Delano Roosevelt was reelected by a landslide. The
comparatively minor support received by Lemke (even though high
by comparison to some other minor party candidates of the past), who
received 892,492 votes and no electoral votes, and whose campaign
was largely ignored by the American people, sealed the fate of the
Union Party. His support had come mainly from German, Roman
Catholic, and elderly Americans. The party also failed to elect any of
its candidates for governor and to Congress under its label alone.

Ironically, perhaps, Lemke did win reelection to Congress running as both a Republican and a Unionist.

Franklin Roosevelt's New Deal policies likewise made the appeals of the Union Party essentially irrelevant to most Americans. Again the American voters rejected the politics of demagoguery for a more pragmatic turn to the left under the policies of Roosevelt and his milder left-of-center programs. The Union Party had attempted to gain the support of the masses by using tactics of the Progressives and other radical elements; these efforts backfired.

The party disappeared by 1939.

Sources/References

Aikman, Duncan. "Lemke's New Party, and Three Key Men." *New York Times Magazine* (March 8), 1936.

Bennett, David H. *Demagogues in the Depression: American Radicals and the Union Party, 1932–1936.* New Brunswick, NJ: Rutgers University Press, 1969.

Blackorby, Edward C. "William Lemke: Agrarian Radical and Union Party Presidential Candidate." *Mississippi Valley Historical Review*, 49 (June), 1962.

_____. *Prairie Rebel: The Public Life of William Lemke.* Lincoln: University of Nebraska Press, 1963.

Congressional Quarterly, Inc. *National Party Conventions, 1831–1984.* Washington, DC: Congressional Quarterly, Inc., 1987.

Johnson, Donald Bruce. *National Party Platforms: Vol. 1, 1840–1956.* Urbana: University of Illinois Press, 1978.

McCoy, Donald R. *Angry Voices: Left-of-Center Politics in the New Deal Era.* Port Washington, NY: Kennikat, 1958.

Rodman, Selden. "The Insurgent Line-up for 1936." *American Mercury* (May), 1935.

Schapsmeier, Edward L., and Frederick H. Schapsmeier. *Political Parties and Civic Action Groups.* Westport, CT: Greenwood, 1981.

United Citizens' Party

Established in 1969 in Columbia, South Carolina.

Creation of the United Citizens' Party (UCP) resulted essentially from the work carried on by the South Carolina Voter Education Project (a group that focused its efforts on increasing voter registration among South Carolina blacks) during the 1960s. Because no black had previously won nomination when running for any office in the Democratic Party primary in that state, the United Citizens' Party was conceived as a vehicle to increase black involvement in South Carolina politics.

The United Citizens' Party was certified as a legal party in South Carolina in September 1970, having received the requisite signatures of 10,000 voters under state law. This was accomplished as a result of work done by United Citizens' Party members and black college students. Even though the party thus had only about two months to choose candidates and organize a campaign, and was unable to get the names of its candidates on the state ballots because the ballots had already been prepared, the party did nominate write-in candidates for the governorship (Thomas Broadwater) and the lieutenant governorship (the Reverend Julius M. McTeer). Some UCP candidates for state legislative offices—those who had run in the June primary and had won as independents, and whose names therefore appeared on the ballot—were also endorsed. Candidates for local offices were also nominated and/or supported by the UCP.

The election results were hardly spectacular, but they were nevertheless significant: although the two candidates for elective office each received fewer than 1,000 votes, three blacks were elected to the state legislature—the first blacks so elected since Reconstruction. United Citizens' Party candidates also won scattered offices on city councils and school boards throughout the state. In a later effort in a campaign for Congress for the seat left vacant by the death of L. Mendel Rivers, the party's candidate, Victoria DeLee, was defeated.

The significance of the United Citizens' Party lay not in its record at winning votes, but in its success at creating an environment in which blacks would be nominated by both the Democratic and Republican parties in South Carolina, as was the case in 1972 and 1976. This, in turn, had an impact on national politics as well.

Sources/References

New York Times. November 24, 1969.

Schapsmeier, Edward L., and Frederick H. Schapsmeier. *Political Parties and Civic Action Groups*. Westport, CT: Greenwood, 1981.

Walton, Hanes, Jr. *Black Political Parties: An Historical and Political Analysis*. New York: Free Press, 1972.

United Labor Party

Established in 1877 in Pittsburgh, Pennsylvania.

The party's objectives were to improve working conditions through the adoption of various economic reforms. Its originators were made up largely of trade unionists.

The United Labor Party met in Cincinnati in 1888 in a convention where it nominated Robert H. Cowdry of Illinois for president and William H. T. Wakefield of Kansas as vice presidential candidate. Before that it had given its support to Greenback Party (q.v.) candidates. Attendance at the convention was limited.

The party's platform advocated in particular the "single tax," under which land would be taxed according to its value and not in accordance with its area. The platform stated:

> We propose so to change the existing system of taxation that no one shall be taxed on the wealth he produces, nor any one suffered to appropriate wealth he does not produce by taking to himself the increasing values which the growth of society adds to land.
>
> What we propose is not the disturbing of any man in his holding or title; but, by taxation of land according to its value and not according to its area, to devote to common use and benefit those values which arise, not from the exertion of the individual, but from the growth of society, and to abolish all taxes on industry and its products. This increased taxation of land values must, while relieving the working farmer and small homestead owner of the undue burdens now imposed upon them, make it unprofitable to hold land for speculation, and thus throw open abundant opportunities for the employment of labor and the building up of homes. We would do away with the present unjust and wasteful system of finance which piles up hundreds of millions of dollars in treasury vaults while we are paying interest on an enormous debt; and we would establish in its stead a monetary system in which a legal tender circulating medium should be issued by the government, without the intervention of banks.

The platform of the United Labor Party concluded with the following two paragraphs:

> We denounce the Democratic and Republican parties as hopelessly and shamelessly corrupt, and, by reason of their affiliation with monopolies, equally unworthy of the suffrages of those who do not live upon public plunder; we therefore require of those who would act with us that they sever all connections with both.
>
> In support of these aims, we solicit the cooperation of all patriotic citizens, who, sick of the degradation of politics, desire by constitutional methods to establish justice, to preserve liberty, to extend the spirit of fraternity, and to elevate humanity.

The party platform also urged monetary reform, doing away with child labor, a shortening of work hours, assistance to the poor, public ownership of transportation and telegraph systems, elimination of convict labor, use of the secret ballot, and aid to the poor.

In 1886 the party had supported Henry George, the advocate of the single tax, for the New York City mayoralty campaign. It was George who was instrumental in preventing the Socialists from moving the United Labor Party to the left and toward the nationalization of capital or doing away with private property at its convention in Syracuse, earlier.

The party suffered a fatal blow when its candidate, Robert H. Cowdry, withdrew from the race even before election day. The United Labor Party was on the ballot in only the states of Illinois, New York, and Oregon, and was able to draw only 2,818 votes. It died shortly thereafter.

Sources/References

Barker, Charles A. *Henry George*. New York: Oxford University Press, 1955.

de Mille, Anna George. *Henry George: Citizen of the World* (Don C. Shoemaker, Ed.). Chapel Hill: University of North Carolina Press, 1950.

Johnson, Donald Bruce. *National Party Platforms: Vol. 1, 1840–1956*. Urbana: University of Illinois Press, 1978.

Schapsmeier, Edward L., and Frederick H. Schapsmeier. *Political Parties and Civic Action Groups*. Westport, CT: Greenwood, 1981.

Stanwood, Edward. *A History of the Presidency from 1788 to 1897*. Boston: Houghton Mifflin, 1924.

Universal Party

Established in Berkeley, California, in 1963 by the Reverend Kirby Hensley.

Hensley had been the founder of the Universal Life Church, an organization that granted minister diplomas for a fee to those who wished to establish churches of their own for whatever reason.

In 1964, Hensley nominated himself as the presidential candidate of the Universal Party, and he selected Iowan John O. Hopkins as the party's vice presidential candidate. The candidates' names appeared only on the California ballot; they received only 19 votes!

In the 1968 election, Hensley ran again. Another Iowan, Roscoe B. McKenna, was picked as vice presidential candidate. In that election, the party again appeared on the ballot of only one state—Iowa—and received only 142 votes.

The party's poor showing continued in 1972, when Gabriel Green of Iowa was the party's presidential candidate, and Californian Daniel W. Fry ran as vice presidential candidate.

The party's "platform" consistently advocated the same objectives: doing away with taxes, the outlawing of lobbying, instituting education founded on the "science of man," and doing away with usury.

Its support in 1972 was again feeble: it received only 21 votes in California and 199 in Iowa. The party ceased to exist after 1972.

Sources/References

See Sources/References under *People's Peace Prosperity Party.*

Wisconsin Progressive Party

Established by Robert M. La Follette, Jr., and his brother Philip, in Fond du Lac, Wisconsin, in 1934.

From its inception, the party was arguably to have been the personal vehicle by which Robert La Follette, Jr., was to be reelected as a U.S. senator from, and Philip was to be elected governor of, the state of Wisconsin. Others maintain that the party was in fact a reflection of a grass-roots effort to establish an organization that would truly and at long last implement the principles for which the Progressives had stood. Many of those supporting the creation of the party—such as the Wisconsin State Labor Federation and the Farmer-Labor Political Federation (a socialist-leaning political group)—hoped that the Wisconsin Progressive Party would ultimately become a nationally recognized third party with more than just regional influence.

Republican Progressives in Wisconsin had supported Franklin Delano Roosevelt for the presidency in 1932 and other Democrats running in the state against former Republican Governor Kohler and other so-called Republican Stalwarts. As a result of this support, for only the second time in its history did Wisconsin cast its electoral votes for a Democrat for president and for the first time in a half century had a Democrat become governor of the state. Even control of the Wisconsin legislature was taken by the Democrats.

But the new governor vacillated in his policies and the Democratic legislature seemed reactionary with respect to the problems faced by the state during the Great Depression. Agriculture in particular was in dire straits, and dairy farmers—led by two somewhat rival factions known as the Farm Holiday Association and the more aggressive Wisconsin Milk Pool—joined forces in announcing the possibility of a strike to prevent milk from reaching the Milwaukee and Chicago markets. Members of the Wisconsin Milk Pool eventually called a strike, and bands of pickets prevented trucks from delivering milk and even dumped the milk in the streets and highways. But the strike was over in only a few days. Other unions, however, expressed support for the exasperated milk producers, and calls for the formation of a farmer-labor party were soon heard. With additional leadership provided by such notable figures as Thomas Amlie (a former Republican Progressive who had served in Congress), Henry Ohl, Jr. (president of the Wisconsin Federation of Labor), and William T. Evjue (the fiery editor of the Madison *Capital Times* newspaper), the movement to form a new party gained further impetus.

Farm leaders, because of their financial problems, were enraged with both Democrats and Republicans. Early in 1934, the political rumor mill produced the word that President Franklin Delano Roosevelt would support for reelection the Progressive Senators Norris and Johnson. At the same time no indication had been given that the president would also support Robert M. La Follette, Jr. La Follette thus faced the difficult political question as to whether he could receive enough Democratic support as a Progressive Republican running on a third party ticket, or whether to attempt capturing the presidential nomination in the regular Republican primary process. A conference of Progressives was therefore called to be held in Madison on March 3, 1934, to discuss matters of consequence—a move that was interpreted by newspapers and commentators throughout the state as an indication that a sincere effort was under way to form a third party.

More than 500 Progressives were represented at the meeting, some of whom were vehemently opposed to the formation of a third party. Even Senator La Follette himself had some doubts about the viability of a third party, recalling his own father's opposition to third party formation as an exercise in futility. In addition, Wisconsin law seemed unclear as to whether a new third party could qualify in time to get on the 1934 ballot. After the courts removed doubts about this, leaders among the Progressives issued a call for a May 19 convention in Fond du Lac to determine whether a third party effort should be undertaken.

Preconvention sentiment was split; a majority of those expressing their views seemed in favor of a new party, however, and by the time the convention actually convened, it seemed a foregone conclusion that a third party effort would be launched. Some 300 delegates appeared. The two major issues discussed involved the procedures to be undertaken to get the new party on the ballot and the name that the new party would assume. The new party was established by a vote of 254 to 44, and, after contentious debate among those who favored a name that would include farmers and laborers, it was finally decided that the title Progressive should be used. Other delegates voted for either Farmer-Labor or a variety of other names.

The convention nominated the two La Follettes for the positions they sought—Robert M., Jr., for senator, and Philip for governor. Moreover, a list of candidates for both statewide and congressional positions was put forth. So excited were potential candidates that almost 200 persons filed nomination papers for the legislature under the Progressive label. Although there were only 10 seats available, some 16 Progressive candidates ran for those seats.

Doing away with its linkages to both the Democratic and Republican parties, the Wisconsin Progressive platform openly declared an attack upon capitalism as the root cause of the nation's ills. Among the party's other demands were calls for public works programs and refinancing of farms and homes by the federal government, a veterans' bonus, increased taxes on the wealthy, unemployment insurance, nationalization of monopoly industries, the introduction of minimum wages and a decrease in the length of the workday, soil conservation measures, the initiative and referendum, and a requirement that all future declarations of war be subject to a direct vote of the people. Among other statements of the candidates were the insistence that farmers be entitled to profits on their investments, that labor have the right to organize, that there be established a government-owned central banking system, and that jobs be guaranteed to all able-bodied persons willing to work.

The degree of success of the new organization was reflected at the polls. Senator La Follette was reelected, carrying 66 of 71 counties and a vote of more than 440,000—over twice the support received by Democratic and Republican candidates combined. Seven of the Wisconsin Progressive Party's candidates were elected to Congress; a majority of Progressives were elected to the Wisconsin Assembly and 13 to the Wisconsin Senate. Philip La Follette was elected to the governor's office, receiving some 373,000 votes, about 14,000 votes ahead of his Democratic rival, and about 200,000 votes ahead of his Republican opponent. Senator La Follette's influence became notable later when, in building his New Deal measures, President Franklin D. Roosevelt used the senator as a major means of allocating federal monies for Depression projects, and particularly those of the Works Progress Administration.

The Progressives once again carried the state in 1936, but clear and unambiguous strains were already beginning to show in the party's performance. In 1938, Philip La Follette ran for a fourth gubernatorial term, but his campaign had aroused the ire of those who felt his policies were bankrupting the state, and he had engaged in public debate with Dr. Glenn Frank, then president of the University of Wisconsin.

La Follette's criticism of Roosevelt's policies likewise angered many supporters throughout the state. A "Stop La Follette" movement began among Democrats and Republicans, who formed a coalition ticket. A Republican was elected governor in 1938. In 1940, when Senator Robert M. La Follette, Jr., ran once more for the U.S. Senate, he faced stiff opposition from the Republican organization. He was reelected by only 55,000 votes. In 1946, La Follette lost the nomination to Joseph R. McCarthy.

On the gubernatorial level, the Progressive candidate lost in 1940 and won in 1942. But before he could take office, the 1942 victor—Orland S. Loomis—died and was replaced by Lieutenant Governor Walter Goodland, a Republican. Goodland, although in his 80s, was reelected in 1944. By 1946, the Progressives appeared to be in an increasingly hopeless position. A Progressive conference held on March 17, 1946, declared its intention to return to the Republican party. Senator La Follette gave a lengthy address at the conference—the rules had been suspended to enable him to present his views—in which he acknowledged that Progressivism had been severely weakened and that although he recognized that there were many liberal Democrats deserving Progressive support, he himself suggested that the Republican party offered the best vehicle for the continued development of Progressive principles and the perpetuation of Wisconsin as a Republican state. He also insisted that Progressives in the Republican party could continue to exercise their independence. As a viable single entity, the Wisconsin Progressive Party had come to an end, its ideals and aspirations diffused and unfocused, but it came to its final rest perhaps in the place where it had begun—the Republican Party of Wisconsin.

Sources/References

Doan, Edward N. *The La Follettes and the Wisconsin Idea.* New York: Rinehart, 1947.

Johnson, Roger T. *Robert M. La Follette, Jr., and the Decline of the Progressive Party in Wisconsin.* Madison: State Historical Society for the Department of History, University of Wisconsin, 1964.

McCoy, Donald R. *Angry Voices: Left-of-Center Politics in the New Deal Era.* Port Washington, NY: Kennikat, 1958.

Schapsmeier, Edward L., and Frederick H. Schapsmeier. *Political Parties and Civic Action Groups.* Westport, CT: Greenwood, 1981.

Young, Donald (Ed.). *Adventures in Politics: The Memoirs of Philip La Follette.* New York: Holt, Rinehart & Winston, 1970.

Workers World Party

Established in 1959 in Buffalo, New York, as an offshoot of the Socialist Workers Party.

Workers World Party is a self-identified revolutionary Marxist-Leninist group that has been involved in demonstrations representing left-wing views on civil rights and antiwar attitudes. It has particularly engaged in what it labels "liberation struggles" with capitalism and imperialism. Although it supposedly supports worker revolution throughout the world, it has nevertheless opposed revolutionary movements by workers against the Communist governments of Czechoslovakia, Hungary, and Poland. It has regarded such attacks on the prevailing regimes of those countries as counterrevolutionary and reactionary efforts largely stimulated by Western imperialism. It has believed that the Soviet Union stood as the model for directing the efforts toward world revolution. Thus it has supported leftist revolutions in Chile, Grenada, Angola, Nicaragua, El Salvador, and elsewhere where it appeared to the party that the struggle was against "Western imperialism." Until the 1980s, it focused its attention mainly on vocally demonstrating against restrictions on civil rights and U.S. involvement militarily, and on such matters as the closing of nuclear plants, a takeover of the oil companies, and greater benefits for workers. The party ran its first presidential ticket in 1980, when it nominated Deirdre Griswold, one of its founders and the editor of the party's newspaper, for its presidential candidate and Larry Holmes, a black activist, for vice president. Their names appeared on the ballot in 10 states. They received only slightly in excess of 13,000 votes.

In 1984, Larry Holmes ran as the party's presidential candidate, his name appearing on the ballot in eight states. He received 15,329 votes.

It should be noted also that both Larry Holmes and Gavrielle Holmes were candidates of the Workers World Party in 1984, but that Larry Holmes's name appeared on the ballots of more states. In Ohio and Rhode Island, moreover, Milton Vera was the vice presidential candidate; he ran with Gavrielle Holmes in those states.

In 1988, Larry Holmes again became the presidential candidate for the party and Gloria La Riva ran as vice presidential nominee.

The party's political objectives involved granting guaranteed jobs for everyone with complete job security, raising the minimum wage to $10 per hour, and raising other benefits such as the basic levels of social security, unemployment, and welfare. The platform emphasized the need for affordable housing for all Americans and urged the imposition of restrictions on the amount of mortgage payments and the activities of landlords. Other "planks" in the list of objectives referred to free health care, free education, doing away with racism by law, equal pay and equal rights for women, and expanding the social and political rights of the young, the old, and the handicapped. It urged paying for the battle against AIDS by using money spent on the so-called Star Wars program, and an end to discrimination against male and female homosexuals. It also called for an end to war-making and the termination of American military intervention in foreign countries.

The party was on the ballot in five states and its candidates received only a minuscule number of votes.

Sources/References

Congressional Quarterly, Inc. *National Party Conventions, 1831–1984.* Washington, DC: Congressional Quarterly, Inc., 1987.

Day, Glenn. *Minor Presidential Candidates and Parties of 1988.* Jefferson, NC: McFarland, 1988.

Smallwood, Frank. *The Other Candidates: Third Parties in Presidential Elections.* Hanover, NH: University Press of New England, 1983.

Workingmen's Party

Founded by William Heighton, a leather worker, in Philadelphia in 1828.

A party confined mostly to the states of the Northeast, its objectives were to elevate the conditions of the workers by drawing them into political activities. The party viewed itself as a party of reform and sought to ride the wave of change occurring during the period of Andrew Jackson's rise to the presidency. The party advocated abolishing imprisonment for debt, free public education, doing away with the militia, and a 10-hour workday, among other objectives.

Although it never ran a presidential candidate, the party did achieve some success with its candidates in places such as New York City, Philadelphia, Boston, and Albany.

The Workingmen's Party was in disarray by 1832. Utopian socialists such as Robert Dale Owen and Frances Wright created internal wrangling in the party, and many of its members crossed over to the Locofoco (Equal Rights) Party (q.v) or other parties, or spent their time working in other areas of the labor movement in general. The party ceased to exist in 1832.

Sources/References

Hugins, Walter E. *Jacksonian Democracy and the Working Class.* Stanford: Stanford University Press, 1960.

Pessen, Edward. *Most Uncommon Jacksonians.* Albany: State University of New York Press, 1967.

Schapsmeier, Edward L., and Frederick H. Schapsmeier. *Political Parties and Civic Action Groups.* Westport, CT: Greenwood, 1981.

Appendix
Years and Places of Origin of Minor Parties

1823   People's Party (Albany, New York)

1824   National Republican Party (Washington, D.C.)

1826   Anti-Masonic Party (Batavia, New York)

1828   Workingmen's Party (Philadelphia, Pennsylvania)

1836   Locofoco (Equal Rights) Party (New York City, New York)

1839   Liberty Party (Warsaw, New York)

1848   Free Soil Party (Buffalo, New York)

1849   American Party (Know-Nothings) (New York City, New York)

1859   Constitutional Union Party (Baltimore, Maryland)

1860   National Democratic Party (Baltimore, Maryland)
        Southern Democrats (Charleston, South Carolina)

1864   Independent Republican Party (Cleveland, Ohio)

1869   Prohibition Party (Chicago, Illinois)

1872   Liberal Republican Party (Cincinnati, Ohio)
        National Labor and Reform Party (Columbus, Ohio)
        Straight-Out Democratic Party (Louisville, Kentucky)

1874   Greenback Party (Indianapolis, Indiana)

1877   Socialist Labor Party (Newark, New Jersey)
        United Labor Party (Pittsburgh, Pennsylvania)

1884   Anti-Monopoly Party (Chicago, Illinois)
        Equal Rights Party (San Francisco, California)

1887   Union Labor Party (Cincinnati, Ohio)

1891   Populist Party (Cincinnati, Ohio)

1896   National Democratic Party (Indianapolis, Indiana)
        National Party (Pittsburgh, Pennsylvania)
        Silver Republican Party (St. Louis, Missouri)

1897   Social Democratic Party of America (Chicago, Illinois)

1901   Socialist Party of America (Indianapolis, Indiana)

1904   National Liberty Party (St. Louis, Missouri)

1908   Independence Party (Chicago, Illinois)

1912   Progressive Party (Albany, New York)

1915   Nonpartisan League (Bismarck, North Dakota)

1916   National Woman's Party (Washington, D.C.)

1919   Communist Party of the United States (Chicago, Illinois)
        Farmer-Labor Party (Chicago, Illinois)

1924   Progressive Party (Cleveland, Ohio)

1932   Jobless Party (St. Louis, Missouri)
        Liberty Party (St. Louis, Missouri)

1934   Wisconsin Progressive Party (Fond du Lac, Wisconsin)

1936   American Labor Party (New York City, New York)
        Christian Party (Asheville, North Carolina)
        Union Party (Royal Oak, Michigan)

1938   National Progressives of America (Madison, Wisconsin)
        Socialist Workers Party (Chicago, Illinois)

1944   Liberal Party (New York City, New York)
        South Carolina Progressive Democratic Party (Columbia,
          South Carolina)

1947   Christian Nationalist Party (Eureka Springs, Arkansas)
        Independent Progressive Party (Los Angeles, California)

1948   American Vegetarian Party (Chicago, Illinois)
        Progressive Party (Philadelphia)
        States' Rights Party (Birmingham, Alabama)

1952   Constitution Party (Los Angeles, California)
        Poor Man's Party (Newark, New Jersey)

1958   National States' Rights Party (Atlanta, Georgia)

1959   American Beat Party (Chicago, Illinois)
        National Socialist White People's Party (Arlington,
            Virginia)
        Workers World Party (Buffalo, New York)

1960   Afro-American Party (Alabama)
        Tax Cut Party (Chicago, Illinois)

1962   Conservative Party (New York City, New York)

1963   Freedom Now Party (Washington, D.C.)
        Universal Party (Berkeley, California)

1964   Mississippi Freedom Democratic Party (Jackson,
            Mississippi)

1966   Black Panther Party (Oakland, California)
        Lowndes County Freedom Organization (Haynesville,
            Alabama)

1967   Peace and Freedom Party (Ann Arbor, Michigan)

1968   American Independent Party (Montgomery, Alabama)
        Freedom and Peace Party (Chicago, Illinois)
        Loyal Democrats of Mississippi (Jackson, Mississippi)
        National Democratic Party of Alabama (Birmingham,
            Alabama)

1969   United Citizens' Party (Columbia, South Carolina)

1970   La Raza Unida (Crystal City, Texas)
        People's Peace Prosperity Party (Modesto, California)

1971   Libertarian Party (Westminster, Colorado)
        People's Party (Dallas, Texas)

1972   American Party (Louisville, Kentucky)

1974   Liberty Union Party (West Rupert, Vermont)

1979   New Alliance Party (New York City, New York)
        Citizens' Party (Washington, D.C.)

1980   National Unity Campaign

1988   Internationalist Workers Party (New Jersey)

Index

Bull Moose Party, 142. *See also*
  Progressive Party (1912)
Burdick, Quentin, 126
Burnham, James, 173
Burroughs, William, 17
Bush, George, 78, 119
Business and Professional Women,
  122
Butler, Benjamin F., 37–38, 73
Byrd, Harry F., 60, 184

Caffrey, Donelson, 111
Calhoun, John C., 35, 113
California, 28
  campaigns in, 22, 40, 46, 60, 70,
    89, 94, 195
  parties established in, 39, 59, 63,
    77, 132, 194
California Black Panther Party,
  126
Camejo, Peter, 176
Cannon, James P., 173
Capone, Al, 152
Capp, Al, 69
Carlson, Grace, 174–175
Carmichael, Stokely, 97, 98
Carriza Springs (TX), 81
Carter, Jimmy, 45, 120
Carter, Reginald, 16
Cashin, John, 106
Cass, Lewis, 67
Catholicism, opposition to, 3,
  27–29
Center for Libertarian Studies, 89
Center for the Biology of Natural
  Systems, 45
Chambers, Benjamin, J., 72
Chambers, Whittaker, 54
*Change and Continuity in the 1988
  Elections,* 10–11
Charity Organizational Society, 122
Charleston (SC), 180
Charlestown (MA), 27
Chase, Salmon P., 67, 84
Cherokee Indians, 113
Chicago, 39, 115, 141
  parties established in, 16, 31, 47,
    63, 69, 74, 148, 157, 173, 186
"Chicago Seven," 39

Chicanos, in politics, 80–82
Childs, R. A., 86
China, 175
Chinese, exclusion of, 72, 73, 108,
  188
Christensen, Parley P., 64, 65
Christian American Patriots, 42, 44
Christian Nationalist Crusade, 42
Christian Nationalist Party, 42–43
Christian Party, 43–44
Christian Social Union Settlement
  of Oxton, 122
Christian Veterans Intelligence
  Service, 42
Christian Veterans of America, 42
Christian Youth of America, 42
Church of God, 133
CIA (Central Intelligence Agency),
  127, 131, 176
Cincinnati, 84, 134, 187
CIO (Congress of Industrial
  Organizations), 23, 50, 54
Citizens' Party
  goals of, 45–46
  and media, 46–47
City council, 81
Civil liberties, 65
Civil rights, 8
  opposition to, 15, 18, 182–184
  support for, 39, 46, 60, 69, 70,
    106–109, 121, 178–180, 199
  See also Equal rights; Suffrage
Civil Rights Act, 18
Civil War, 38, 103, 149, 181, 182
Clark, Edward E., 90
Clark, Mark, 39
Clay, Henry, 35, 93, 112, 113
Cleage, Albert, 70
Cleaver, Eldridge, 39–40, 126–127
Cleveland (OH), 77, 115, 141
Cleveland, Grover, 38, 105, 158
Clinton, DeWitt, 128
Coalitions, 11–12, 127
Cochrane, John, 78
Coin's Financial School, 94
Colorado, 60, 81, 86
Columbia (SC), 178, 191
Columbus (OH), 107
Cominform, 52–53

218   *Index*